The Economy of Glory

THE ECONOMY OF
GLORY

From Ancien Régime France to the Fall of Napoleon

ROBERT MORRISSEY

Translated by Teresa Lavender Fagan

The University of Chicago Press : Chicago and London

Robert Morrissey is the Benjamin Franklin Professor of French Literature in the Department of Romance Languages and Literatures at the University of Chicago and executive director of the France Chicago Center.
Teresa Lavender Fagan is a freelance translator living in Chicago. She has translated numerous books for the University of Chicago Press.

The University of Chicago Press, Chicago 60637
The University of Chicago Press, Ltd., London
© 2014 by The University of Chicago
All rights reserved. Published 2014.
Printed in the United States of America

23 22 21 20 19 18 17 16 15 14   1 2 3 4 5

ISBN-13: 978-0-226-92458-8 (cloth)
ISBN-13: 978-0-226-92459-5 (e-book)
DOI: 10.7208/chicago/9780226924595.001.0001

Originally published as *Napoléon et l'héritage de la gloire*, © Presses Universitaires de France, 2010.

The University of Chicago Press gratefully acknowledges the generous support of the Division of the Humanities at the University of Chicago toward the publication of this book.

Avec le soutien du

Library of Congress Cataloging-in-Publication Data

Morrissey, Robert, 1947–
    [Napoléon et l'héritage de la gloire. English]
    The economy of glory : from ancien régime France to the fall of Napoleon / Robert Morrissey ; translated by Teresa Lavender Fagan.
        pages cm
    Includes bibliographical references and index.
    ISBN 978-0-226-92458-8 (cloth : alk. paper) — ISBN 978-0-226-92459-5 (e-book)
    1. Napoleon I, Emperor of the French, 1769–1821. 2. Napoleon I, Emperor of the French, 1769–1821—Influence. 3. France—History—Consulate and First Empire, 1799–1815—Historiography. 4. Emperors—France—Historiography. I. Title.
    DC203.9.M6813 2014
    944.05—dc23

                                                            2013014450

CONTENTS

v

ACKNOWLEDGMENTS (2010)

I wish to thank all those who, nearby or from far away, have contributed to this book. First, I am grateful to all my colleagues at the University of Chicago, in particular to the greatly missed François Furet, with whom I had the pleasure of conducting a seminar — one of his last — on *Les Misérables*, a course that was influential in the development of this book. I am also grateful to those who took the time to read the manuscript, either in its entirety or in part, and who gave me their advice: Philippe Borgeaud, James Redfield, Claude Duchet, Peter Dembowski, and Paul Cheney. My editor at Presses Universitaires de France, Paul Garapon, was extraordinarily patient and supportive throughout; I thank him for all his work on the project. I also thank Stéphane Douard, who was always available to discuss, suggest, read. The affection of my entire "tribe" was constant, Marie-Claire's support indispensable; I thank them all from the bottom of my heart.

TRANSLATOR'S NOTE

I must begin with an enormous "thank you" to my longtime friend Robert Morrissey. Robert painstakingly reviewed the early drafts of the translation, making stylistic and more substantive changes to the text, which I gratefully incorporated into the final version. Robert's collaboration and help have been invaluable.

Regarding translations of cited French texts, I have used, where possible, existing published English-language translations, occasionally modifying them slightly. All other translations from the French are my own. The author has chosen to include the original French of many translated quotations within the body of the work; for most of the others, the French appears in brackets in the endnotes.

Given its greater length, the original chapter 4 of the French edition has been divided into two chapters in this translation.

At the Confluence of Reality and Myth

"Your glory is immense: the Universe can scarcely contain, and posterity will hardly believe, the most authentic events of your illustrious career," exclaimed "soldiers of every rank" in a letter addressed to Napoleon and published in *Le Moniteur* of 19 June 1804 (30 Prairial Year XII). To dispel any suspicion of flattery, they added: "We know not the language of flattery! The language of the heart is the sole language worthy of the Great NAPOLEON."[1] In his *Histoire du Consulat et de l'Empire*, Antoine-Claire Thibaudeau, an active player in the events of the period, attempts to make sense of it all while remaining faithful to his republican values. Reflecting on the inflated language that characterized the Napoleonic moment, he notes that on great occasions, from the very beginnings of the consular government, laudatory missives poured in from every corner of the land, and he decries that "dangerous trend, where truth is indistinguishable from flattery, hypocrisy from good faith."[2] Although convinced that most of those outpourings were spontaneous, he observes that, because of their overwhelming similarity, they appeared artificial, as if solicited,

> and indeed they were, not by the government, but by courtiers who took pride in doing so, and even by citizens and functionaries who in good faith believed that it was a means of forming public opinion, and promoting in people an even greater respect and love for the Head of State.

et elles l'étaient en effet, non par le gouvernement, mais par des courtisans qui s'en faisaient un mérite, et même par des citoyens et des fonctionnaires qui croyaient de bonne foi que c'était un moyen de former l'opinion, et de recommander encore plus le chef de l'État au respect et à l'amour du peuple.[3]

For Thibaudeau, who, moreover, clearly denounces Napoleon's despotic tendencies, this panegyrical inflation was neither simply the mark of absolute power nor the result of some kind of mystification of the people, unwitting victims of diabolical propagandist machinations. In his opinion, such expressions were a phenomenon of collective exultation. This effervescent solidarity rested, of course, on the glory of Napoleon, a glory of such power that it seemed to eclipse even the feats of the heroes and demigods of antiquity. Indeed, one might even suggest that after attempting to erase time, to begin everything anew, revolutionized France collectively projected itself into the realm of myth.

Seen in this light, the Napoleonic moment can be understood as the final battle in the long quarrel between the Ancients and the Moderns; almost as if, to overcome the prestige of the Ancients, modern France needed an adventure worthy of the epic so many French authors, since the sixteenth century, had been seeking in vain to write, the better to prove that France was as great as the greatest civilizations of antiquity. In this brave new world the collective imagination was not to be burdened with a subtle use of language, nor did the thorny issue of Christian marvels need to be raised; the French had only to open their eyes; the truly marvelous was happening right in front of them. On 6 January 1806, *Le Moniteur* published an *Ode sur les victoires de Napoléon-le-Grand* that described a Frenchman deep in thought before the tomb of Homer. In the ensuing dialogue between the ancient poet and the modern Frenchman, the man asserts that although Homer's poetry remains unmatched, the exploits of the great Achilles have indeed been surpassed by those of a modern hero.

In the vast fields of victory,
This conqueror has harvested
More laurels and more glory,
Than you ever imagined.
Nowadays prodigious feats are very real.
There are no more wonders to behold;
I have seen the supernatural quality
Of the feats of antiquity vanish;

Fables have ceased to be fables;
There is nothing more incredible
Than the events taking place before our eyes.

Aux vastes champs de la victoire,
Ce conquérant a moissonné
Plus de lauriers et plus de gloire,
Que tu n'en as imaginé.
Il n'est plus pour nous de prodiges;
J'ai vu des antiques prestiges
S'évanouir le merveilleux;
La fable a cessé d'être fable;
Il n'est plus rien d'invraisemblable,
Que les faits passés sous nos yeux.[4]

This sense of living at the confluence of reality and myth had begun before the advent of Napoleon. Early on, seeking a legitimacy in harmony with all that it owed to the thinking of ancient republicanism, the new French Republic emphasized the parallel with the Roman Republic, in which glory played a primary role. "We must also," asserted Bertrand Barère, "*revolutionize glory* and distribute it *like wealth* over the many battalions, over the humble citizens who battle every day for the Republic."[5] Thus, glory as a reward would function as a currency of a different kind. In a sense, Bonaparte fulfilled Barère's wish while himself inheriting the glory of the Republican armies. This "revolution" of glory was facilitated by a vision of Bonaparte as a hero literally surpassing the imaginable. We know all that the man did to create and maintain his heroic image, and the extent to which his fate was connected to it.[6] But although his rule is commonly said to have depended on his glory, and his authority explained by invoking the notion of the charismatic leader, much less attention has been paid to the uniquely Napoleonic concept of an *economy of glory*.

For it was through glory that Napoleon Bonaparte planned to escape from the impasse of revolutionary contractualism, since glory elicited immediate and spontaneous adherence and motivation that were anchored in emotion rather than in rational abstraction. As an affirmation of the individual in his or her relationship with the collectivity, glory enabled a reconciliation of the irreconcilable, personal interest with the general interest, precisely because a concern with self could and should take the path of emulation. In a context in which Jacobin logic stressed the equality of all citizens, glory provided a means to create distinctions on bases other than wealth. Because of the structuring position it had within both the monarchic and aristocratic systems of values, glory was at the very heart of the politics of fusion, which Napoleon pursued with true consistency and which aimed to unite the old and the new, to overcome the revolutionary fracture and reconcile a divided France. It was by experiencing reality as if living on the level of the greatest myths that the nation could undertake a return to history. "I was vanquished by glory" ("Je fus vaincu par la gloire"), explained Las Cases regarding his conversion after the campaign of Austerlitz; "I admired, I recognized, I loved Napoleon, and at that moment I became fanatically French."[7]

Of course, Napoleon's glory manifested itself so clearly that it is not difficult to understand its immediate attraction and power of seduction. But if we attempt to see it only as a temporary crystallization, from which Napoleon improvised—like a magician or a sorcerer—in order to have the people believe in and adhere to what was nothing more than an elaborate, enormous sham, it is difficult to appreciate fully his politics of fusion, precisely because that politics depended, in its very principle, on the mirage of glory. And we find ourselves, suddenly, like Alice in Wonderland, astonished by things that seem to fly in the face of basic common sense: a whole people mystified by a master charlatan who had come under the spell of his own illusion. Of course, the hypothesis of a collective delusion provoked and maintained by that master of propaganda both exonerates the people, who thus regain their purity as victims, and discredits the sorcerer by emphasizing his own self-delusional limitations. Such reasoning nevertheless serves to illustrate the profound ambiguity that has characterized France's relationship with the Emperor even to the present, and helps explain why, for example, Napoleon appears in Pierre Nora's well-known *Les Lieux de mémoire* only after he has been reduced to ashes.[8] In such a perspective, the Napoleonic moment is often seen as a strange parenthesis, a delusional blip in the long course of national history, whether that history was viewed as invested with all the prestige of progress or, on the contrary, experienced as a movement of corruption and loss of values.

My goal is quite different, for I aim above all to understand what we might call the *Napoleon effect*. I am not looking at the man himself, nor at his history, if by that we mean the unfolding of his adventures, the events of his life and his reign: all this has already been abundantly and eloquently told.[9] Rather, I will attempt to understand the workings and function of the figure of Napoleon within the French cultural landscape. This book, then, is not so much a history of representations of Napoleon—here, too, the list of such studies is extensive[10]—as a study of the mechanisms at work in the formation of a cultural reality. Within that reality is an awareness of the collective self, in other words, a "national identity," what Montesquieu called "the general character" of a nation or the "genius" of a people.[11]

Beyond the Uniqueness of the Individual

Any study of Napoleon risks falling into the trap of "for or against,"[12] which is all the more difficult to avoid since both the personality and the legend evoke strong emotional reactions of admiration or revulsion. Added to this, more or less explicitly, are various political and ideological positions. Even what we call him — whether Napoleon or Bonaparte — has been subject to that electrical polarization of positive or negative reactions. The challenge is to escape that binarity and to raise the question in another way. Reflecting on the Napoleon effect enables us to acquire a critical distance, and to place the arguments for and against in perspective. Looking at questions of cultural effect no doubt also involves dangers and blind spots. But to adopt this approach cautiously offers clear advantages because it *necessarily* extracts Napoleon from his uniqueness as an individual — however attractive or repulsive — and places him within the context of the enduring collectivity known as "France." In this perspective we can better grasp the profound logic of his politics of fusion and can locate more precisely his position in the French cultural landscape of the nineteenth century, and beyond. To understand this profound logic does not mean singing Napoleon's praises once again, or denigrating him. It means attempting to understand a dynamic relationship in its essential components, beginning with those that were formed in the seventeenth century, and even earlier, and continued to develop and evolve throughout the eighteenth century. Looking back in time enables us to see how Napoleon Bonaparte was in some way fashioned, "traversed" if you will, by strong currents of thought on glory and how it functions, on what we might call the economy of heroism and glory.

The idea of seeing the eighteenth century as the moment when a politics of heroism and glory began to blossom might, however, be surprising. We recall these oft-cited lines of Voltaire, which sum up a very widespread vision that was hostile to the idea of military glory:

I hate all heroes, both Nero and Cyrus,
And that brilliant king who trained Lentulus.
The world admires in vain their undefeatable valor,
I flee far away from them all, and send them all to the devil.

Je hais tous les héros, et Neron et Cyrus,
Et ce roi si brillant qui forma Lentulus.
Le monde admire en vain leur valeur indomptable,
Je m'enfuis loin d'eux tous, et je les donne au diable.[13]

Paul Bénichou, in *Morales du Grand Siècle*, argues that the "demolition" of the hero occurred in the seventeenth century; that thesis served as a point of departure for Albert Hirschman's *The Passions and the Interests*.[14] Hirschman, an economist, traces the emergence in the eighteenth century of the ideology that replaced heroic morality: the ideology of interest. In this new paradigm, interest—the desire for profit and wealth—was the passion best suited for reining in others. The very constancy and predictability of a love of profit, linked to productivity and to rational commercial values, led to its being seen both as a virtue and as a brake on unlimited political power. For Pierre Rosanvallon, the fundamental problem is not so much a mechanism for balancing economic passions and political passions as a conception of society that sees economics as the *only realm* possible in which to achieve social harmony.[15] In short, where an economic model prevails that assumes the automatic and structural harmonization of individual interests with the general interest of society, the Rousseauist opposition between general will and individual interest loses its relevance.

We know the importance of this opposition during the French Revolution and, more generally, the degree to which the entire eighteenth century was marked by the complex links maintained by each term of the opposition with various moral, ethical, and political positions. This binary relationship between the general interest and particular interests constitutes one of the principal axes of our understanding of the philosophical and political evolution of the Enlightenment and the advent of the Revolution. And the underlying antinomic *virtue/interest* dyad provided a structure for eighteenth-century thinkers in a gamut of reflections aiming better to understand the nature of man in his relationship with a society that had become a finality in itself.[16] The conflict between virtue and interest was at the heart of religious, philosophical, economic, and political debates in the eighteenth century. It was natural that it should become a key element in our understanding of the times, especially since those two terms continue to resonate in our contemporary debates between partisans of a commercial society and defenders of a moral society.[17] At other times the opposition between virtue and interest took different turns, in matters of religion, for example, or court society.[18] With respect to interest the most commonly used terms include "vanity" (*amour-propre*), "self-love" (*amour de soi*), "particular interest" (*intérêt parti-culier*), and "personal interest" (*intérêt personnel*). With respect to virtue, the general thinking and vocabulary tended to distinguish between a morality of intent and a morality of effect, or between a natural virtue and a willful and ascetic virtue. But, as we shall see, there was a dialectical relationship at work, and the eighteenth century was continually drafting solutions that would allow those two terms to be reconciled, the opposition to be reduced or eliminated. We need only follow Adam Smith from his *Theory of Moral Sentiments* to the "invisible hand" of the *Wealth of Nations*. From Fénelon and Montesquieu to Helvétius, Rousseau, and even Robespierre, countless attempts were made to bring virtue and interest together.[19]

For our understanding of the eighteenth century, the many positions with regard to these two poles enable us to generate a range of coherent visions of the path leading from what Paul Hazard calls the *crisis of European conscious-ness* up to the Revolution. But this binary opposition is less useful when we seek to understand the Napoleonic moment. In the figure of Napoleon we can certainly see an incarnation of the general will, and even in the empire the hyperconcentration of a representative system. Seen from that point of view, Napoleon's reign indeed finds its place within what Pierre Rosanvallon has called "the catalogue of pathologies," which the French established in their practices of democracy in the nineteenth century and beyond.[20] It is part and parcel of a long historical movement leading to the gradual triumph of the ideology of interest in a globalized commercial society — ours, in fact — but one in which the ideal of virtue continues to resonate in counterpoint. In today's world, however, the ideal of glory no longer resonates with us; it is, as it were, a discourse that has gone silent.

Reconciling the Ancients and the Moderns

This was not the case in the eighteenth century when, alongside the first models legitimizing interest — formulated most vividly by Mandeville's bees (private vices, public good) and Smith's "invisible hand"—another model grew and prospered, that of glory. For if interest could be defined in such a way as to make the problem of virtue simply disappear (thanks to the invis-ible hand, to the idea of enlightened self-interest, or even to a certain notion of the general interest), the notion of virtue did not lend itself to any auto-matic elimination of the problem of interest. In France, it was often the no-tion of glory that enabled virtue to transcend the interest/virtue opposition. The concept of glory had the advantage of being deeply rooted in the heroic mores and traditions of the aristocracy. This rootedness allows us to integrate the Napoleonic ideology of glory into the *longue durée* of the history of France and, in so doing, to explore a fundamental element of French identity. But it also helps us understand how Napoleon might have seen it as a model powerful enough to serve as the basis for national reconciliation, one sufficiently rooted in French consciousness to serve as an anchor for political legitimacy and as a means for overcoming the instability inherent in revolutionary logic.

A close look at the eighteenth century confirms that, in spite of assertions to the contrary, the hero — whether in civil or military life — not only survived but figured preeminently in the discourse on glory that developed to huge appeal in France. Several factors account for this appeal. While the economic model tended to establish a regime of the impersonal, the heroic model emphasized the personal. While the economic model was concerned rather with society's functioning and did not consider its origins to be of great importance, the heroic model, though concerned with social functioning, reserved an important place for the originary or foundational moment. Contrary to the economic model, which emphasized the regular movement of things, heroism implied a rupture with common reality, with the banal continuity of everyday life. It opened the possibility of a new order or a radical reaffirmation of primary values. Finally, the model of heroic glory was solidly anchored in an immemorial vision of France, conveyed both by the monarchy and by the nobility. Similarly, in the world of letters, glory constituted a constant value — certainly not the only one — on which both the Ancients and the Moderns could agree.

The economy of glory was thus not a new invention: the eighteenth century, like Napoleon, inherited a long tradition. To understand the discourse on glory as it unfolded at the end of the seventeenth century and was developed in the eighteenth, we must identify its constitutive elements. The best way to do this is to outline, however broadly, a genealogy of the idea of glory.[21] Following its course from antiquity, we will surely better understand the great strength this ideal held, but also the ambiguities and contradictions it contained. For it was in large part thanks to those ambiguities and contradictions that the *topos* of glory in the eighteenth century gained a discursively strategic position, where apparently incompatible tendencies could draw together, where warriors, poets, and philosophers could meet. It is precisely because it represented a common ground for very different currents that the vision of an economy of glory acquired so much force and ideological traction.

We begin by looking at a few important moments in pagan antiquity before moving on to the role of Christian thought in the representation of glory. Chapter two is devoted to the insertion of the ideal of heroism and glory into a France being formed under an ever more assertive monarchy. In the third chapter, we come to the moment in the Enlightenment when the various elements of the discourse on glory came together to constitute a powerful ideology. Chapters four and five examine the establishment of an economy of glory that enabled France to escape the impasse of contractualist voluntarism and establish fusional legitimacy on other bases, until the collapse that sent the Emperor to Saint Helena. Out of that exile would come the *Mémorial de Sainte-Hélène*, a hybrid and unclassifiable work, whose complexity we will attempt to analyze in chapter six. Though nineteenth-century France became a political laboratory that cultivated pathological forms of government, it rethought itself through literature in its particular identity and in relation to universalist principles. Hence, in the Conclusion we will explore some of the "Napoleon effects" in several well-known works of literature. This journey will, I hope, help us to understand the logic of continuity and the roots of the Napoleonic moment deep in the history of France.

Jean-Auguste-Dominique Ingres, *Apotheosis of Homer* (1827). Oil on canvas. 386 × 512 cm. (5417). Louvre, Paris, France. Photograph by Thierry Le Mage. Photograph © RMN-Grand Palais / Art Resource, New York.

CHAPTER 1

From Pagan Antiquity
to Christian Thought

Between Dependence and Autonomy:
From Homer's Achilles to Aristotle's Magnanimous Man

From time immemorial, glory has been the supreme reward for heroes and the subject of epics. In Homer, who is often cited in the *Mémorial de Sainte-Hélène*, the hero is a liminal figure, somewhat of an asocial individual whose principal duty is to defend society. He fights above all for the glorious renown (*kleos*) that the collectivity is expected to confer upon him. And so the hero has every reason to defend society, because the survival of his renown depends upon the survival of society. But internalized glory becomes self-awareness, an awareness of one's own greatness.[1] Thus it is possible that in the name of his own greatness the hero endangers the very society he is supposed to defend. Take, for example, Achilles, the hero whose glory — according to the *Moniteur* poet — Napoleon had surpassed. To assert his greatness in the face of Agamemnon, Achilles refuses to fight. To assert his independence and autonomy he scornfully refuses all the gifts that Agamemnon offers him. In his magisterial study of the ideal of magnanimity, René-Antoine Gauthier sums up the functioning of glory among warriors and politicians in pagan antiquity:

> Magnanimity is primarily the courage that leads the warrior into the thick of battle; it is also the spirit of enterprise, the spirit of conquest, the insa-

tiable appetite to conquer and dominate, to demonstrate one's strength
and superiority. And the reward for greatness thus achieved is honor and
glory. Magnanimity is therefore the exclusive thirst for honor and glory.
The magnanimous one dreams only of glory, and he fears only dishonor; he
stops at nothing to achieve glory, he is ready to sacrifice everything, even his
life; and to keep dishonor at bay, to erase the blot of a misstep, he shies away
from nothing. Magnanimity conceived in this way belongs to men of action,
whether they are warrior heroes like Achilles and Ajax, or statesmen such as
Alcibiades and Evagoras, Demosthenes and Philippus. In Aristotle's termi-
nology, this is the magnanimity of "Politicians."[2]

This conception of glory always implies a strong connection to the values
of the collectivity, a fundamental dependence with regard to the opinion of
those one holds in esteem—the *aristoi*—precisely because they are esteemed
by the collectivity. The hero is motivated by emulation (*zelos*), a passion that,
as we will see, was of great importance in France in the classical age as well
as in the Enlightenment.

"Emulation," explains Jaucourt in the *Encyclopédie* article devoted to the
subject, "is a voluntary, courageous, sincere sentiment that renders the soul
fecund, causes it to benefit from great examples, and often carries it beyond
that which it admires." The great man asserts his worth and his greatness in
the agnostic imitation of others who wear the halo of glory. And it is certainly
no coincidence that Jaucourt cites these lines by Pierre Corneille, the poet par
excellence of heroism and glory (in a dedicatory letter to *La Suivante*):

> I observe with a steady eye the rise of the reputations of others,
> And try to raise myself as high as they,
> Without attempting to make them descend.
> Glory has treasures that cannot be exhausted:
> And the more it lavishes them in our favor,
> The more it retains for others to claim.

> Je vois d'un œil égal croître le nom d'autrui,
> Et tâche à m'élever aussi haut comme lui,
> Sans hazarder ma peine à le faire descendre.
> La gloire a des trésors qu'on ne peut épuiser:
> Et plus elle en prodigue à nous favoriser,
> Plus elle en garde encore où chacun peut prétendre.

Far from being limited to the warrior or the political hero, glory is accessible to many activities, ranging from those of the sword to those of the pen. For poet and warrior heroes alike, in the age of the heroes of classical antiquity as in seventeenth-century France, glory depended on the collectivity and on public recognition. The French poet Thomas Corneille, Pierre's brother, emphasizes this point in his 1697 translation of the famous epilogue with which Ovid concludes his *Metamorphoses*:

> Mon Nom, par mes Ecrits devenu si fameux,
> Passera d'âge en âge à nos derniers Neveux,
> Partout où les Romains ont conduit la Victoire,
> En lisant ces Ecrits on publiera ma gloire,
> Et si ce que j'augure a quelque vérité,
> Je puis me tenir sûr de l'immortalité.[3]

> My name, by my writings made so famous,
> Will pass from age to age through the last generation,
> Everywhere that Romans ride to Victory,
> Anyone reading these writings will publish my glory,
> And if what I predict has any truth,
> I can be sure of my immortality.

It would be impossible to avoid that fundamental dependence with regard to others, unless heroic self-awareness emanated from oneself or from a connection with a superior truth. Glory would then be either a value inherent in the individual himself, or a transcendent value; in either case, it would depend little on others. This is the ideal Aristotle seems to suggest in his famous portrait of the "great-souled man" in *Nicomachean Ethics*. Here, he who is magnanimous, the person of great soul, judges his own value justly, independently, and in spite of what others think of him. All tokens of honor, all the laurels of which he could—or indeed *should*—be the recipient may go without saying. They are merely a testimony to his virtue; for one cannot be magnanimous "without the excellence that unites the beautiful and the good." In this aristocratic vision, the magnanimous one derives some moderate amount of pleasure only from great honors; the praise of the masses leaves him indifferent. But fundamentally the magnanimous man derives no true satisfaction from honors, precisely because he is above good or bad fortune. In a sense, Aristotle is abandoning the gift/counter-gift cycle that characterizes the economy of glory. Rather than being a significant reward in itself, glory is a natural consequence — but not a necessary one — of magnanimous gestures.

Because he rejects the idea of glory as an exchange, the philosopher, in search of truth rather than public approval, can be assimilated into the heroic world of the magnanimous. Being also a liminal figure, comparable to the warrior or the political hero, the philosopher — like Plato's Socrates — can also become a danger to the social order. The two types of men, so different in so many respects, do, however, have traits in common. Whether a man of action or a philosopher, the magnanimous, great-souled person has the courage to confront great dangers without concern for his own safety:

> He must be open in his likes and dislikes, since hiding one's feelings is characteristic of a fearful person, and *he cares more for the truth than for what people think.* And he must speak and act openly; for the fact that he is inclined to look down on people and to speak the truth, except when he speaks self-deprecatingly to the masses, makes him free in his speech.[4]

His need for independence makes him incapable of living "in dependence on another" (with the exception of a friend), and "he is the kind of person whose possessions are noble but unprofitable, rather than profitable and useful, since *this is more indicative of self-sufficiency.*" It is also this assertion of self-sufficiency that leads him to benevolence whereas he "is ashamed to be a beneficiary himself,"[5] because giving is the mark of superiority; receiving, that of inferiority. Gauthier stresses the importance of the difference between the two types of magnanimity described by Aristotle: that of action and that of contemplation. But in our perspective, this portrait of the magnanimous person enables us to distinguish between a glory emanating from the collectivity, and a more absolute glory emanating from a truth detached from opinion.

The magnanimous person in *Nicomachean Ethics* can be a great politician as well as a philosopher, and Aristotle takes obvious pleasure in confounding the two. In a context in which the principal values are those of truth and autonomy, glory loses its strength as a reward — its exchange value — and does not in itself confer any sort of legitimacy. This is not a logic of recognition, and, for that very reason, glory is not constituted as a reward for truth.[6] The notion of greatness of soul becomes a means of thinking about the autonomous hero, of perceiving a glory that is all the greater for being the result of disinterested action, detached from any idea of exchange or reward, but that nevertheless retains elements of a spectacular strategy.

This portrait would have considerable impact in the Renaissance, a time when conceptions of *translatio imperii* and *translatio studii* reappeared with new vigor. On the one hand, then, there was the glory of the sword, of weapons; on the other, that of the pen, of letters, and, rising above all other forms, the glory of the king, a conduit for the glory of God.[7]

Between *Cupiditas Gloriae* and Republican Glory: Cicero and the Disconnect of Glory

The humanist reflection on the hero and glory often relies on the Aristotelian ideal of magnanimity. But it is also inspired by other important texts, notably Cicero's treatise *De Officiis* (On Duties), whose influence would continue throughout the eighteenth century. The Roman philosopher also paints a portrait of the magnanimous man. In his conception of an aristocratic republicanism, he attempts—as Fénelon would do at the end of the seventeenth century—to redefine glory by placing it in a sphere other than that of military glory, so essential to Roman political life. In the context of eighteenth-century France, the strength of the model of glory is due precisely to its fundamental plasticity. The components of that model are constantly reconfigured and placed in the service—depending on circumstances—of the warrior, the politician, the wise man, the poet, and the orator. Though literature may provide content for the concept of glory, it is always the warrior's glory that serves as a fundamental point of reference, if only to provide a point of contrast. As Vauvenargues noted in the mid-eighteenth century: "There is no other glory than military glory."[8]

For Cicero, the psychology of greatness can only be that of the attainment of honors, power, and glory. In Stoic logic, the magnanimous man should, in principle, be indifferent to this. But the great orator recognizes that in practice quite the opposite is true.

> We are now, to be sure, on very slippery ground; for scarcely can the man be found who has passed through trials and encountered dangers and does not then wish for glory as a reward for his achievements.[9]

For Cicero glory is a reward, a moral currency in a system of individual recognition. One offers great undertakings, one obtains glory. The orator goes so far as to draw a parallel between money and glory:

> But as there is a method not only of acquiring money but also of investing it so as to yield an income to meet our continuously recurring expenses—both

for the necessities and for the more refined comforts of life — so there must
be a method of gaining glory and turning it to account.[10]

Like money, glory is accumulated and saved because it is useful. It constitutes
symbolic capital. Considered from that angle, glory renders one more free
and more autonomous, in the sense that it provides greater freedom of action, which is essential in the *vita activa* Cicero so admires. But such freedom
can become a danger to society because a desire for glory (*cupiditas gloriae*),
which characterizes the greatest of souls, incites them to neglect justice.
Caesar followed this path, which led to tyranny. And this occurs when, in
the pursuit of glory, one battles not for the salvation of all but for one's own
interests ("non pro salute communi, sed pro suis commodis").[11] It is exactly
what Chateaubriand and Madame de Staël would denounce in Napoleon.

If, according to Cicero, glory plays an undeniable role in the psychology
of the individual, it is also at the heart of the psychology of the collectivity
from which it emanates:

> The highest, truest glory depends upon the following three things: the affec-
> tion, the confidence, and the mingled admiration and esteem of the people.
> Such sentiments [. . .] are awakened in the masses in the same way as in
> individuals.[12]

Benevolence, or even that which is perceived as the intent to be benevolent,
elicits the goodwill of the crowd. Justice and prudence inspire confidence.
Greatness and superiority elicit admiration. Men are made in such a way that
nature "constrains" them to love those in whom they see those virtues, because they are in the common interest. But what the multitude perceives as a
virtue is above all a matter of reputation (*opinio libertatis, beneficientae, justi-
tiae*, etc.). And so one can manipulate the crowd "by pretense, by empty show,
by hypocritical talk and looks,"[13] by appearing virtuous when one is not. One
then acquires merely a false, ephemeral glory. Only good (*boni*) people are
able to distinguish between false glory and *vera Gloria*, to understand and
practice the aligning of both the real and the apparent with the *honestum*
and the *utile* in a chain of virtue in which the interests of the individual are
in harmony with those of the collectivity, a chain that extends to the interests
of all of humanity, to Nature, to Reason, and to God. True glory falls to the one
who carries out great deeds with a view to assuring this universal harmony.

Yet glory as Cicero conceives it remains fundamentally ambiguous: at
times he associates it with the multitudes, at others only with those who are

"good."[14] And if Cicero manages to define a glory that isn't military but "republican," he is unable to resolve the problem raised by the psychology of the great man: the desire to conquer, the *cupiditas gloriae*. In the eighteenth century Montesquieu summed this tension up well when, in the *Considérations sur les causes de la grandeur des Romains et de leur décadence,* he borrows from Sallust to develop a comparison between Cicero and Cato:

> I believe that if Cato had focused on the Republic, he would have given things a completely different turn. Cicero was well equipped to play a secondary role, but incapable of playing the leading role: he was quite intelligent, but had an often ordinary soul. For Cicero, virtue was an accessory; for Cato, it was glory; Cicero always saw himself first; Cato always forgot himself. Cato wanted to save the Republic for its own sake; Cicero, to boast about it.

> Je crois que, si Caton s'était réservé pour la République, il aurait donné aux choses un tout autre tour. Cicéron, avec des parties admirables pour un second rôle, était incapable du premier: il avait un beau génie, mais une âme souvent commune. L'accessoire, chez Cicéron, c'était la vertu; chez Caton, c'était la gloire; Cicéron se voyait toujours le premier; Caton s'oubliait toujours. Celui-ci voulait sauver la République pour elle-même; celui-là, pour s'en vanter.[15]

Paradoxically, to act in the name of the collectivity with no thought for oneself is the best way of asserting one's true value, the surest path to true glory; it is more naturally a consequence of one's deeds and actions than a goal to be sought for itself. In such a perspective and in conformity with Stoic thought, intent plays a fundamental role; but so does the state of the Republic, because the virtue of the individual and the virtue of the collectivity must be aligned. Only then does glory provide both immediate recompense and survival in posterity.

Cicero himself seems to incarnate the disconnect that threatened the ideal of glory, for rarely does one see such evidence of an appetite for glory alongside a critique of the dangers of that kind of appetite, especially in Rome as it had become. Cicero, like Sallust, constantly returns to the essential question: what is glory worth in a Republic prey to decadence, corruption, the worst self-serving interests? The same question was raised continually throughout the eighteenth century. For Cicero, as for Sallust, glory acquired in such a context can only be false — unless it is attained through philosophical contemplation. The "Platonic" solution that Cicero suggests, depending on the circumstances, incorporates both the ideal of origins — the *mos majorum* — and that of "the fortunate survival in an incorruptible beyond."[16]

The question of glory is thus at the crossroads of two radically different orientations: self-assertion on the one hand, and self-abnegation on the other. In the very surpassing of oneself that glory entails, there is always the implication of a movement beyond the self, whether beyond one's clan (Latin *gens*), the community as a whole, or further spheres. When immanence is not enough, there remains the path of transcendence. The emulation of past models leads to an appeal to future generations: by aiming to be worthy of one's predecessors and ancestors, one also seeks one's own survival in the memory of others to come, arriving thus at what Étienne Tiffou so aptly characterizes as "a sort of transcendence in immanence."[17] It was Sallust who, observing the loss of values in Rome, developed the important notion of glory as an ascesis of which the historian and posterity would become the arbiters.

The Courage of the Warrior and of the Christian: Saint Ambrose

Contemplating the Roman ideal of glory, whose most "transcendent" formulation remained anchored in the immanence of an earthly future, Christian thinkers attempted to construct an image of transcendence that was both more radical and more reassuring. To assert that the advent of Christianity upset the ideal of earthly glory is a commonplace. But we may not have fully recognized all that the Church Fathers did to transmit the heritage of Greco-Roman glory to Christian culture — within which the Carolingian and Holy Roman Empires as well as later national monarchies blossomed — and, in doing so, paradoxically established an important place for that heritage in the functioning of the earthly City.

To understand the resulting amalgam, Saint Ambrose's *De officiis* is particularly useful. The bishop of Milan (374–397), who was Saint Augustine's teacher, borrowed Cicero's matrix to reflect on morality and the duties of a Christian. Ambrose, whose father was the praetorian prefect of Gaul, raises the question of glory in the context of Christian courage:

> Let us at this point move on to deal with courage. Since it belongs higher
> up the scale, as it were, than all the other virtues, courage gets divided into
> two types: one has to do with the business of war, the other with ordinary
> domestic life. But a taste for the affairs of war appears to be quite alien to
> the kind of duty which concerns us now, for our interest is in the duty of the
> soul rather than the body, and our activity has to do not with arms but with

the business of peace. *All the same*, it has to be said that our ancestors, men like Joshua son of Nun, or Jerubbaal, or Samson, or David, won great glory in the affairs of war as well.[18]

His "all the same," which enables Ambrose to reintroduce a warrior glory that he had just dismissed, is emblematic of the entire approach of this Church Father: his description of the courage of the soul of the true "athlete of Christ" is shaped in terms of courage in battle.[19] Indeed, the very structure of Ambrose's *De officiis* can be seen as a struggle between classical and biblical *exempla*, in which the biblical always wins in terms of valor, values, and precedence. For, as Ambrose saw it, Tullius, Panaetius, and even Aristotle derived their truths from the lessons of the Bible. Among the heroes of the Ambrosian pantheon, the exemplary and heroic King David, like Moses, doesn't hesitate in his waning years to wage battle against the "Titans"—the bishop's term for Philistines—putting himself "right in the thick of it, fighting like a true warrior amidst the fierce columns, eager for glory, and quite unconcerned for his own safety."[20] Here, the grandeur of the Bible story is conveyed within a framework and a language marked by the Roman ideal of glory.

Ambrose expands on the notion of courage, which manifests itself in the inner struggle to conquer oneself, in a disdain for external goods—especially money, because "greed is the root of all evils"[21]—and in the search for the *honestum*. Quickly, however, he returns to courage in war: "but it may be that glory won in war holds some people so enthralled that they imagine courage cannot be found anywhere except in battle; they may feel that I have gone off on this last track simply because that particular quality was missing in our people."[22] As proof of the contrary, the bishop evokes the military exploits of "our ancestors" Joshua, Gideon, and above all Judas Macabee, whose tale he embellishes, the better to stress "strength of soul" and its effects. Thus the soldier Elzear sacrifices himself by throwing himself under the enemy king's elephant to kill the fearsome animal. According to Ambrose, that heroic act impresses the enemy, who flees, whereas in the story of the book of the Macabees, it is the Jews who run away, intimidated by the royal forces. Confronting the army of Demetrius, Judas Macabee advises his soldiers "to die with glory rather than flee and bring shame on themselves."[23] These examples lead Ambrose to a conclusion that inscribes them in a Ciceronian problematic: courage in war "offers no small expression of what it means to act in a way that is honorable and seemly, for it prefers death to slavery and disgrace."[24] The author then moves on to the courage of martyrs, so close to that of warriors, which has its own dangers, notably the "excessive desire for glory." The ambiguity of the way in which Ambrose deals with glory is revealed in his warning to those who, through excessive desire and lack of restraint, seek martyrdom by provoking the powers that be, thereby endangering the lives of others. As regards courage, the concept of glory enables Ambrose to perform now in the arena of Roman values, now in terms of Christian values. In this way, heroes of the faith are able, so to speak, to beat the Romans on their own turf while enjoying the rewards of the glory of God.

It is only much later, when he defines moral beauty (*honestum*) by associating a happy life (*vita beata*) with an eternal life (*vita aeterna*), that Ambrose abandons the ambiguity from which he has derived so much benefit:

> A person's life is indeed happy if, instead of being measured by the judgments of other people, he is assessed by his own inner convictions—if he is, as it were, his own judge. Such a life does not court popular opinion as some kind of reward, nor is it afraid of it as a punishment. And so it is that the less it pursues glory, the more it rises above it. In fact, those who go after glory find that the reward it brings in the present is only a shadow of the glory to come, and it is an obstacle to eternal life, as it is written in the gospel: "Verily I say unto you, They have their reward."[25]

Here the idea of autonomy is reformulated within the context of faith, because one is one's own judge in function of an ideal of *honestum* and of *utile* established not by philosophers but by Scripture. A happy life is maintained with a view toward eternal life,[26] and any human glory can only be false glory, an obstacle to future salvation. Ambrose uses this argument to assert the duty of humility in the exercise of Christian virtues. Whether acting with generosity or mercy, or in the practice of fasting, any ostentation must be carefully avoided. However, when he speaks of a man's duties as a member of the earthly City, glory returns—as does war. Here

> our natural instinct, after all, prompts us to be ever-vigilant in the interests of everyone around us, to put up with real troubles for them, and to go to great lengths to serve them. And *we all think it a glorious thing* if an individual is prepared to face personal dangers in order to guarantee peace for all.[27]

Thus for Ambrose, the very plasticity of the notion of glory enables a certain fusion of Stoicism and Christianity, the courage of the warrior and that of the Christian, glory and humility. Ciceronian Stoicism lends itself well to the parallel that Ambrose establishes between the moral duties of clerics and the moral duties of politicians, so as better to establish the legitimacy of Christianity in the very heart of the Roman Empire.

The Romans on the Verge of Human Greatness: Saint Augustine

This happy cohabitation no longer exists when Augustine picks up his pen to defend Christianity against the accusation of having contributed to the collapse of the Empire. Cicero remains very present in his writing, as does Sallust. Rather than blending values, Augustine establishes his well-known distinction between the heavenly City and the earthly City. Dealing with the latter, in book 5 of *The City of God*, Augustine raises the question of the "ancient virtues of the Romans." Asserting the role of divine providence in history, he takes aim at Cicero, who had defended the free will of man and denied any sort of determinism imposed by destiny. While agreeing with Cicero that it is not destiny that determines man, Augustine undertakes to reconcile free will—which allows man to *choose* to turn away from God—with divine prescience. For Augustine, God's providence is universal and encompasses everything under its laws. Having taken this position, however, Augustine can't avoid explaining why God would have allowed a pagan Rome to achieve its extraordinary domination of the world. He affirms that, after the rise of the kingdoms of the East, God wanted a *translatio imperii* toward the Western Empire, with the aim of "overcoming the grave evils which had afflicted many other nations."[28]

Inviting us to "consider the virtues of the Romans and the reason why the true God [. . .] deigned to help them in enlarging their empire," the bishop of Hippo emphasizes the effectiveness of glory; he asserts that "it was therefore this avidity for praise and passion for glory that accomplished so many wondrous things: things which were doubtless praiseworthy and glorious in the estimation of men."[29] Citing Virgil, Horace, Cicero, and above all Sallust, the former professor of rhetoric explores in detail the economy of glory that enabled the Romans to practice virtue.[30]

> So also, the Romans held their own private interests in low esteem for the sake of the common good [*pro re communi*], that is, for the commonwealth [*hoc est re publica*]. For the sake of its treasury they resisted avarice, and they took counsel for the good of their fatherland with unfettered minds; nor were they guilty of any offence against its laws, or of any unwholesome desires. By all these arts did they seek honour and power and glory, as by a true

way. They were honoured among almost all the nations; they imposed the laws of their empire upon many races; and they are glorious among almost all peoples to this day, in literature and history. They have no reason to complain of the justice of the highest and true God: "They have their reward."[31]

In Augustinian eschatology, Rome appears as a borderline case, providing Augustine with an opportunity to explore the ideal of human greatness and to ponder the heroism of Christian humility in relation to the heroic abnegation that enabled the Romans to dominate the world. Through the ascesis of glory, the Romans were able to scorn many pleasures, endure much suffering, stifle many passions; they practiced virtue of a sort. And, in a sense, the Romans were paid with their own currency. They sought glory and obtained it. Through glory, and thanks to it, they succeeded in dominating the world. But it was not only out of a spirit of justice,

> it was not only for the sake of rendering due reward to the citizens of Rome that her empire and glory were so greatly extended in the sight of men. This was done also for the advantage of the citizens of the eternal City during their pilgrimage here. It was done so that they might diligently and soberly contemplate such examples, and so see how great a love they owe to their supernal fatherland for the sake of life eternal, if an earthly city was so greatly loved by its citizens for the sake of merely human glory.[32]

Augustine goes on to cite lines from Virgil on the famous example of Lucius Junius Brutus, who condemned his two sons to death for their role in a plot against the Republic: "But love of country drove him, and the immense love of praise [*laudumque immensa cupido*]"; he concludes once again that "these, then, are the two things which drove the Romans to perform such wondrous deeds: love of liberty, and the desire for human praise."[33] The devotion shown by the Romans to their earthly City is thus an example of the devotion that each Christian should show to the heavenly City. The power of the Christian ideal is asserted through its martyrs, who surpass Roman heroes not so much by their numbers as by their virtue.[34] What more did they want, those children of the greatest of earthly Cities, than some sort of afterlife? "What else were they to love, then, but glory, by which they sought to find even after death a kind of life in the mouths of those who praised them."[35] The Romans' error was precisely in seeking transcendence in immanence.

If Augustine concentrates so heavily on glory, it is because glory gives the measure of what man is capable of, of the greatest he can do without God.

But that collective greatness does not end in man's autonomy with regard to the collectivity; quite the opposite, because it is only a matter of the power of opinion: "That glory which the Romans so ardently desired to possess is the judgment of men thinking well of other men."[36] The glory that Christianity proposes allows the ideal of autonomy — *in relation to the earthly world*—to be achieved. For the Christian is no more dependent on others than on the state of affairs in the earthly City. Indeed, virtue is now measured only in relation to one's conscience. To support this assertion, Augustine goes from the accounts of pagan historians to the authority of Saint Paul's epistles: "For our rejoicing is this, the testimony of our conscience" (II Cor 1:12). "But let every man prove his own work, and then shall he have rejoicing in himself alone, and not in another" (Gal. 6:4).[37] We know what follows: freed from the opinion of others, bound to the only true glory, that of God, one can finally practice true virtue and love men benevolently without needing them to confirm one's own value.

Nevertheless, for Augustine the love of earthly glory cannot be eradicated; in the asymmetrical relationship that he establishes between the two Cities,[38] he grants a privileged place to that passion precisely because it stifles other passions leading to greater vices. Thus earthly glory can function as a tool for the wise government of the earthly City. "Certainly," writes the bishop of Hippo in a passage that helps explain all the power that the *topos* of glory would have for eighteenth-century thinkers,

> there are, then, those who bridle their baser desires by means of the desire for human praise and glory, and not with the faith of godliness and the love of intelligible beauty given by the Holy Spirit. These are not, therefore, yet holy; they are only less vile. Cicero himself was not able to conceal this fact in those books which he wrote called *De republica*. For, having spoken of the education of the city's ruler, who ought, he says, *to be nourished on glory*, he goes on to add that the men of old did many wonderful and famous deeds because of their desire for glory.[39]

In the context of the earthly City, Augustine recognizes the opposition between the *vera gloria*, which represents a surpassing of self in the name of the collectivity, and false glory, which serves only personal interests. The common point between the love of "true" earthly glory and the love of heavenly glory lies in self-denying behavior. One might think of two points in an asymptotic relationship in which perfection would imply total self-denial. And it is through self-denial that a heroism of humility, submission, and

resignation is conceivable, of which the martyr represents only the most extreme point. Images of this kind encouraged the development throughout the
Middle Ages of a language of war within the context of faith.[40] As Augustine
sees it, Rome, a borderline example of the greatness of man without God, is
one stage in the movement toward the heavenly City.

Between Glory and Vainglory: Saint Thomas Aquinas

It was only in the thirteenth century, with the Aristotelianism of Thomas
Aquinas, that the notion of man's grandeur recovered its legitimacy and man
could aspire to conquer the earthly world through reason. Here the portrait
of the magnanimous "great soul" regained its place of honor; and glory, if
not an end in itself, could be considered useful. True beatitude was found
in participation in the glory of God, but there was also a place for some kind
of human fulfillment. Just as God did not seek his own glory for himself but
for us, humans could commendably desire their own glory in the service of
others, as said in the gospel: "Let your light so shine before men, that they
may see your good works, and glorify your Father who is in heaven" (Matt.
5:16).[41] Early on, Saint Thomas defines glory as resulting from the honor and
the praise bestowed by the many:

> Glory means a kind of radiance, so that in Augustine's words *being the recipi-
> ent of glory is the same as being radiant with light*. Now radiance implies both
> a certain beauty and its manifestation. So the term *glory* strictly connotes
> the manifestation by someone of a thing which in our eyes seems beautiful,
> whether it is a physical or spiritual good. Now what is unquestionably bright
> can be seen by many, even by people far away; so strictly speaking the term
> "glory" means that the good of a person comes to the notice and approval of
> many people. As Livy says, *one cannot win glory from one single person*.[42]

But Thomas then adds that glory can also result from the knowledge of a small
number, "or by oneself alone, provided that one's own good is considered
praiseworthy." Here again we discover a Christian resolution of the tensions
at work in Aristotle's description of the magnanimous man. In this scenario,
autonomy and truth coincide; glory can be the inner testimony of individual
conscience — a fully interior glory, so to speak. This strange insistence on
the possibility of glory as only a form of self-awareness can be understood in
relation to the role that Thomas reserves for glory in general. For it testifies

to the good and the perfection of which man is capable. What man seeks is perfection, not glory. And yet, one may also desire glory:

> it can be sought in so far as it has a useful purpose. This may be the glorification of God by men, or improvement in men as a result of the good which they recognize in another; or a man may recognize his own good qualities as a result of the laudatory testimony of others, and therefore eagerly persist in them and advance to higher things.[43]

Here we find the three ways in which glory can be useful: for God, for others, for oneself. Thomas removes it from the system of finalities and anchors it within the logic of means for human perfectibility. It retains its spectacular aspect, but that aspect is related more closely to monstrance than to staging. Significantly, Thomas does not evoke glory within the context of war and does not use the warrior metaphor to explain it. Related as it is to perfection and excellence, the notion of glory becomes more abstract, encompassing a wide range of activities. Since it must always be useful, it is never an end in itself, which removes it from the realm of reward and connects it to a behavior of disinterestedness born of charity. In this sense, the glory of men must function like that of God: "God seeks his own glory not for himself but for us. In the same way a man can commendably seek his own glory for the benefit of others."[44] The parallel to the glory of God reveals the effective power that Thomas attributes to the glory of men:

> Now amongst the goods by which a person attains outstanding distinction, glory appears to be especially effective, in so far as it implies the revelation of his goodness, for what is good is naturally loved and esteemed by all. So just as a man, by the glory which God confers, achieves outstanding distinction in the things that are God's, so too by human glory he achieves pre-eminence in human affairs. Hence because glory is closely related to pre-eminence, which men desire most of all, it logically follows that it is greatly desirable and that many vices arise from a disordered desire for it. Thus vainglory is a capital sin.[45]

In short, vainglory, born of pride, inverses values. In the unbridled desire for glory seen as an end in itself, the end is no longer the good; it is glory itself. The evils engendered by vainglory are many: discord, a thirst for novelty, disobedience, dispute, stubbornness, hypocrisy. Instead of opening oneself up to progress and perfection, whose only limits are those imposed by man, the economy of vainglory becomes a zero-sum game, as illustrated by the mechanisms of envy, which aims above all for the benefits associated with glory. "Envy is about another's glory insofar as it diminishes the glory a man desires to have."[46] And we envy only those to whom we are near. We don't seek to surpass in glory those who are far superior: the common man does not envy the king. Rather, society reveals itself to be a cascade of proximate envies. But for Thomas, as for so many others, the appetite for vainglory can lead to virtuous actions, even if the one who carries them out cannot be described as virtuous. This is probably why Thomas classifies vainglory among the major vices rather than among mortal vices. Between the legitimate pleasure in one's own glory and an unbridled appetite, everything becomes a matter of degree, and the Middle Ages was constantly concerned with striking a happy medium (*mesura*).

While Christianity tried to redefine glory by connecting it to transcendent and absolute truth, it was unable to resolve the tensions inherent in the notion of glory. Yet it was these insurmountable tensions themselves that endowed the ideal of glory with all its polyvalence, for they enabled the happy medium to be placed in a space defined in relation to two axes: one extending from the individual to the family, to the collectivity, and on to universal truth; the other evolving along a line of human activities — from those of the warrior at one extreme, to those of the wise man or the cleric at the other. The space was that of an ideology of distinction: individual, rank, City, leader, God were all possible seats of glory. A space sufficiently vast to accommodate the inversions of mentalities: from resignation and escape from the world, to optimism in man's ability to grasp that world, to thrive in it and give it meaning. A space where self-denial and self-affirmation were in perpetual contact, where the virtuous heroism of true glory was always shadowed by its doubles: egotistical self-interest and false glory. This opposition between true and false glory opened up a critical distance within the same discourse, giving it a powerful dynamism of its own. For glory was to be constantly redefined, and ceaselessly reconstructed.

Pierre Mignard, *Louis XIV on Horseback, Crowned by Victory, before Namur* (1692).
Oil on canvas. 359 × 260 cm. (MV2032). Châteaux de Versailles et de Trianon,
Versailles, France. Photograph © RMN-Grand Palais / Art Resource, New York.

CHAPTER 2

Kings, Warriors, Poets

On the Cusp of Modernity

From Charlemagne to Saint Louis

Medieval Europe was steeped in the complex configuration of glory inherited from the Ancients, teeming with ambiguities. We know that Saint Augustine's *City of God* was very important for Charlemagne, whom Einhard, for his part, felt compelled to portray with the Suetoninan hues of a thirteenth Caesar. The fusion of Frankish and Gallo-Roman mores provided particularly fertile soil for the ideology of glory. The crowning of Charlemagne and the creation of the Western Empire achieved a new form of *translatio imperii*, but the authority and power tenuously shared by the Church and the State, by the papacy and the monarchy, increasingly necessitated a continuous appeal to a legitimizing glory. It was within this context that the individualism of the feudal system was born and flourished, a system that constantly sought to achieve balance within an economy of glory. Jacques Le Goff has well summed up the diversity of the possible evolutions of a system that could be regarded as "a stimulus for the protection of the individual (the English case) or as an obstacle to this protection that favored a hierarchical system in which equality only existed in the heart of the privileged upper echelon of society (the French case)."[1] In the French case, this balance might be achieved at any given point between excessive domination by the privileged class, in which the royal house was only one among others, and an extreme assertion of monarchical power.

In many respects the *chansons de geste* may be understood as a portrayal of the tensions inherent in this mode of self-conception. While the word "glory" was reserved for God, there were terms to express earthly "glory": *honor, los, renom, renommée*.[2] In one of the most famous scenes in the *Chanson de Roland*—a masterpiece of the ideology of feudal monarchy, developed in the context of Augustinian theocentrism[3]—the wise Olivier turns toward the gallant Roland and implores him to sound his horn in order to alert Charlemagne, so he will come to their aid:

> Answers Rollanz: "A fool I should be found;
> In France the Douce would perish my renown.
>
> [. . .] Never, by God, I say,
> For my misdeed shall kinsmen hear the blame,
> Nor France the Douce fall into evil fame!
>
> Roland répond: "Ce serait une folie!
> En douce France j'en perdrais ma gloire
> [*En dulce France en perdreie mon los*]
>
> [. . .] Ne plaise à Notre Seigneur
> Que mes parents, par ma faute, soient blâmés
> Et que la douce France soit déshonorée!
> [*Ne France dulce ja cheet en viltet!*][4]

Three times Roland refuses to follow the good advice of his friend and comrade-in-arms. "Never shall my kin be reproached," he cries, after encouraging Olivier to fight well, so that "no evil song shall e'er be sung or said."[5] This scene exemplifies both the forceful allure and the dangers of vassalic glory, a profoundly individual value but linked firmly, in a sometimes contradictory chain of logic, to the family, to the collectivity France, to the king, and to heaven. And, as we know, it is the heavenly link to the glory of God that makes possible—in the face of those valiant infidels the Saracens—the fragile balance that the *Chanson de Roland* seeks to herald. "Pagans are wrong; Christians are right" ("Paien unt tort e chrestiens unt dreit"), according to Roland's famous saying in line 1015. Indeed, it was through the heroic epic of the Crusades that the West subbornly sought peace for itself: "futile but necessary gestures," as Alphonse Dupront called them,[6] an age-old safety valve that enabled princes and knights of Christendom to maintain a certain balance by seeing themselves as military heroes of Christian peace. Through the ideology of the Crusades, those wars in the Holy Land and elsewhere, the feudal barons expressed themselves—and were absolved. The same was true for royalty. The Crusades' imaginary projected itself backwards in time to an originary moment, that of the emperor-king Charlemagne. Saint Louis promoted the double ideal of sovereignty and holiness and, in doing so, uniquely reinforced monarchical power while forcefully promoting the heroism of Christian abnegation through the Crusades themselves.[7] These two pillars of royal mythology instituted at the core of French identity a universalist drive and the paradox of a king who was supposed to incarnate both self-affirmation and self-denial.[8]

Although the kings of France stopped participating in Crusades, they did not stop believing in them—or using them. As Alphonse Dupront explains:

> A royal Crusade and a purging operation for the internal prosperity of the kingdom: there was no disparity between glory and usefulness. The Crusades had the extraordinary virtue of reconciling conflicting values. At once exaltation and social service, [they were] the work of Christian peace, the highest form of peace.[9]

The nobility, even at the end of the seventeenth century, continued to practice that "commerce of glory, with holy war as a source of values":[10] in 1685, against the wishes of Louis XIV, the princes of Conti and de Turenne placed themselves in the service of the emperor to battle the Turks in Hungary. More than a century later, Bonaparte's Egyptian expedition, which was in no sense a Crusade, nonetheless played on the multiple registers inherited from what had resonated as a basso continuo throughout the history of France. Like the Crusades, the expedition that Bonaparte led functioned as a kind of safety valve, beginning with his own security; for the young general was able to pursue both his own glory and that of a republican army—and to do so elsewhere—in a campaign that was as grandiose as it was futile. Chateaubriand understood better than anyone the deep historical resonances of this episode:

> Throughout time the French have dreamed of the East; knights paved the way for them; though they no longer had the faith that led them to deliver the Holy Sepulcher, they had the fearlessness of the crusaders, the belief in the kingdoms and beautiful sights described by the chroniclers and the

troubadours singing of Godfrey. The conquering soldiers in Italy had seen
a rich land for the taking, caravans to rob, horses, weapons, and seraglios
to conquer; writers had glimpsed the princess of Antioch, and scholars
added their reveries to the enthusiasm of the poets. At first even the *Travels
of Antenor* was taken for a learned study: they were going to penetrate into
mysterious Egypt, descend into the catacombs, explore the Pyramids, find
forgotten manuscripts, decipher hieroglyphics, and awaken Thermosiris.

[D]e tous les temps les Français ont rêvé l'Orient; la chevalerie leur en avait
tracé la route; s'ils n'avaient plus la foi qui les menait à la délivrance du saint
tombeau, ils avaient l'intrépidité des croisés, la croyance des royaumes et
des beautés qu'avaient créées, autour de Godefroi, les chroniqueurs et les
troubadours. Les soldats vainqueurs de l'Italie avaient vu un riche pays à
prendre, des caravanes à détrousser, des chevaux, des armes et des sérails
à conquérir; les romanciers avaient aperçu la princesse d'Antioche, et les
savants ajoutaient leurs songes à l'enthousiasme des poètes. Il n'y a pas
jusqu'au *Voyage d'Anténor*, qui ne passât au début pour une docte réalité:
on allait pénétrer la mystérieuse Égypte, descendre dans les catacombes,
fouiller les Pyramides, retrouver des manuscrits ignorés, déchiffrer des
hiéroglyphes et réveiller Thermosiris.[11]

The disappointment of the men who confronted the miserable conditions
they found there must have been fully as great as their earlier hopes. But
in an interpretation that is as surprising as it is significant, Chateaubriand
turns Napoleon into an instrument of history. Seen in this perspective, Napoleon's adventure in Egypt somehow represented the end of an age-old story
that had been edited and corrected by the Enlightenment. While in no respect
an expansion of faith, it was certainly an expansion of civilization. For in
spite of the appearance of failure, in spite of the injustice and suffering, "in
Egypt the French sowed the seeds of civilization that Mehmet then cultivated:
Bonaparte's glory increased; a ray of light shone into the darkness of Islam,
and barbarism was breached."[12] Chateaubriand understood perfectly the
role of the writers and scholars accompanying the soldier who was to become
emperor of France; it was the alliance of knowledge and power that Chateaubriand himself, at various moments in his life, also attempted to embody, one
that had accompanied the establishment of the French monarchy since the
reign of Charlemagne. Indeed, Einhard wrote his *Vie de Charlemagne* both to
preserve the memory of the great emperor and to repay, through writing, a
debt—that of having been "nourished" by him.[13]

Heroic Peoples: From the French to Cannibals

While medieval writers rarely spoke of their own glory, writers in the Renaissance and beyond became cognizant of their power as guardians of memory and arbiters of glory. "Behold the honor of the Prince, King, and Captain," wrote the poet and historian François de Belleforest in a passage that merits citation in its entirety, for it encompasses all the themes characterizing this relationship:

> Behold the honor of the Prince, King, and Captain to have a trumpet to sing his praises, which truly and without embellishment or flattery sounds the illustrious and heroic deeds of these valiant men. Alexander bemoaned not having a Homer, whose muse filled the universe with the glory of his deeds and the memory of his name in accordance with their merit and grandeur. Our Princes, I hope, will accomplish no less. But be it in brandishing their arms in the shadows of castles, in the midst of their dubious dealings, or in the paradise of their delights, they will befriend writers and men of knowledge, particularly of history, which will serve in the future as a painting and a lively portrait, expressing much more of them than the outward lines of their bodies, that is to say their virtues, prowess, and magnanimity. For the deed is but an outline of memory, whose trace is erased by a brief lapse of time; but when the writing is full of color and depth, fame takes its sound from it to shower posterity with the glory and valor if its predecessors.

> Et voilà l'honneur du Prince, Roy & Capitaine que d'avoir une trompette de ses loüanges, qui veritablement & sans fard ou flatterie publie les illustres & heroics faicts des homes vaillans. Ce fut la cause que Alexandre se plaignoit de n'avoir un Homere, la muse duquel fist resonner par l'univers la gloire de ses gestes & memoire de son nom, selon le merite & grandeur d'iceux. Moins n'en feront i'espere noz excellens Princes: ains avec le maniement des armes à l'ombre des pavillons, au milieu de la tourbe de leurs affaires, au paradis de leurs delices ils caresseront les lettres, & hommes addonnez au sçavoir: & principalement l'histoire laquelle servira à l'advenir d'un tableau & vive painture, qui pourra exprimer d'eux beaucoup plus que les lineaments exterieurs du corps: c'est asçavoir leurs vertus, proüesse & magnanimité. Car le faict n'est que le crayon de la memoire, lequel s'efface par un petit laps de temps, là où l'escrit est la couleur adaptée vivement, & laquelle s'enracine si bien que la fame prend d'elle le son avec lequel elle abreuve la posterité de la gloire & valeur des predecesseurs.[14]

From Machiavelli to Ronsard, the heroic ideal flowed through the entire Renaissance. Those who reflected on power, those who held it, and those who
sang its praises refashioned glory to attest to the rediscovered greatness of
man. The strength of this discovery made the first half of the sixteenth century
the golden age of the panegyric. The legendary Trojan origins of the French
made them an eminently epic people. Belleforest aptly describes the new state
of things: the poet, the historian, and also the artist enabled great men and
heroes to outlive themselves, as it were: it was through these new "clerics"
that one could attain transcendence in immanence; and this union of oppo-
sites would remain one of the constants of Napoleon's glory. In the name of
their new calling — to assure the survival of those they praised — these clerics
demanded in turn their share of glory. In France the specific nature of the relationship between these complicit and agonistic dyads — power and knowledge,
weapons and letters — played a major role in the reconfiguration of the ideal of
glory, adapting it to a society that would long continue to draw its legitimacy
from the past while turning increasingly toward the future. Beginning with
Francis I, the image of the kings of France was that of a Gallic Hercules, of
inspired heroic eloquence, who held crowds spellbound at his lips.[15] The path
that led from Fontainebleau to Versailles may not have been direct, but it was
illuminated with an ever brighter light by the earthly immortality that glory
offered. It was now up to the new learned class to maintain that brilliance with
their arts and letters, which continued to gain importance in a society where
civility and *politesse* were becoming basic and, indeed strategic values in the
maintenance of social harmony.[16] No longer in the service of the Church, these
new clerics set up shop, so to speak, on their own behalf and on that of their pa-
trons. Henceforth they worked for their own glory as much as for that of their
protectors. We know how adamantly the crown sought to "nourish" them, to
watch over them, to integrate them into the logic of the *raison d'État*.

   If Michel de Montaigne so resolutely sought to establish himself within
a different logic, it was largely because the discoveries of humanism and the
Renaissance liberated moral philosophy from the clutches of religion. He declared his independence and stood apart in this period of civil wars, which
ravaged the country in the sixteenth century. Wars of religion, of course, but
also, in fact, baronial revolts. If the gesture of withdrawing so visibly from the
scene at that time appeared somewhat heroic, the self that Montaigne constructed did not claim to be heroic, and his wisdom of "mediocrity" did not
feed on glory, neither that of the court nor that of war. Still, he often returned
to the question of glory. While his anthropology seems to have left little room

for it because it depended on vulgar opinion and was in no way the measure of a man's virtue, being merely a form of vanity, Montaigne nevertheless did admit that glory could be politically useful.

> However, if this false opinion is of service to the public in keeping men within their duty; if the people are thereby roused to virtue; if princes are touched by seeing the world bless the memory of Trajan and abominate that of Nero; if it moves them to see the name of that great gallows bird, once so frightful and so dreaded, so freely cursed and reviled by the first schoolboy who deals with it, let it grow boldly and let it be fostered among us as much as possible.

> Si toute-fois cette fauce opinion sert au public à contenir les hommes en leur devoir: si le peuple en est esveillé à la vertu: si les Princes sont touchez de voir le monde benir la memoire de Trajan et abominer celle de Neron: si cela les esmeut; de voir le nom de ce grand pendart, autres-fois si effroyable et si redoubté, maudit et outragé si librement par le premier escolier qui l'entreprend: qu'elle accroisse hardiment et qu'on la nourrisse entre nous le plus qu'on pourra.[17]

In fact, Montaigne — whose family could hardly be counted among the old nobility — remained nostalgic for a primary, original heroism, such as that which was manifested in wars among cannibals, those "savages" still living in a pure economy of glory:

> If their neighbors cross the mountains to attack them and win a victory, the gain of the victor is glory, and the advantage of having proved the master in valor and virtue; for apart from this they have no use for the goods of the vanquished, and they return to their own country where they lack neither anything necessary nor that great thing, the knowledge of how to enjoy their condition happily and be content with it.

> Si leurs voisins passent les montaignes pour les venir assaillir, et qu'ils emportent la victoire sur eux, l'acquest du victorieux, c'est la gloire, et l'avantage d'estre demeuré maistre en valeur et en vertu: car autrement ils n'ont que faire des biens des vaincus, et s'en retournent à leurs pays, où ils n'ont faute d'aucune chose necessaire, ny faute encore de cette grande partie, de sçavoir heureusement jouyr de leur condition et s'en contenter.[18]

Montaigne's cannibals perform actions with no other purpose than to display courage and virtue, actions whose only reward was glory. The ethnological perspective that the essayist brings to these "others" leads him to see the natural grandeur of savages in much the same light as that which the ancient Greeks drew upon even in defeat. To die rather than to be humiliated before the conqueror, to resist with pride until the end, such was the grandeur of both the savages of the New World and the Ancients. It was precisely this kind of grandeur that an overrated and fragmented civilization had lost. In his text on the social usefulness of glory (even though glory was only a "false opinion") as reward and incentive for virtue, as well as in his description of the glory that results in a refusal to submit, a refusal to admit to being conquered, Montaigne reveals a range of motivations and behavior that would characterize both the policies of the monarchy and the *Frondes* of the noblity.

The Return of the Magnanimous

And so in France, with the coming of the Renaissance, reflections on the hero that borrowed from the concepts of grandeur and glory proclaimed by the Ancients melded with traits inherited from the vassal-monarchic tradition. In *Héros et Orateurs* Marc Fumaroli reveals how much the development of this ideal owed to a Catholic Reformation marked by a rather optimistic vision of human nature, one that saw the tribulations of the profane hero as an edifying prefiguration of those of the saints.[19] The texts of antiquity found their place in the philosophy and rhetoric courses in the colleges of the Company of Jesus. This blending of Christian values, classical culture, and noble individualism inherited from feudal society is at the heart of the Cornelian hero.

Dedicated to Richelieu, Corneille's *Horace* illustrates this amalgam of values in which glory and virtue are aligned, and self-sacrifice, in the name of the collectivity, becomes the best means to assert one's true worth, the surest path to true glory. As Fumaroli notes, the young Horatius sacrifices "his singular individuality to transfer all his energy to the service of Rome: he became the *actor Romae*."[20] But the same ardor of the heroic impulse leads Horatius to commit — as King Tullus stresses — "an offense against nature" ("outrage à la nature") by killing his sister. Only a royal pardon permits an escape from heroic excess and the reestablishment of a balance between the values of the City and those of the family:

> You may live, Horatius, too great-hearted warrior:
> Your loyalty sets your glory above your crime.

Vis donc, Horace, vis, guerrier trop magnanime:
Ta vertu met ta gloire au-dessus de ton crime.[21]

This scene, within a context in which the earthly City has recovered its respectability, repeats the themes we saw at work in the *Chanson de Roland*, but inverts them. Horace asserts himself in his abnegation, but his identification with the City goes too far; without the intervention of the king he would break the chain of logic connecting the individual, the family, the collectivity, and the king. Even while protecting society, the hero endangers it.

In our own perspective, the politics of absolutism may be understood as aiming to overcome the problem posed by the heroic ideal when, in the name of grandeur and glory, the hero becomes a threat for the very society he is meant to defend. This can happen when he tries to assert his own grandeur, but also when he identifies completely with the values of the collectivity, as in the case of the young Horace. By making the prince the unique earthly source of glory, absolutism remains fundamentally anchored in an economy of glory, while seeking to put an end not only to the abuses of heroic individualism but also to those that would come out of an erroneous interpretation—that is, any interpretation other than that of the prince—of the needs and the values of the community. From this point of view, the only true glory consists in being recognized by the prince. In his *Honnête homme, ou l'art de plaire à la cour*, a work that was reprinted nine times between 1630 and 1681, Nicolas Faret underlines the importance of the "desire for glory" for the *honnête homme*—a polished, cultivated man worthy of respect—, and summarizes in very Aristotelian language its functioning in the absolutist context:

> The good of the Prince is not separated from that of the State, of which he is the soul and the heart, as well as the head: and the good of individuals is important in general only insofar as it is useful to the person of the Prince, from whom alone one expects all the good and all the ill that exist in the body of the Monarchy. That being veritable, and it also being true that each thing seeks an end, as at the peak of its perfection, what more worthy object may the wise courtesan have than the glory of serving his prince well, and of loving his interests more than his own. That is the only goal he should set himself.

> [L]e bien du Prince ne se separe point de celuy de l'Estat, dont il est l'ame & le cœur, aussi bien que la teste: et le bien des particuliers n'est considerable au general, qu'entant qu'il est utile à la personne du Prince, de qui seul on at-

tend tout le bien & tout le mal qui se respand dans le corps de la Monarchie.
Cela estant veritable, & estant vray aussi que chaque chose tend à une fin,
comme au comble de sa perfection quel plus digne objet peut avoir le sage
Courtisan, que la gloire de bien servir son prince, & d'aymer ses interests
plus que les siens propres. C'est là le seul but qu'il se doit proposer.[22]

An essential element of this configuration: the glory of the king of France is
the reflection of that of God. Much has been said about the two bodies of the
king,[23] but it was Louis XIV himself who, in his *Mémoires pour l'instruction du
dauphin* (Memoranda for the education of the heir apparent), best explains
the moral consequences of this doctrine of the "double" self of the king:

> If there is legitimate pride in our rank, there is a modesty and a humility
> that are no less praiseworthy [. . .]. But if I may explain my thinking to you,
> it seems that we must at the same time be humble for ourselves and proud
> for the position we occupy.

> S'il y a une fierté légitime en notre rang, il y a une modestie et une humilité
> qui ne sont pas moins louables [. . .]. Mais si je puis vous expliquer ma pen-
> sée, il me semble que nous devons en même temps être humbles pour nous
> mêmes et fiers pour la place que nous occupons.[24]

This is a vision that was perfectly compatible with the ideal of the profane
hero developed by the Catholic Reformation, where, as we have seen, outward grandeur and magnanimity were counterparts to inner humility.[25]

Within this context, and shortly after the publication of Vaugelas's celebrated translation of Quintus Curtius Rufus's biography of Alexander, *His-
toriae Alexandri Magni*,[26] Jean de Lartigue, in his *Politique des conquérants* of
1662, focuses on the author of *Nicomachean Ethics* to rethink the place of the
nobility in the light of the ambitions of Louis XIV. For it was Aristotle, "that
most excellent production of the mind and the most extraordinary of all time,
who certainly and principally trained Alexander, and who made him Master
of the World."[27] In a strange amalgam of Aristotelianism, Machiavelianism
("the greatness of a Prince strictly speaking is nothing other than the ruin or
the diminution of his neighbors"), Christianity, and the ideology of the nobility, Lartigue (in his "Dédicace au Roy" in the same work) aspires to enunciate,
"as if it were Aristotle himself who was addressing the audience," the politics
that should govern the entire reign of the conqueror, whose goal is to com-

mand those who must obey. The conqueror acts through virtue, the greatest, the most excellent of which aims for the public good. To that end, there is nothing better than war. Not only because it is a good means to maintain calm within a State, but also because, in itself, it is superior to peace. "For there is no condition or type of life that comes closer to a severe and perfect Virtue,"[28] that more strongly urges us to scorn the pleasures of the senses, to conquer the fear of death, and to demonstrate courage. The conquering prince would incite "people with heart" to embrace the profession of war through rewards and prizes, but also "by barring them access to the greatest titles by any other path than that of Weapons, as has been seen among Nations where domination and power have been sought."[29] This is the logic of the hereditary nobility: because these warriors have risked their lives "for the Nation and the service of the Republic through extraordinary virtue, we wanted to have their merit and their virtue be reborn in their Children."[30]

The conqueror steeps himself in philosophy that "inspires lofty thoughts in him through the general principles that are all the more excellent in that they are more universal, and more separated from useless particularities or inappropriate matter."[31] While it may be that interests constitute the ordinary bond linking civil society, they cannot serve to bind "the society of all men" that the conqueror aims for, that is, his "domination over the whole Earth." This domination, Lartigue affirms, is to be established by armed force and maintained also by reputation, that is to say, "the present opinion that nations have of the affairs of State, of its power, of its weapons, of its good conduct, and of the good disposition in which it finds itself today."[32] From this point of view, History becomes "the mouth of Renown," which publishes the deeds and actions of the conqueror, and "the eyes of all [past] wars," thus helping to determine strategies necessary for conquest. By publicly announcing the exploits of warriors, History

> serves as reward for fine actions by giving them glory and the advantage they deserve, which, being the first and the most worthy of all the rewards, is given to those who might not have received it through the generosity and magnificence of the Prince.

> sert de récompense aux belles actions en leur donnant la gloire & l'avantage qu'elles meritent, & qui estant la premiere et la plus digne de toutes les récompenses est donnée à ceux mesmes qui n'en auroient pas receü par la liberalité & magnificence du Prince.[33]

In this republic of warrior virtue, all policies based on wealth, the daughter of interests, leads only to corruption and dissipation:

> Man, having gotten outside of himself through love, and having thus established bonds to his family, from the family to the city, from cities to the Republic, it is necessary that his progress and consummation be achieved through love and friendship.

> L'homme estant sorty hors de luy-mesme par l'amour, & s'estant ainsi communiqué à sa famille, de la famille à la ville, des villes à la Republique, il faut que ses progrez & sa consommation se fasse par l'amour et l'amitié.[34]

A superior man, the great conqueror harnesses his subjects' love of country in order to impose a universal ideal. While informed by philosophy, he also draws that ideal directly from Nature, which in itself possesses "something immortal and divine." This ethico-religious truth, the foundation of all other truths, has "the universal consent of all Nations and all peoples, not only the most ancient and the most enlightened, but also the most savage and most stupid, the Philosophers and the vulgar have approved it in one voice."[35] The only truly virtuous politics is the politics of conquest that aims to impose an ideal of universal harmony through domination.

The second part of the work exists only in the form of manuscripts in two copies, addressed respectively to Colbert and to Le Tellier Louvois. Here Lartigue mobilizes a host of nobiliary values—often manifested in stands *against* mercantilism, *against* luxury with its dissipating and feminizing effects, *against* the uniformization of customs imposed by the court—in order to show how essential these values are in a France whose government is military in its very essence. Lartigue/Aristotle makes explicit the parallel between Alexander and Louis XIV. France, Latigue believes, needs a glorious undertaking:

> This is where my reasoning leads: and it is no longer the conquest of Flanders, nor of Upper Navarre, but the conquest of the universe that I hope for and that I propose to Your Majesty as a worthy object of his concerns.

> C'est où tendent mes raisonnemens: et ce n'est plus la conqueste de la Flandre, ny de la haut[e] Navarre; mais celle de l'univers que je souhaite et que je propose à Vostre Majesté, pour un digne objet de ses occupassions.[36]

While this project might seem excessive, it is not so, asserts Lartigue rediscovering his Aristotle, for it is "at the mean and in just proportion in relation to the qualities of the prince."[37] In short, the greatness of the undertaking corresponded to the greatness of the soul of Louis XIV. Thus the right to conquest was acquired in function of the qualities of King Louis, described above all as a heroic individual endowed with multiple virtues. In the execution of this project of universal monarchy, the nobility of the sword — like the warriors of Greece and Rome — would rediscover its entire raison d'être, as well as the virtue of self-sacrifice. In this vision of things, the glory of the king would not be established at the expense of the nobility. But it is a vision of a world without eschatology, characterized rather by a continual struggle, with moments of stability depending on domination imposed by a heroic leader.

Not surprisingly, the age of Louis XIV marked the beginning of the quarrel of the Ancients and the Moderns. For the Sun King it was not just a matter of placing himself on the level of ancient heroes — Hercules or Alexander, for example — in order to communicate the brilliance and the mystery of royal power, but also of imposing a glorious vision of modernity with its Christian and dynastic foundations, of which he himself represented the culminating point. In such a system, the only true glory that the greatest of subjects could enjoy was being recognized by the king, who himself was freed from, and above, any motivation of emulation. This logic soon led to the inability of the muses to express his glory, precisely because it was incomparable. The celebrated poet Boileau well translates this feeling into verse: "Great king, cease your conquering, or I will cease writing [. . .]. / I am stopping now, I am admiring, and I am silent."[38] In the *Mercure galant* an anonymous poet cries out: "One must, daring no more, watch, remain silent, and admire."[39] In 1686, yet another expresses the weakness of language confronted with the overpowering force of Louis XIV's deeds:

> To rightly sing the praises of an invincible hero,
> Under whom all other kings tremble,
> Charming for his friends, terrible for others,
> There is no voice strong enough.

> Pour chanter dignement un Héros invincible,
> Sous qui tremblent les autres rois,
> Charmant pour ses amis, pour les autres terrible,
> Il n'est point d'assez forte voix.[40]

The very same year—which also witnessed the erection of the famous equestrian statue of Louis XIV on the Place des Victoires—Guyonnet de Vertron published his *Nouveau Panthéon, ou le rapport des divinités du paganisme, des héros de l'Antiquité et des princes surnommés grands aux vertus et aux actions de Louis-le-Grand*.[41] In this work we find the same sentiments uttered in terms that already evoke the quarrel between the Ancients and the Moderns:[42]

> All of Antiquity proves unworthy of the task:
> To place our conqueror among all those heroes,
> Is not to raise him up, but to lower him;
> And if what I say of him may be said of others,
> Be it Hercules, Caesar, or the Great Alexander,
> The praise, I admit, is unworthy of him.

> Toute l'Antiquité s'offre mal à propos:
> Placer notre vainqueur parmi tous ces héros,
> Ce n'est pas l'élever, c'est le faire descendre;
> Et si ce que j'en dis se peut dire d'autrui,
> Soit Hercule, César, ou le Grand Alexandre,
> L'éloge, je l'avoue, est indigne de lui.[43]

In the presence of this modern hero, the only appropriate response is to be found in the silence of contemplation. While the *topos* of incomparable glory goes back at least to the time of Augustus, when Horace admiringly said of him: "From whom nothing's born that's greater than he is, and there's nothing that's like him or near him,"[44] the stakes are quite different in the period extending from Louis XIV to Napoleon—from the "pleasures of the enchanted isles" to the tribulations of the island of Saint Helena—because the culture of modernity is now seeking to affirm its superiority over that of antiquity.

The impossibility of singing the praises of the incomparable king no doubt created conditions in which "glory" could be—indeed needed to be—visualized; and in this sense, nothing could better serve the cause than the establishment at Versailles of a spectacular culture, with great festivals occurring in marvelous gardens, enabling people to see and to live in a state of enchantment, to evolve in a landscape infused with the fabulous. As early as 1664, the "pleasures of the enchanted isle" invited the court to live a fabulous modern history, that of Charlemagne revised and corrected by Ariosto. In that context, explains Jean-Pierre Néraudau, "the difficulties of expressing

the King are all the greater for literature in that carousels are now demonstrating that the visual is triumphing over the written." The *Grand Divertisse-
ment* of 1674, celebrating as it did the history of the reign of Louis XIV and
his military glory, also became a way of going beyond mythology, as Olivier
Chaline says, to "announce the overwhelming defeat of the Ancients."[45] But
all of this was only the first battle in a long war that would not end before the
early nineteenth century.

From the Brilliance of the Sun King to "Enlightened Self-Interest": A World without Glory

Absolutism represented a new point of equilibrium in the economy of glory.
Beginning in the 1680s, however, in the face of military defeats and growing,
ever more visible poverty, the model of Louis XIV, hero-king of modernity,
lost its power to enchant. The political undermining had begun much earlier,
in the wake of the *Fronde* and in a culture favoring civility and *politesse*, a
taste for *esprit*, language, and repartee. In that context, the dynamics inherent in the discursive economy of glory inspired a critical movement that Paul
Bénichou has described as "the demolition of the hero" and that borrowed
from a long tradition of false glory, acquired through *cupiditas gloriae* rather
than through true virtue. By assimilating a desire for glory with self-serving
interest—a form of *libido dominandi*—Jansenists and moralists who were
influenced by Jansenism sought to delegitimize the very idea of glory, for
"the desire for glory is of no more worth than greed."[46] The principal victim
of this amalgam was the heroic concept situated at the heart of the identity
that the nobility had created for itself in the course of the Middle Ages. And
it was precisely the tensions inherent in this heroic conception of self that La
Rochefoucauld, among others, would exploit. In the preface to the 1678 edition of his *Maximes*, the moralist specifies that when he refers to *interest*, he
is not talking about an "interest in profit" ("intérêt de bien") but an "interest
in honor or glory" ("intérêt d'honneur ou de gloire").[47] The destruction of the
hero involves attributing a *moral* significance to a metaphysical or structural
egotism, the mere fact of being onself, of having an *ego*. In short, there is
nothing noble in debased man; there exists no form of disinterestedness that
could be invoked to counter a reasoning attempting to reveal and denounce
the egotism inherent in any moral attitude.[48] In this vision of debased man,
even renunciation and resignation are only illusions enabling personal satisfaction.

If, on the one hand, the quest for glory is no better than greed because it is merely a masked form of self-interest, the opposite also becomes true: if everything is reduced to *amour-propre*, or self-love, the profit motive may be no worse than other forms of self-interest. Pierre Nicole describes the extent to which *amour-propre* resulting from the *libido dominandi* is "boundless and vast," "a tyrannical disposition," which causes a man to desire "all sorts of goods, honors, pleasures [. . .]. He becomes the center of everything: he wishes to dominate everything, and all creatures are there only to make him happy, to praise him, to admire him."[49] Nicole affirms that there are two fundamental axes of self interest: the *amour-propre de vanité*: being acclaimed, praised, honored by others; and the *amour-propre de commodité*, or comfort:[50] conserving one's life and enjoying "comforts" and "leisure." This same egotistical interest incites all of us to seek to maximize our goods and pleasures at the expense of others, but also teaches us that we need others and that we must thus find common ground. This is the famous *amour-propre éclairé*, or enlightened self-interest, tamed by reason producing the same effects as if one were acting out of Christian charity or love:

> One must consider that men, being devoid of charity through the disorder of sin, nevertheless remain full of needs, and are dependent upon each other in infinite ways. Greed has thus taken the place of charity to fulfill those needs, and it does so in a manner that is too little admired and cannot be attained by common charity.

> Il faut considérer que les hommes, étant vides de charité par le dérèglement du péché, demeurent néanmoins pleins de besoins, et sont dépendants les uns des autres dans une infinité de choses. La cupidité a donc pris la place de la charité pour remplir ces besoins, et elle le fait d'une manière que l'on n'admire pas assez, et où la charité commune ne peut atteindre.[51]

Here we recognize the same argument with regard to greed that we saw in Augustine with regard to glory:

> There are, then, those who bridle their baser desires by means of the desire for human praise and glory, and not with the faith of godliness and the love of intelligible beauty given by the Holy Spirit. These are not, therefore, yet holy; they are only less vile.[52]

The same psychological mechanism is at work on the two axes of *amour-propre*: vanity and comfort. If comfort naturally borrows the path of wealth, vanity borrows the path of glory. The same utilitarian paradigm enables the development of two types of "economies," whose means and consequences are radically different: commerce and glory. This fundamental distinction, established from the same schema of human psychology, became in the French context an essential element in the rise of a model of glory capable of overcoming the problems posed by the glory / false glory antinomy. For, as we will see, the more the opposition to absolutist politics relied on an appeal to public opinion, the more that opinion would be understood to be a source of legitimacy in itself, and the more the model of a glory based on public opinion would acquire ideological strength.[53]

In a period when the disastrous military policies pursued by Louis XIV aroused a barrage of criticism, his mercantilist policy — with its heroic ideal of a national autarchy — also came under fire. Seen as an aspect of absolutist Machiavelianism, mercantilism was denounced not only for its immorality but also for its ineffectiveness. In his *Détail de la France*, Pierre Le Pesant de Boisguilbert decries the ruin of France by a system of taxation that favored a privileged class — especially the *Fermiers généraux* — and inhibited consumption and the free circulation of goods, the largest amount of which came from the realm of agriculture. This criticism, in which one senses the influences of Stoicism as well as Jansenism, is of particular interest to us, because to my knowledge it is the first to develop the model of *amour-propre de commodité* to the extent of seeing the profit motive as a structural egotism that served the general interest:

> There is a reflection to be made that all business on earth, both wholesale and retail, and even agriculture, is governed only by the interest of entrepreneurs who have never dreamed of being of service or of obliging those with whom they deal for their business; and every innkeeper who sells wine to passersby has never intended to be of use to them, nor do the passersby who stop in his shop do so for fear that his provisions might be wasted. It is this reciprocal usefulness that creates the harmony of the world and the stability of States; each person dreams of furthering his own interests to the greatest extent possible and with the greatest facility possible.

> Il y a une réflexion à faire que tout le commerce de la terre, tant gros qu'en détail, et même l'agriculture, ne se gouverne que par l'intérêt des entrepreneurs qui n'ont jamais songé à rendre service ni à obliger ceux avec qui ils contractent pour leur commerce; et tout cabaretier qui vend du vin aux passants n'a jamais eu l'intention de leur être utile, ni les passants qui s'arrêtent

chez lui à faire voyage de crainte que ses provisions ne fussent perdues. C'est cette utilité réciproque qui fait l'harmonie du monde et le maintien des États; chacun songe à se procurer son intérêt au plus haut degré et avec [le] plus de facilité qu'il lui est possible.[54]

Boisguilbert's radical turn consisted in replacing moral criterion with that of general utility.[55] Freed from having to try to act virtuously, each person can act according to his own interests — an activity rooted in the very nature of man, as he is and not as one would like him to be — and, in so doing, serve the general well-being. The universal harmony that resulted is both providential and natural. The structural balance that characterizes this very perfect whole

> is destroyed as soon as the solidity of interest of an infinity of workers is in any way threatened in any one of its parts, for this becomes a contagion spreading to all the rest: so that this union, which forms the happiness and wealth of a State when it is but one body, once ground to dust by a continual disjunction [. . .] remains only as an infinity of parts good for nothing.

> périt aussitôt du moment que la solidité d'intérêt d'une infinité d'ouvriers reçoit la moindre atteinte en quelqu'une des parties, ce qui devient contagieux à tout le reste: en sorte que cette union, qui forme la félicité et la richesse d'un État tant qu'elle ne fait qu'une masse, étant mise en poussière par une disjonction continuelle [. . .] il ne résulte qu'une infinité des parties propres à rien.[56]

As we can see, we are very close here to the "invisible hand" that Adam Smith would describe decades later in *An Inquiry into the Nature and Causes of the Wealth of Nations* (1776).

During the time when Boisguilbert was writing in France to denounce the systemic abuses characterizing contemporary fiscal policies, a debate was unfolding in England around the creation of the Bank of England, which saw the desire for profit as belonging to the sphere of national glory. In a publication attributed to Sir Humphrey Mackworth and known under the title *England's Glory by a Royal Bank* (1694), the author declares that the nation is like a great family: "if a particular Person gets, the Nation gets."[57] In this schema, there is no opposition between individual interests and the general interest. As an emblem for a kingdom endowed with a central bank, the author cites the industrious bee — which, moreover, Napoleon would later put to use. "Methinks the Bees, by all possible means of preserving their King, because their very Being depends upon him, are a perfect Emblem of a People honouring such a rich Prince."[58] The American historian Steven Pincus argues that the establishment of the Bank of England was a key element in a certain publicity and set of practices based on the collaboration of merchants and manufacturers, as well as on an exchange of information that allowed the public to have confidence in the bank, to deposit their money there, and to accept its notes.[59]

The creation of the Bank of England served as a catalyst in that country for the formulation of a discourse that was supported by a range of practices. By integrating a general desire for profit and national glory, this discourse was founded on the principle of a basic compatibility between the interests of each person and the solidarity of all. It was only ten years after the creation of the national bank that Mandeville, in his famous satire, borrowed the bee metaphor to exploit brilliantly the paradox of individual vices that served the general interest ("private vices, public good"). In France, on the other hand, the formulation of structural harmony based on the profit motive was developed in quite another context. Instead of taking the form of an appeal to national solidarity around a project in which, in principle, everyone could participate, and which would profit everyone, Boisguilbert's vision developed in the framework of a moral and political critique of a society fractured by a division between a "nation" of the privileged and "an unknown country of merchants and workers."[60] Boisguilbert denounces a society of *politesse*, in which the essential "consists of continually disguising one's true feelings, betraying one's awareness of truth, calling white black, and black white, when currying favor at court, so as to contribute to one's fortune."[61] A fortune which, according to the very rules of that society of *politesse*, fed only "an extraordinary magnificence," so that people could keep up appearances. *Politesse*, that "perpetual insincerity" ("mauvaise foi perpétuelle"), allowed the real truth of the kingdom, that is, its economic ruin, to remain hidden. "It is *politesse* alone that has produced all the disorder, that eliminates the line of communication that must exist between all the members of a State."[62] Whereas, in the land of merchants and workers, people agree to buy and sell on the basis of generalized, recognized, and tacitly accepted individual interests,

> what sort of trade and what wealth might a merchant acquire who would
> expect only lies from his correspondents and would receive that sort of
> information from them, and if, when he had sent merchandise to a distant

land that could not be sold there, they did not immediately write to him that the goods were no longer bought there, and that he should get rid of what was in his stores.

Quelle sorte de commerce et quelle richesse pourrait acquérir un marchand qui ne manderait que des mensonges à ses correspondants et qui recevrait d'eux des avis de pareille nature, et si, lorsqu'il a envoyé de la marchandise dans un pays éloigné qui ne s'y est pu vendre, on ne lui écrivait pas aussitôt qu'il n'en achetât plus sur le lieu, et qu'il se défît même de celle qu'il pourrait avoir dans ses magasins.[63]

"Polite" people disguise the misfortune of that "unknown land of merchants and workers," disseminating only "impostures born of the interest" they have in maintaining their position and their fortune.[64] Instead of facilitating communication and the free circulation of goods, they create barriers to truth, just as they do to wealth. Boisguilbert positions himself as ambassador and interpreter for the people of that unknown land of workers and merchants, with the intention of speaking "a very new language" and announcing that

nature, or Providence, alone can make us observe this justice, provided once again that no one other than them be involved, and this is how they manage it. They first establish in transactions of all kinds an equal need to sell and to buy, so that *the desire for profit alone is the soul of all transactions*, both for the seller and the buyer; it is with the help of this equilibrium and balance that each person is equally forced to see reason and to submit to it.

[la] nature donc, ou la Providence, peuvent seules faire observer cette justice, pourvu encore une fois que qui que ce soit d'autre qu'elles ne s'en mêle, et voici comme elles s'en acquittent. Elles établissent d'abord une égale nécessité de vendre et d'acheter dans toutes sortes de trafics, de façon que *le seul désir de profit soit l'âme de tous les marchés*, tant dans le vendeur que dans l'acheteur; c'est à l'aide de cet équilibre et de cette balance que l'un et l'autre sont également forcés d'entendre raison et de s'y [sou]mettre.[65]

There is no exception to this truth, even in the name of virtue or Christian charity; "the desire for profit" alone becomes the soul of a system that is self-regulating and upon which depends the well-being of the people as well as of the crown, whose principal duty becomes that of aligning its policies with the principles of nature and Providence.

From *Amour-propre* to Pure Love and Disinterestedness

If Boisguilbert's criticism resonated in his time — and earned him exile in Auvergne[66]—it gave too much play to the spirit of commerce, which then becomes, so to speak, the soul of society. His criticism profoundly questioned the very premises of the French society of *politesse*, whether that of the court or of the aristocracy. Denouncing a moral vice, Boisguilbert proposed a remedy that would imply a societal revolution, but the remedy consisted in setting the moral question aside. In this kind of "utilitarianism," glory became a superfluous question because it was in some way synonymous with wealth. By contrast, in the reasoning centered on the *amour-propre* of vanity, questions of glory and heroic morality maintained their relevance.

Thus, given the destruction of the hero on the one hand and the monopolization of the concept by the monarchy on the other, we might be led to conclude that the ideal of glory had lost its power, that it was no longer relevant. Yet, nothing could be further from the truth; for, there soon emerges, from a whole cluster of immemorial values, two currents of thought that would prove to be quite compatible with the critical thinking of the Enlightenment and would have immense importance for the establishment of the Napoleonic economy of glory. One of these currents aimed resolutely to detach glory and heroism from a morality of intention and to integrate them into a "structural" vision of the collectivity seen as a finality unto itself. The other involved a reflection on the individual, which envisioned a behavior and a psychology of true disinterestedness: it took aim, so to speak, at the pessimistic view of extreme corruption, and rejected the vicious cycle that reduced every moral attitude to a form of self-interest. The vision of an economy of glory that would take hold in the eighteenth century represented the fusion of those two currents. In many respects, this fusion occurred under the pressure imposed by the power of the rival model, the one predicated on the *amour-propre* of comfort and a desire for profit.

It was Fénelon — more on the side of the Ancients in the realm of aesthetics, but deeply connected to the nobiliary opposition to the monarchy on a political level — who formulated the psychology of disinterestedness that would resonate throughout the eighteenth century. In his *Explication des maximes des saints sur la vie intérieure*, he develops the idea of pure or disinterested love:

> The most disinterested love must want what God wants for us, as well as
> what he wants for others. An absolute determination to want nothing would

no longer be disinterestedness but the extinction of love, love being a true desire and will.

> L'amour le plus désintéressé doit vouloir ce que Dieu veut pour nous, comme ce qu'il veut pour autrui. La détermination absolue à ne rien vouloir ne serait plus le désintéressement, mais l'extinction de l'amour, qui est un désir et une volonté véritables.[67]

Fénelon here makes an essential point, which is all too often ignored: he clearly affirms that disinterestedness does not imply an absence of will but, on the contrary, a strong will that is beyond the concern of interested will and is entirely in harmony with that of God. Quietude and action are perfectly compatible:

> This disinterested love, always inviolably attached to the written law, performs all the same acts and employs all the same distinct virtues as interested love, with the single difference that it employs them in a simple, peaceful way, detached from any motive of self-interest.

> Cet amour désintéressé toujours inviolablement attaché à la loi écrite fait tous les mêmes actes et exerce toutes les mêmes vertus distinctes que l'amour intéressé, avec cette unique différence qu'il les exerce d'une manière simple, paisible, et dégagée de tout motif de propre intérêt.[68]

Another essential point: for all his insistence on disinterested love, Fénelon is careful not to condemn the interested love of God. Rather, he attempts to distinguish different types of such interested love, which can lead to pure love, for one must "never deprive a soul of the support of interested motives when, following the attraction of its grace, one begins to show it pure love."[69] This is true of the Ignatian type of meditation, which, unlike Salesian contemplation, is made up of discursive and reflective acts, freely admits interested love, and thus often has recourse to "the whole interest-based vocabulary of hope and fear."[70] Fénelon's system, while formulating the ideal of disinterested love, leaves a lot of room for spiritual practices characterized, to varying degrees, by interested love, that is, by a concern with self. As we will see, the idea of putting "the support of interested motives" in the service of a transcendent ideal sometimes called "society," sometimes "nation" or "fatherland," sometimes even "mankind" or "humanity" was to constitute a key element in eighteenth-century reflections on glory. Furthermore, and very quickly, the image of true disinterested love found its way into the political realm, where it would become a key element of anti-absolutist ideology. Perfectly compatible with the idea of a certain magnanimity and unburdened by Stoic austerity, disinterestedness then became one of the basic components of glory in the eighteenth century, and it was Fénelon himself who carried out its transfer from the realm of theology to that of politics.

In the *Explication des maximes des saints sur la vie intérieure*, the archbishop of Cambrai stresses the idea of the necessary attachment to sacred laws; in *Les Aventures de Télémaque*, he maintains that those in the world who govern must themselves "submit to the laws."[71] Above all, Mentor/Minerva tries to teach the young Telemachus that a king "is no further worthy of royalty, than as he forgets himself in order to sacrifice himself to the public good."[72] We know the degree to which *Les Aventures de Télémaque* was a war machine designed to reconceive the notion of glory as Louis XIV had understood it.[73] And much has been written about the Fénelonian ideal of the moderate monarch who seeks the happiness of his peoples and sees war as the curse of the human race. But perhaps too little emphasis has been given to the fact that Fénelon, while denouncing absolutism and the Louis XIV idea of glory, in no way opposed the military nobility's concept of glory. On the contrary, in this epic tale, the young Telemachus doesn't lack opportunities to prove his prowess, whether in slaying a lion, winning in all forms of battles proposed in the tournament organized for the candidates for the crown of Crete, or leading an army to victory in a campaign in which he "showed himself indefatigable in the discharge of all, even the most [arduous] duties of a commander."[74] The tutor of the duc de Bourgogne condemns wars of conquest and the "false glory" that accompanies them, but he supports the importance of warrior training for the nobility:

> You know what bodily exercises I [Mentor] have already ordained; the prizes I have appointed to excite emulation; the maxims of glory and virtue that will be infused into the minds of the youth by singing from their earliest infancy the great actions of heroes [. . .]. But besides all these, as soon as any nation in alliance with yours is engaged in war, the flower of the youth ought to be sent to it; those especially that reveal a military genius, and are most likely to profit by the experience [. . .] and without having a war to carry on at your own expense, or in your own country, you will have a gallant and intrepid youth. Even in the midst of a profound peace you must not neglect to treat with great distinction those who are possessed of military talents; for the surest way to prevent war and to secure a long peace is to have your

people trained to arms; to distinguish those who are eminent in the profession.

> Vous avez déjà vu, explique Mentor, les exercices du corps que nous établissons, les prix qui exciteront l'émulation, les maximes de gloire et de vertu dont on remplira l'âme des enfants, presque dès le berceau, par le chant des grandes actions des héros [. . .]. Mais ce n'est pas tout: aussitôt qu'un peuple allié de votre nation aura une guerre, il faut y envoyer la fleur de votre jeunesse, surtout ceux en qui on remarquera le génie de la guerre et qui seront les plus propres à profiter de l'expérience. [. . .] Sans avoir la guerre chez vous et à vos dépens, vous aurez toujours une jeunesse aguerrie et intrépide. Quoique vous ayez la paix chez vous, vous ne laisserez pas de traiter avec de grands honneurs ceux qui auront le talent de la guerre: car le vrai moyen d'éloigner la guerre et de conserver la paix, c'est de cultiver les armes; c'est d'honorer les hommes excellents dans cette profession.[75]

Fénelon sought the middle ground between unbridled ambition and the dissipation engendered by wealth and idleness; it was called *measure* in the Middle Ages and constituted the very ideal praised in the *Chanson de Roland*. Thus, *Télémaque* represents the fusion of classical aesthetics and morality with French nobiliary ethics. The self-forgetting that is a necessary trait of a good king implied vigorous policies, where warrior heroism had its place just as did the poetry that praised it. The king was to identify himself completely with the nation, his own self with the well-being of the collective self of his subjects. He "is not to have more wealth and pleasure, but more wisdom, virtue, and glory than other men."[76] This power of paternal identification with the collectivity functioned according to the same psychological mechanisms that characterized pure love, and in this sense the glory of the king was indeed in the image of that of God, just as the monarch's manifest disinterestedness played an essential role in the politico-moral training of his people. "But would you prevent the ingratitude of men? [. . . Then] exert yourself to the utmost to reform their morals."[77] If the prince works "by his example and authority to make them good," he will find the fruit of his work in their virtue.[78] In this political vision of the pure love that the king is supposed to incarnate, he loses all concern with self in his identification with the well-being of his people, and in doing so becomes the source of emulation of virtue and true glory.

Henri de Boulainvilliers, Fénelon's friend and a pillar of aristocratic oppositional thought, links the psychology of disinterestedness to one of the great oppositional mythologies of the eighteenth century, a mythology of which Napoleon would in turn make ample use: that of Charlemagne.[79] In de Boulainvilliers's political idyll, this "hero of the first order, and without contradiction the greatest King [. . .] to have reigned until now in France," was a great conqueror like Caesar—but without the despotism—and a great legislator like Lycurgus—but without the severity. This providential man was great especially in character: "the genius of the sovereign" was above all that "personal disinterestedness, which became, so to speak, the particular character of the century of Charlemagne; that Prince wanted nothing for himself that was not to the advantage of the entire Nation." Disinterestedness—the union of his will and that of the nation—did more than confer moral authority upon him, it assured him the ability to go against the grain of history and establish the rule of a political version of pure love in France; "this union of feelings and will"[80] constituted the very foundation of this ideal monarchy. This strange amalgam of a pessimistic view of history seen as a process of usurpation and decline, on the one hand, and the heroic disinterested figure depicted as a possible remedy and a source of hope, on the other, constantly returns in eighteenth-century narratives of the history of France. From the aristocrats Boulainvilliers and Montesquieu to the "republican" Mably, from the parliamentary ideologue Le Paige to the physiocrat Le Trosne, they all interrupted their historical narratives to focus on the reign of Charlemagne, a moment of collective enchantment that was located not in a distant antiquity, but in the history of France; a moment when a monarch endowed with genius and power that transcended all others demonstrated a disinterestedness that created his glory and that of the nation. Thus, to the ideology of this version of absolutism an ideal of pure disinterestedness was contrasted, often driven by a psychology of the hero and the notion of a kind of glory above any suspicion of individual interest.

Set in diametrical opposition to the Machiavellian machinations of reason of State, as well as to the greed of the merchant economy, the pole of heroic disinterestedness attracted those who wished to be situated neither on the terrain of a will for power and distinction nor on that of chrematistics. It offered a third way, the transcending of oneself, not being reduced to the impersonal calculations of making money or to the strategies of political or social ambition. Lucien Karpik has stressed how, among the magistrates and the lawyers in the *parlements*, "disinterestedness participates in the formation of a new economy of the mind."[81] The same logic applied to the encyclopedists. Making utility the foundation of a certain legitimacy, they contrasted their own attitude to the "sordid interest" motivating those who were working within the State—in the academies, for example—and sought to "prolong the works ordered by kings."[82] D'Alembert, who considered disinterested-ness the highest of all virtues, invokes it to characterize the involvement of the encyclopedists in their enterprise, calling upon the solidarity of men of letters:

> We beseech them again to join with us to create a work which we want to make into that of the nation, and toward which our disinterestedness and our zeal will gain the approval of all honest people.

> Nous les conjurons de nouveau de se réunir avec nous pour l'exécution d'un ouvrage, dont nous voudrions faire celui de la nation, et auquel notre désin-téressement et notre zèle doivent rendre tous les honnêtes gens favorables.[83]

L'Encyclopédie would be a "monument to the glory of France and its letters." In the heroic vision that the editors reveal in this "work of the French nation," the highest of virtues and the universalist concern with the well-being of humanity go hand in hand. By placing themselves under the sign of truth and the collectivity—whether it be called the fatherland (*patrie*) or the nation, or even the great community of all humanity—and by voicing their disinter-estedness, those intellectuals proclaimed themselves free from submission to the great. What might be called the ideology of heroic disinterestedness gained durable and efficient traction in very different realms. From religion to politics, from jurisprudence to scholarship, it offered a plausible explana-tion, an understandable motivation, and clear moral justification. Having acquired a true discursive force for those who claimed to follow it, however, it still did not provide a general model that could be applied to society as a whole.

Marie Nicolas Ponce-Camus, *Napoleon before the Tomb of Frederick the Great*
(early nineteenth century?). From a lithograph by Jean-Pierre-Marie
Jazet. 31 × 44 cm. (N2306/E4). Châteaux, Fontainebleau, France.
Photograph © RMN-Grand Palais / Art Resource, New York.

CHAPTER 3

Motivation and Leadership
in the Enlightenment

Distinction and Emulation

Though the idea of heroic disinterestedness provided a powerful model for generous and virtuous action, it certainly was not enough to define a sociology of heroism and glory. While this idea might help us to understand certain aspects of what Napoleon was striving to incarnate, and to explain the attraction that such a figure could hold, it sheds little light on the economy of glory that this conqueror/legislator aspired to put in place. Here, more than any other, it is Montesquieu who allows us best to grasp what was at stake. For by making honor not a moral but a political principle, the very foundation of the monarchy, Montesquieu changed the way glory and heroism were thought about. Clearly, the president of the Parlement of Bordeaux takes a sly pleasure in integrating — and inverting — the terms of the argument used by Jansenists and moralists when he stresses that honor is a principle whose goal is political utility for the collectivity and not the moral foundation of the individual:

> True it is that, philosophically speaking, it is a false honour which moves all the parts of the government; but even this false honour is as useful to the public as true honour could possibly be to private persons.

> Il est vrai que, philosophiquement parlant, c'est un honneur faux qui conduit toutes les parties de l'État; mais cet honneur faux est aussi utile au public que le vrai le seroit aux particuliers qui pourroit l'avoir.[1]

Montesquieu illustrates the mysterious power and majesty, as well as the fundamental coherence, of the monarchy by comparing it to the system of the universe, where each planet is held in place by a set of centrifugal and centripetal forces. "Honour sets all the parts of the body politic in motion, and by its very action connects them; thus each individual advances the public good, while he thinks only of promoting his own interest."[2] It is easy to see how the universe described by Montesquieu is close to Mandeville's beehive because in many respects the private vices in it lead to public good.[3] According to Montesquieu, a republic holds virtue as a principle and freedom as a goal, whereas European monarchy — rooted in feudal laws — has honor as its principle and glory as its goal:

> The monarchies we are acquainted with have not [. . .] liberty for their direct view: their only aim is the glory of the subject, of the state, and of the sovereign. But hence there results a spirit of liberty, which in those states is capable of achieving as great things, and of contributing as much perhaps to happiness as liberty itself.

> Les monarchies que nous connoissons, n'ont pas [. . .] la liberté pour leur objet direct; elles ne tendent qu'à la gloire des citoyens, de l'état et du prince. Mais de cette gloire il résulte un esprit de liberté, qui dans ces états, peut faire d'aussi grandes choses, et peut-être contribuer autant au bonheur que la liberté même.[4]

We find ourselves here in a planetary system utterly different from that of the Sun King. The modernity of the hero-king cedes its place to a systemic modernity based on an economy of glory in which, in principle, everyone may participate.

Montesquieu's emphasis on the importance of the civilizing function of commerce has been widely noted: among nations, commerce tends to lead to peace. Inside the collectivity, however, the effect is much less salubrious:

> But if the spirit of commerce unites nations, it does not in the same manner unite individuals. We see that in countries where the people move only by the spirit of commerce, they make a traffic of all the humane, all the moral virtues; the most trifling things, those which humanity would demand, are there done, or there given, only for money.

Mais, si l'esprit de commerce unit les nations, il n'unit pas de même les particuliers. Nous voyons que dans les pays où l'on n'est affecté que de l'esprit de
commerce, on trafique de toutes les actions humaines et de toutes les vertus
morales: les plus petites choses, celles que l'humanité demande, s'y font ou
s'y donnent pour de l'argent.[5]

In Montesquieu's opinion, the beauty of the modern monarchy is its ability
to prevent, *through the structured effect of the system*, the moral debasement
of people as members of a society. For it requires them "to perform the most
difficult actions, such as require an extraordinary exertion of fortitude and
resolution, without other recompense than that of glory and applause."[6]
Thus by separating honor from a morality of intent, Montesquieu manages
to place the monarchical system within a moral economy based on what he
calls "that general passion of the French for glory."[7] The efficacy of glory is
rooted in the culture of a nation. Its strength depends on customs, but it is
linked in a general way to a certain idea of freedom:

> The desire for glory does not differ from that instinct which all creatures
> have for their self-preservation. It seems that we extend our very being
> when we can exist in the memory of others. We acquire through it a new
> life, which becomes as precious to us as that which we have received from
> the creator. But, as all men are not equally attached to life, so they are not
> equally affected by the prospect of glory. This noble passion is, indeed,
> always engraved in their hearts, but imagination and education modify it
> in a thousand various ways. This difference, which is found between man
> and man, makes itself also felt between people and people, and that in a
> higher degree. It may be laid down as a maxim that, in every state, the desire
> of glory is proportional to the growth and diminution of the liberty of the
> subject: glory is never the companion of slavery.

> Le désir de la gloire n'est point différent de cet instinct que toutes les
> créatures ont pour leur conservation. Il semble que nous augmentons notre
> être lorsque nous pouvons le porter dans la mémoire des autres: c'est une
> nouvelle vie que nous acquérons, et qui nous devient aussi précieuse que
> celle que nous avons reçue du ciel. Mais, comme tous les hommes ne sont
> pas également attachés à la vie, ils ne sont pas aussi également sensibles
> à la gloire. Cette noble passion est bien toujours gravée dans leur cœur;
> mais l'imagination et l'éducation la modifient de mille manières. Cette

différence, qui se trouve d'homme à homme, se fait encore plus sentir de peuple à peuple. On peut poser pour maxime que, dans chaque État, le desir de la gloire croît avec la liberté des sujets et diminue avec elle: la gloire n'est jamais compagne de la servitude.[8]

Each word of this passage from the *Persian Letters*, in which we find all the power and nuance of Montesquieu's thinking, should be examined carefully. The transcendence in immanence that characterizes glory has the same universality as the instinct for survival, but also the same psychological and cultural relativity. This is precisely why it exercises a profound and lasting influence on the cultural and national level rather than on the intercultural and international level. Far from any spectacular strategy and based on practices of reciprocity, the spirit of commerce "produces in the mind of a man a certain sense of exact justice, opposite, on the one hand, to banditry, and on the other to those moral virtues which forbid our always adhering rigidly to the rules of private interest, and suffer us to neglect this for the advantage of others."[9] As regards international relations, what matters is the understanding of the other, and peace, whereas for peoples and nations there exists a whole range of balanced cultural possibilities. Nevertheless, Montesquieu asserts that when it functions like the moderate monarchy it should be, the French monarchy—which seeks "the glory of the subject, of the state, and of the sovereign"[10]—produces systemically not only as much happiness and freedom as a regime whose goal is freedom itself, but also a certain grandeur. Whereas the spirit of commerce reduces us to negotiating all actions and all moral and human values, the spirit of glory avoids this reduction of our being. In short, the spirit of glory leads to viewing these values in a way that, while perhaps not *truer*, is certainly much more *worthy* of humanity.

In our current perspective, we should retain two fundamental aspects of Montesquieu's thinking: on the international level, a denunciation of the spirit of conquest in favor of *le doux commerce*, and on a "national," specifically *French* level, a forceful defense of a regime whose goal is glory and whose principle is honor. Montesquieu tends generally to devote more attention to the principle than to the goal; that is, he spends more time discussing the mechanisms of honor, while glory occupies a secondary place, never at the forefront. In his analysis of the monarchic system, it is the concept of honor that occupies center stage. His entire vision of the proper functioning of the monarchic system rests on the association of the aristocracy with a kind of honor which, from a philosophical and moral point of view, is, as he himself admits, *false*. At the same time, Montesquieu, baron de La Brède, indelibly connects the aristocracy/honor dyad to ideas of luxury and *politesse*.[11] The effect of linking luxury and *politesse* to honor detached from morality is to contaminate the very notion of honor.[12] By turning honor into a systemic principle, Montesquieu saps its legitimizing strength as a fundamental value of the aristocracy. Honor ends up being "dishonored," so to speak, because it is associated with privilege, hypocrisy, a very rich and spendthrift nobility, and the "honors" of court.

A young Jean-Paul Marat sums up this current of ideas well in *The Chains of Slavery*, published first in English in 1774, then in French in 1793. The future revolutionary journalist denounces the abuses of princes who pay for services rendered only to themselves rather to the State or the nation:

> their creatures are covered both with infamy and marks of dignity, and these marks of note are soon valued at the expense of merit, virtue and talents [. . .]. Disgraced by the use they are made of, and the persons on whom they are bestowed, to become worthy of them is no more the pursuit of noble souls. When once honours are discredited, an incentive to generous actions, to great deeds, is wanting; and the love of glory, for want of [fuel], is extinguished in every heart.

> leurs créatures sont seules couvertes de marques d'honneur, et ces nouvelles distinctions sont bientôt accordées sans égard au mérite [. . .]. Décriées par l'usage qu'on en fait et l'indignité des personnes qu'on en décore, l'honneur de les mériter n'a plus d'attraits: or une fois avilies, il ne reste rien dans l'État pour exciter aux belles actions [. . .]. Ainsi, faute d'aliments, l'amour de la gloire s'éteint dans tous les cœurs.[13]

For Marat, the distinctions of honor, bestowed by princes and granted without consideration of merit, lead to "rooting out the love of glory."[14] Such thinking helps us understand the rising influence of the idea of "merit," whose influence extends all the way into the heart of the nobility's opposition to absolute monarchy.[15] In this context, precisely because it comes even more from the domain of the individual or the national collectivity, the notion of glory acquires a discursive *federative* power. Whereas honor is tangled up in its associations with a privileged caste and increasingly contested monarchic policies, glory remains both perfectly compatible with individual merit and success, and profoundly anchored in the immemorial values of the French collectivity.

As an ideal, glory is all the more powerful in that it is a recognition accorded by men, and thus fits well into a logic emphasizing public opinion, which becomes its foundation and its legitimacy. Thus the concept of glory proves to be discursively powerful in that it establishes itself as common ground for these very different registers and helps to harmonize the aspirations of the individual with those of the collectivity. The idea of an economy of glory as it was developed in the eighteenth century posits the ability of a government to set up and maintain a policy of emulation aiming to take advantage of what Fénelon called the "support of interested motives" (see chapter 2, note 67). Borrowing from the archbishop of Cambrai elements such as the refusal of luxury and the praise of agriculture, in the famous *Ami des hommes* (1756–1760) the marquis de Mirabeau proposes a program for managing passions, redirecting them from greed and personal interest toward virtue and public utility. Like a "talented engineer" facing the threat of a raging flood, the political leader, while unable to contain passions, can channel them toward moral good.

For Mirabeau, government possesses the ability to "make us all virtuous."[16] To do that, it must first of all know how to leverage *amour-propre*, for "the desire to distinguish oneself in one's profession appears the most natural of ambitions."[17] Government policies must work to make merit, not wealth, the basis for distinction. A society structured around self-interest and industry is a society in which "emulation turns toward wealth, and the emulation of wealth is nothing other than greed."[18] If the advancement of an honorable magistrate or a courageous soldier depends on wealth,

> if the profession of glory and disinterestedness is—like that of self-interest and industry—ultimately concerned with gold, then any type of virtue and any idea of glory will be but vain words, forgotten like the mace and the spear; and all that remains of the citizen's strength of soul will be directed toward a desire for gold.

> si la carrière enfin de la gloire et du désintéressement est occupée par l'or, comme celle de l'intérêt et de l'industrie: dès-lors toute espece de vertus et toute idée de gloire ne seront plus que de vains noms, oubliés comme la masse d'armes et la lance; et tout ce qui restera de forces à l'ame du citoyen, se portera vers le desir de l'or.[19]

Over the course of the eighteenth century, then, a general reflection on glory emerged as a regulating principle in society. It found its most "natural" formulation in the discourse of classical republicanism, whose influence continued to develop and expand throughout the eighteenth century.[20] It goes without saying that all those who denounced luxury and the power of money, those who advocated a return to civic virtue, granted a favored place to benevolence and, above all, emphasized the social and political utility of glory. We have already mentioned *The Chains of Slavery,* which Jean-Paul Marat wrote during a stay in England. In it he describes how luxury and opulence stifle the love of glory and pave the way to despotism.[21] In a litany typical of ancient republicanism, Marat lists the virtues that enable nations to preserve their liberty: activity, frugality, disinterestedness, vigilance, a love of glory and of the nation.[22] If love of the nation in its purest form becomes true disinterestedness, it is impossible to imagine a well-functioning society based solely on disinterested love of nation. Marat certainly does not suggest that a concern for the self could be replaced by any sort of Rousseauist identification of each member of the collectivity with the general interest. While he makes a distinction between virtue and interest, he does not take the next step, that is, suggesting the simple suppression of one or the other by imagining a society ruled and regulated, either by virtue or by personal interest. Rather, it is thanks to a third concept—glory—that he conceives of a society capable of exploiting a complex ensemble of more or less self-interested, individualistic motivations. The economy of glory that Marat invokes is thus in some respects very close to the one described by Montesquieu.[23] Indeed, Marat's point of departure might well be attributed to the maxim formulated by the author of the *Persian Letters,* that "glory is never the companion of slavery."[24] But—and this point is essential—unlike what we find in Montesquieu, the freedom-glory dyad in Marat is entirely detached from the luxury-honor dyad, for which, so to speak, it constitutes a remedy.

The search for a social system founded on something other than profit and luxury, and which would encourage the conception of some kind of human grandeur, continued to grow in strength and resonance in the eighteenth century. The appeal to glory was seen as an essential leveraging mechanism for an economy that would combine politics and morality. Montesquieu had spoken of a planetary system; Mirabeau evoked the work of an engineer; the académicien Antoine-Léonard Thomas, in his *Essai sur les éloges,* explains that "in mechanics, we prefer machines that produce the greatest effects with the least effort. In politics, the same should be true."[25] Each of these authors evokes a mechanism that would enable society to manage itself, not by denying the role of individual interest, but by giving a person the means to go beyond it—to go beyond *oneself*—in the name of the collectivity. "Do you wish to know what the sentiment of glory can accomplish?" asks Thomas:

Remove it from the face of the earth and everything changes: man's opinion no longer animates man; he is alone in the crowd; the past is nothing: the present is now; the future disappears; the instant that passes perishes eternally, of no use for the instant that must follow.

Voulez-vous savoir ce que peut le sentiment de la gloire? Ôtez-la de dessus la terre; tout change: le regard de l'homme n'anime plus l'homme; il est seul dans la foule; le passé n'est rien: le présent se resserre; l'avenir disparoît; l'instant qui s'écoule périt éternellement, sans être d'aucune utilité pour l'instant qui doit suivre.[26]

We should not be surprised to find the thematics of transcendence in immanence being reiterated by an "Immortal," as members of the Académie française are known. Consider, after all, the motto inscribed on the seal of the Académie—*À l'immortalité.* But the key to understanding the centrality of the *topos* of glory in Thomas is to be found in its fundamental reliance on the idea of public opinion. Recognition can be conceived alternatively as a political instrument wielded by enlightened elites aiming to instruct a people or as a legitimizing seal of approval emanating from that people. The emulation that it inspires thus becomes the favored means for society to improve itself, to reform itself, to maintain itself. Both a means and an end, glory allows the resolution of contradictions that oppose particular interest to the interest of all, love of self to love of the nation, and, by extension, love of the nation to love of humanity. It becomes the simultaneous affirmation of the individual and the collectivity, and above all, a means to assert human grandeur.

If, in France, luxury and the pursuit of profit are associated with a certain moral and political decadence, with privilege rather than merit, then the passion for glory becomes an assertion of a freedom that could be envisioned in terms of individuals, societies, and peoples:

Do not expect it from a people for whom self-interest rules: glory is the currency of States, but glory represents nothing where gold represents everything. Do not expect it from a pleasure-loving people: such people have only their senses, they deprive themselves of nothing, they know not how to lose a day to gain centuries. Do not expect it from an enslaved people; glory is proud and free, and the slave is corrupted by his slavery.

Ne l'attendez pas d'un peuple chez qui domine l'intérêt: la gloire est la monnoie des États, mais la gloire ne représente rien où l'or représente tout.

Ne l'attendez pas d'un peuple voluptueux: ce peuple n'a que des sens, il ne sait renoncer à rien, il ne sait pas perdre un jour pour gagner des siècles. Ne l'attendez pas d'un peuple esclave; la gloire est fière et libre, et l'esclave corrompu par sa servitude.[27]

At once a mechanism of social control and the manifestation of a fundamental freedom, glory shone like a ray of hope for regeneration and consensus at a time when dissensions and conflict weighed ever more heavily.

Probably because it allows virtue to be reconciled with personal interest, the Baron d'Holbach places the passion for glory at the heart of his *Morale universelle* (1776). Rejecting Mandeville's idea that individual vices result in a benefit to society, the materialist philosopher describes a society in which virtue based on properly understood personal interest prevails. His utilitarian morality fully authorizes a love of self in a society that favors the passion for glory in order to bridle other passions. In this perspective, a desire for glory is the manifestation of a love of self:

> The passion for glory, which is often seen as a vain cloud of smoke, is but the desire to be esteemed by other men; this desire is necessary to society, within which it gives birth to courage, a sense of honor, charity, generosity, and all the talents that contribute either to well-being or to the pleasures of humankind.

> La passion de la gloire, que l'on regarde souvent comme une vaine fumée, n'est que le désir d'être estimé des autres hommes; ce désir est nécessaire à la société, dans le sein de laquelle il fait naître le courage, le sentiment d'honneur, la bienfaisance, la générosité, & tous les talents qui contribuent, soit au bien-être, soit aux plaisirs du genre humain.[28]

Aligning love of self, love of the nation, and love of humanity in one harmonious, noncontradictory chain, d'Holbach describes a society in which even the hero who sacrifices his life does so only out of a love of himself that prompts a desire to be esteemed by others. Thus the practice of virtue that arouses the esteem of others leads them to accept that he who is the object of their esteem should exercise over them "a power that they approve."[29] The power based on this esteem can in turn encourage and compensate what the author calls "public spirit." Thus a sort of mutual dependence emerges, whereby the value of the individual is fundamentally associated with the opinion of others, even if d'Holbach sometimes limits valid opinion to that of *the good* (*les bons*). Curiously, however, according to this staunch materialist, some individuals rise above any constraint to attain a moral autonomy such as that described by the Ancients. In a text that focuses entirely on personal interest as a universal motivation, the figure of the magnanimous man and the theme of disinterestedness both find a place. Invoking Plutarch and Seneca, d'Holbach describes grandeur of the soul, which by nature is frank—that is, *free*—and beneficent. Characterized by great "energy," it enables the man who is endowed with it to sacrifice his own interests to those of others and to achieve true generosity: a virtue that has no need of the recognition of others, endowed as it is with freedom:

> Greatness of soul gives the acts of a man inviolably attached to virtue that vigor which is considered heroic disinterestedness.

> La grandeur d'âme donne aux actions de l'homme inviolablement attaché à la vertu cette vigueur que l'on regarde comme un désintéressement héroïque.[30]

As we can see, d'Holbach describes a whole gamut of motivations that seem to echo, but in a materialist and secular key, those described earlier by Fénelon. The highest of values, then, is greatness of soul, which, as in the case of Boulainvillier's Charlemagne, enables you to rise above the constraints and contingencies of your time. This heroic and virtuous consciousness understands its own true value independently of the judgment of others. It gives the individual the freedom to act *for others*, but also *in spite of others*. Yet, as d'Holbach notes, placing yourself above opinion often fosters a bad image of yourself, and you must sometimes suffer the consequences. But the injustice to which the hero falls victim is then transformed into an edifying display, which reinforces the social connection:

> The well-founded consciousness of a good man thus places him above the judgments of the public and exempts him of its iniquities. There is no one to whom a virtuous man appears greater when he endures with courage the injustices of the mighty; he then seems to measure his strengths against those of destiny, in hand-to-hand combat. Seneca said, "There is no greater spectacle for gods and men than to see a good man struggling with fate." But that spectacle [. . .] serves to interest and greatly affect mortals that are themselves buffeted by the blows of fate.

La conscience assurée de l'homme de bien le met alors au dessus des jugements du public & le dédommage de ses iniquités. Il n'est personne à qui l'homme vertueux ne paroisse plus grand, lorsqu'il supporte avec courage les injustices du fort; il semble alors mesurer ses forces contre celles du destin, & lutter avec lui corps à corps. Sénèque dit "qu'il n'est pas de spectacle plus grand pour les dieux & les hommes, que de voir l'homme de bien aux prises avec la fortune." Mais ce spectacle [. . .] est fait pour intéresser & toucher vivement les mortels qui sont eux-mêmes en butte aux coups du sort.[31]

From the island of Saint Helena, Napoleon would describe himself with these same traits to illustrate the injustice of his imprisonment, but also to stress that the act of making himself a prisoner of the British was essentially an act of free will:

> We read in the papers that we had been made prisoners, we who had come so freely and with so much magnanimity! That we had been forced to turn ourselves in, we who had disdained, by greatness of soul, to benefit from the chances of war on the ground, and who would have been able to test the fate of arms at sea!

> Nous lisions dans les papiers qu'on nous avait faits prisonniers, nous qui étions venus si librement et avec tant de magnanimité! Que nous avions été contraints de nous rendre à discrétion, nous qui avions dédaigné, par grandeur d'âme, de profiter des hasards de la guerre sur terre, et qui eussions pu tenter le sort des armes par mer![32]

The Power of Imagination and the Secular Marvelous

The politico-moral system that d'Holbach describes is in keeping with profoundly rationalist principles. In this natural world, we act according to our own interests and, with reason as a guide, use our passions to cultivate a morality whose principle is utility. To disengage us from immediacy, from contingencies of the moment, and from the lure of appetites as well as instincts, the idea of transcendence in immanence plays a crucial role. For the concept of glory enables those of us too burdened by the present to imagine, by way of our own esteem for those who have preceded us, the consideration and praise of those to come. It is by leaving the present, through a projection of the self in time, that we accede to a moral grandeur and a rationality that are different from those of the present. Antoine-Léonard Thomas is making this precise point when he asserts that "often oppressed virtue and genius take refuge far from the real world, in an imaginary world, as in a haven where justice is reestablished."[33] For the economists of glory, society as a whole should function through emulation and recognition; but they always reserve a favored place for exceptional persons who rise above their condition and can be judged on the scale of immortality.

In that society, a love of the public good and an inclination to defend the rights of society are rendered habitual "through example, and through public opinion which, lending continual strength to ardent imaginations, inspire them to actions that often appear supernatural."[34] At first glance, the appearance of the supernatural in the materialist world of d'Holbach might seem surprising, but in fact it is a remarkably constant element in eighteenth-century reflections on glory. Though the world is only natural, nothing prevents us from imagining it otherwise. In d'Holbach's case, only people endowed with a "greatness of soul that reasons" are open to a "fortunate enthusiasm," which renders them capable of forgetting themselves and of achieving deeds that surpass comprehension.

Indeed, in the eighteenth century, glory was often explained through the liberating strength of the imaginary. Associated as it was with the idea of grandeur and genius, it contained an element of exception that was not easily reduced to a purely rational explanation. Granted, the passion for glory could be a restraint on other passions and serve social rationality, but unlike the laws of commerce and a quest for profit, it is difficult to calculate the value of glory; even the Philosophes had difficulty defining its weight and measurements. It was all well and good to keep repeating that exploits appearing to be supernatural were the result not of some divine intervention but of quite natural human strengths, yet those deeds and actions continued to arouse astonishment. In the preceding century the defenders of the *Christian marvelous* were routed;[35] the same would not be true of what might be called the *secular marvelous* of the Enlightenment—a marvelous that found its raison d'être in a thinking eager to reconcile natural laws—to which all men are subject—with exceptional beings who went beyond the constraints imposed by material circumstances, historical conditions, customs, and prejudices of a particular society.

In an article in the *Encyclopédie,* which d'Holbach clearly knew well, Jean-François de Marmontel explains that glory is "the unanimous and sustained chorus of universal admiration." With the article by Voltaire devoted to the same subject, the *Encyclopédie*, in volume 7 (published in 1757), sets out to redefine glory in the spirit of the Enlightenment. In it, Marmontel develops a reflection on the nature and functioning of glory whose basis would be *"the marvelous,"* or that which *"rises or seems to rise above the forces of nature."*[36] For Marmontel, truly glorious actions are those in which the disinterested hero deploys superhuman force, virtue, or talent that he puts in the service of the happiness of mankind:

> The great sacrifices of personal interest for the public good require an effort that raises man above himself, and glory is the only prize worthy of being associated with it.

> Les grands sacrifices de l'intérêt personnel au bien public, demandent un effort qui élève l'homme au-dessus de lui-même & la gloire est le seul prix qui soit digne d'y être attaché.[37]

For Marmontel, however, glory is very much dependent on public opinion and therefore varies throughout the centuries, depending on the degree of enlightenment. "Men born for glory have sought it where opinion has placed it";[38] the essential role of men of letters—and let us not forget that the *Encyclopédie* defined itself as being the "work of a society of men of letters"— was, then, to establish and maintain that opinion in conformity with right reason. The very notion of the marvelous contains an element one might call mythico-poetic, which strikes the collective imagination and elicits a unanimous surge of admiration. The secular marvelous thus constitutes an essential element in an economy of glory defined by an opinion that is awestruck by a kind of grandeur that seems to exceed the forces of nature. Seen in that light, it becomes clear that without the regulating vigilance of intellectuals, "organs of glory," this economy could very quickly turn into a vicious cycle. The role of the new "clerics" was to assure the survival of worthy renown by encouraging new heroes to be inspired by history and orienting them toward future generations, in which their afterlife would reside.

While recognizing that intellectuals could indeed accede to glory, Marmontel focuses on two specific cases: the king and the soldier. The king, benefactor of his people, assures the prosperity of the nation not through conquest but by encouraging agriculture, commerce, and the arts. And so "glory, like light, is transmitted without losing strength: the glory of the sovereign flows over the nation." The encyclopedist categorically condemns conquest, which represents the "darkest sort of marvelous." But he nonetheless sings the praises of military glory. War is a curse on humanity, but an unavoidable one, and "there is no glory comparable to that of warriors; for that of legislators perhaps demands more talent, but many fewer sacrifices."[39] The role of great and heroic officers is incontestable but does not prevent the existence of a collective glory:

> There must be a mass of *glory* for the corps that distinguishes itself [. . .]. A legionnaire thinks as a man, a legion thinks as a hero; and what one calls *esprit du corps* can have no other sustenance, no other motive, than *glory*.

> Il doit y avoir une masse de *gloire* pour le corps qui se distingue [. . .]. Un légionnaire pense en homme, une légion pense en héros; & ce qu'on appelle *l'esprit du corps*, ne peut avoir d'autre aliment, d'autre mobile que la *gloire*.[40]

And Marmontel includes a few anecdotes illustrating the heroic behavior of the simple soldier, which are in full accord with an essential aspect of the spirit of the *Encyclopédie*. For this work aims to give voice to a whole class of men all too often ignored or even scorned, who are engaged in the mechanical arts associated with manual labor and are "enslaved [. . .] to a type of routine."[41] An officer in the Champagne regiment asks three times for twelve men of goodwill to volunteer to lend a hand. In the lengthy silence he grows angry: "What is it," he says, "don't you hear me?" "*We hear you*, cries a voice; *but what do you mean by twelve men of goodwill? We are all such men, you have only to choose.*" "In the flooded trenches of Philippsburg the soldiers march in water up to their waists. A grenadier offers to carry a young officer on his back: '*Put him on my back*, he said; *at least if there is a bullet to be had I will spare him from it.*'"[42] In tone and content these anecdotes resemble those of the soldiers in Napoleon's Old Guard, stories that would proliferate under his reign. Marmontel notes that the French soldier has a thousand traits of this kind, which a Plutarch or a Tacitus would have taken pains to reveal but which France in the eighteenth century considered unworthy of the "majesty of history." This vision of a democratized glory accessible to all ranks was at the heart of the idea of "revolutionizing glory" that we saw in the writing of Bertrand Barère.[43] Thus in their own way the encylopedists had already begun the work of projecting glory toward classes who had never had access to it before.

To Conquer and Enlighten

It is often pointed out how adamantly the conquering Enlightenment rejected the spirit of conquest. Marmontel's text is an illustration of this. We have seen, however, that the conquests of Charlemagne did find a place in the logic of heroic disinterestedness. The key, then, was to go beyond the idea of conquest as an end in itself. But this idea could certainly be put in the service of an ideal that transcended it. Such was the case of Charlemagne in the modern era; in representations of antiquity, portrayals of Alexander morph from a figure who incarnated military genius, as we saw him described by Lartigue in the time of Louis XIV, to one who carried the flame of a higher purpose, that of civilization. As Montesquieu explains: "A conquest may destroy pernicious prejudices, and place, if I dare say so, the nation under a better genius."[44] For the Baron de La Brède, the conqueror's genius—notably in the cases of Charlemagne and Alexander—is the ability to reconcile the irreconcilable, to impose by force a state of affairs approaching what should be the true spirit of the laws. In Charlemagne's case, "everything was united by the strength of his genius [which] flowed through every part of the empire."[45] In Alexander's case, the "greatness of his genius" enabled him to overcome pernicious prejudices and forge a union of the Greek and Persian peoples by abolishing the divide between conqueror and conquered:

> He thought only of uniting the two nations, and of abolishing the distinctions between a conquering and a conquered people. Upon achieving his conquests, he relinquished all those prejudices that had helped him to obtain them.

> il ne songea qu'à unir les deux nations, et à faire perdre les distinctions du peuple conquérant et du peuple vaincu. Il abandonna, après la conquête, tous les préjugés qui lui avaient servi à la faire.[46]

To achieve that union, he built "an infinity of cities" and cemented all parts of the new empire. But he was careful to allow the conquered peoples to retain their customs, their civil laws, and sometimes their existing governors. "He paid great respect to the ancient traditions, and to all the public monuments of the glory or vanity of nations."[47] Respecting the customs, laws, and traditions of peoples, while at the same time ridding them of pernicious prejudices, the conquering genius thus arrives at a new synthesis: a transformation that is both preservation and advancement, totally unlike the Roman model, in which conquest aimed only to "destroy everything." Thus Montesquieu turns Charlemagne and Alexander into heroes of moderate grandeur, of enlightened and enlightening conquest.

We find a similar vision, more explicitly linked to the philosophical project of the Enlightenment, in the important article Denis Diderot devotes in the *Encyclopédie* to Greek philosophy ("Grecs, philosophie des"). Insisting on the fact that the proud Greeks described other societies as being made up of "barbarians," Diderot notes that it was the so-called barbarians who "planted the first seeds of Philosophy in Greece." Out of that fertile ground there grew "a huge tree whose branches extended from age to age and from land to land" and ultimately covered the entire globe.[48] Generally, in his articles on the philosophy of the Ancients, Diderot's strategy is to establish a parallel between various manifestations of superstition and intolerance throughout the history of antiquity, and those which the philosophers had been heroically confronting in Europe since the Renaissance.[49] According to Diderot, the triumph of philosophy among the Moderns verged onto a new path, that of eclecticism.[50] But, in the article devoted to the Ancient Greeks, the triumph of philosophy leads, surprisingly, to the conquests of Alexander. At the end of the article, Diderot gives the floor to Plutarch—with whose writings Napoleon was quite familiar—to support the idea that Alexander exploited and enacted the lessons of Zeno: men in general are citizens of the world; the interests of the human species goes beyond those of the divisions into cities, peoples, and nations. Thus, the conquests of Alexander stemmed directly from the triumph of philosophy, notably the Stoic current, which, by viewing human beings in general and going beyond the division of the world between Greeks and barbarians, attained a certain universality:

> for [Alexander] did not do what his tutor Aristotle advised him to do, to
> act toward the Greeks as a father, and toward the barbarians as a lord, and
> to take care of the first as his friends and relations, and use the others as
> plants or animals [. . .]; being regarded as having been sent from heaven as
> a common reformer, governor, reconciler of the universe, those he could not
> assemble through the remonstrances of reason, he forced through strength
> of arms, and gathering them all together, having them all drink, so to speak,
> from the same cup of friendship, and bringing together lives, customs,
> marriages, and ways of life, he ordered all living men to regard the inhabited
> earth as their land.

car [Alexandre] ne fit pas comme Aristote son précepteur lui conseilloit, qu'il se portât envers les *Grecs* comme pere, & envers les barbares comme seigneur, & qu'il qu'il eût soin des uns comme de ses amis & de ses parens, & se servît des autres comme de plantes ou d'animaux; [. . .] ains estimant être envoyé du ciel comme un commun réformateur, gouverneur, réconciliateur de l'univers, ceux qu'il ne put rassembler par les remontrances de la raison, il les contraignit par force d'armes, & assemblant le tout en un de tous costés, en faisant boire tous, par manière de dire, en une même coupe d'amitié; & meslant ensemble les vies, les moeurs, les mariages & façons de vivre, il commanda à tous hommes vivans d'estimer la terre habitable être leur pays.[51]

Following this quotation from Plutarch (as translated by Amyot), Diderot continues in his own voice to describe a strategy that would be none other than that of Napoleon:

To legitimize this policy among the peoples, he then called upon the most famous philosophers in Greece; he sent them out to the nations after he had conquered them.

Pour accréditer cette politique parmi les peuples, il appela à sa suite les philosophes les plus célèbres de Grece; il les répandit chez les nations à mesure qu'il les subjuguoit.

In fact, Napoleon would seek to integrate, to fuse together, so to speak, elements from Montesquieu — conquer to preserve while going beyond pernicious prejudices — and from Diderot/Plutarch — shed the light of universality in order to overcome the contradictions that divide men. In both cases, disinterestedness is manifested in the grandeur of the vision, which could be that of the nation just as well as that of humanity as a whole. In both cases, glory results from grandeur without being an end in itself.

A "Mirror for Princes" for Modernity

If reflections on glory in the eighteenth century attempted to redefine glory in order to turn it into a political instrument or a societal principle, the military reference nonetheless continued to hold sway; it constantly reappeared, even if only as a foil for other forms of glory. Indeed, for producing spectacular

heroism nothing is better than the theater of war. As regards military heroism, however, the Moderns were obliged to bow before the Ancients, whose
superiority was difficult to contest, especially after the humiliating setbacks
of the Seven Years' War, when the need to reform the army became obvious.
Calls for this reform were often formulated in terms of merit, which, in spite
of its egalitarian potential, was embraced by a segment of the aristocracy that
was fundamentally hostile to the nobility of the court. In this perspective,
the military nobility — through its traditions as well as its education — would
constitute the most capable element in society to lead armies. Among those
pushing for drastic reform was Jacques-Antoine-Hippolyte de Guibert, a
friend of the encyclopedists and of Buffon and the lover of Julie de Lespinasse.
He was the author of *Essai général de tactique* (1770), which had a profound
influence on Napoleon.[52] Voltaire's famous line "I hate all heroes" comes
from the poem he composed about Guibert's *Tactique*. Though the philosopher opens the poem with a rant against war, he ends it by recognizing the
legitimacy of Guibert's position.

Guibert's thinking was at the crossroads of very divergent tendencies: the
Enlightenment, absolutism, ancient republicanism, and military culture all
came together to produce a deeply original work linking the political to the
military. Decrying the abuses of a regime "in which success no longer means
acquiring a reputation but amassing wealth,"[53] the great tactician denounces
a tendency that he traces back to the efforts of Richelieu to destroy or degrade
the nobility and continued with those of Louis XIV concerning "pompousness
as power, luxury as wealth, shine as glory."[54] Guibert contrasts the decadence of the politics practiced in modern Europe to the greatness of ancient
Rome:

> I think there may have been, in some corner of the Universe, an obscure
> and peaceful nation, whose members were happier; but certainly there was
> never a people that had more grandeur, as much glory, so richly deserved by
> its courage and virtues.

> Je dis que peut-être il y a eu, dans quelques coins de l'Univers, une nation
> obscure et paisible, dont les membres ont été plus heureux; mais que certai-
> nement jamais peuple n'a eu autant de grandeur, autant de gloire, et n'en a
> autant mérité par son courage et par ses vertus.[55]

The author attempts at the same time to stress the realism of his arguments:

I am not describing men above humanity. I am lowering heroes to the highest possible level of perfection that the human heart may contain.

Je ne me peins point les hommes au-dessus de l'humanité. Je rabaisse les héros à la mesure possible de perfection que le cœur humain comporte.[56]

Advocating a constitution indissolubly connecting politics and the military to create a "national discipline" resulting in "that confederation of all hearts and all forces" in which the interests of the people and those of the government would be the same, Guibert argues for public education, which, he believes, would lead to the blossoming of "superior and universal minds, which make the glory and destiny of empires."[57] Gradually, there would thus emerge

that enlightened mass which illuminates the whole administration. In the midst of these men there need only rise up—and one surely will—some vast genius. He seizes, if I may express myself thus, the accumulated knowledge of all and creates or perfects the political system, placing himself atop the machine, and steering it.

cette masse de lumières qui éclaire toute l'administration. Au milieu de ces hommes, il suffit qu'il s'élève, et il ne peut manquer de s'élever quelque génie vaste. Celui-là s'empare, si je peux m'exprimer ainsi, des connaissances de tous, crée, ou perfectionne le système politique, se place au haut de la machine, et lui imprime le mouvement.[58]

But France was degenerating to an extent that it was quite unable to put such a system in place. Throughout his treatise Guibert continually calls for a regeneration, speculates on the necessary conditions for it—and glory appears as a constant:

Alongside the frightening picture of their ills, let us constantly present the encouraging possibility of their cure. It may be that at the head of nations men will rise up who will not despair of their salvation, who will desire good, who will love glory, and for whom these two sentiments will make everything easy. Genius and virtue may arise on thrones.

Mettons sans cesse auprès du tableau effrayant de leurs maux, la possibilité encourageante de leur guérison. Peut-être il s'élèvera à la tête des nations des hommes qui ne désespéreront pas de leur salut, qui désireront le bien,

qui aimeront la gloire, et à qui ces deux sentiments rendront tout facile. Le
génie et la vertu peuvent naître sur les trônes.[59]

Guibert then describes the figure of the hero capable of standing up to the
tide of history and the corruption of morals, someone who would restab-
lish the greatness and harmony of the nation. The following lengthy passage
shows remarkable prescience; Guibert seems to sketch the tactical scenario
that Napoleon would adopt. Even the ideology of the Hundred Days is here,
for the hero finally promises to return to his people the excessive rights he
had claimed, and to govern according to the laws:

> O my nation! This picture may not always be a fantastic dream. You can
> achieve it: you can become that fortunate State. One day perhaps, escaping
> the vices of his time and placed in more favorable circumstances, a prince
> will ascend your throne who will carry out this great revolution. From the
> writings of some of my fellow citizens, perhaps from my own, he will draw
> the desire and the means. *He will change our mores, he will give our souls new*
> *strength; he will inspire the government again; he will carry the torch of truth into*
> *all parts of the administration; he will substitute for our strict and complicated*
> *politics the vast and sublime knowledge that I have attempted to describe* [. . .].
> He will make the nation what it can become [. . .]. He will gather his peoples,
> who have become his children, around the throne [. . .] and say to them: "I
> restore to you the too extensive rights of which I have not taken advantage
> and which I don't want my successors to abuse [. . .]. I will retain the honors
> of the crown, the right to propose to you wise laws, the power to have them
> enacted when you have ratified them [. . .]. Here are the statutes of this new
> government, here are its laws: I will henceforth reign only according to them
> and through them. May my family, who will swear with me, succeed me in
> these conditions. Receive our oaths as we will receive yours."

> Ô ma patrie! Ce tableau ne sera peut-être pas toujours un rêve phantastique.
> Tu peux le réaliser: tu peux devenir cet État fortuné. Un jour peut-être,
> échappant aux vices de son siècle et placé dans des circonstances plus
> favorables, il s'élèvera sur ton trône un prince qui opérera cette grande révo-
> lution. Dans les écrits de quelques-uns de mes concitoyens, dans les miens
> peut-être, il en puisera le désir et les moyens. *Il changera nos mœurs, il retrem-*
> *pera nos âmes; il redonnera du ressort au gouvernement; il portera le flambeau de*
> *la vérité dans toutes les parties de l'administration; il substituera à notre politique*

étroite et compliquée, la science vaste et sublime que j'ai tenté de peindre. [. . .]
Il rendra la nation ce qu'elle peut devenir. [. . .] Il appellera autour du
trône ses peuples, devenus ses enfants. [. . .] Je vous remets des droits trop
étendus, dont je n'ai point abusé, et dont je ne veux pas que mes successeurs
abusent. [. . .] Je me réserve les honneurs de la couronne, le droit de vous
proposer des lois sages, le pouvoir de les faire exécuter, quand vous les aurez
ratifiées, [. . .]. Voici les statuts de ce gouvernement nouveau, voici ses lois:
je ne vais plus régner que selon elles et par elles. Que ma famille, qui va jurer
avec moi, me succède à ces conditions. Recevez nos sermens comme nous
allons recevoir les vôtres.[60]

Elected in 1785 to the Académie française, where he replaced Antoine-
Léonard Thomas, Guibert, in his inaugural speech, echoed the theme of a
love of glory defined as a general emulation "which animates all the Arts,
which inspires all professions: because they all reflect the glory of a nation,
either in grandeur, or in public usefulness."[61] But the cornerstone of Guibert's politico-military edifice remains the brilliant leader, a man of genius,
the warrior-legislator.[62] One can only be struck by the depth of feeling and
the precision of his analysis of the impasse in which Europe — and France in
particular — found itself. For Guibert, only the magnanimous hero who rises
above all others, who grants himself a power beyond all other powers and
imposes a reign nothing less than "marvelous," would be capable of pulling
the nation from the abyss in which it was languishing.

If Guibert's thinking did not fall into an intractable pessimism on account of the historic conjuncture, it was because Frederick II of Prussia had
just proved that modernity was capable of producing a man for the occasion.
Guibert's encomium to Frederick, which he published in London in 1787, is a
true "mirror for princes." In it Bonaparte would have been able to contemplate at his leisure the image of the man he would strive to be. All elements
of the figure the future emperor of France sought to emulate, all the great
themes of the public persona he would create for himself, are to be found in
condensed form in Guibert's text. In the picture Guibert presents, the all-
embracing genius of the king of Prussia enabled him to carry out great public
works, to embellish his capital with monuments and palaces that gave it "a
sort of public dignity that was missing in his land," for "he indeed had to
provide his nation, his factories, his artists with examples and models."[63] In
the midst of this splendor, Frederick demonstrates great simplicity in all that
is associated with him: his dress, his table, his inner life. Philosopher-king

and legislator-king, recognizing the primordial place occupied by justice, he "conceives and executes the project of creating a general code of laws, which he then introduces simultaneously and in a uniform way across so many disparate lands"[64] over which he reigns.

But it is first and foremost as a modern military officer that Guibert's Frederick II reveals his ability to act on the level of his genius; it is in war and through war that he acquires a status sufficient to impose his vision on the society to which he devotes his life and all his strength. Through increased discipline and instruction within the army, he has managed to build "that amazing machine out of what appeared to be a collection of odds and ends, ready to fall apart."[65] Guibert describes how the power of Frederick's genius enables him to take the army in hand and "steer it successfully, as if it had been composed of the most perfect, homogeneous materials."[66] The "informal" visits that this great general constantly pays his troops play an important role in inculcating in them the motivation, the unanimity, and the emulation so essential to their effectiveness. Unlike the mumbo jumbo emanating from the diplomatic bureaux, Frederick's political communiqués "are almost all dated from his camps, and composed amid the tumult of fighting; they all have that tone of strength and simplicity, that straightforward, noble logic that is so natural to a warrior-king but at the same time can belong only to a man of great character and a distinguished mind," such as had not been seen since antiquity.[67] Thus, it is by borrowing the strength and simplicity of the language of the Ancients that this Modern is able to speak directly to his peoples as well as to his enemies. Reflecting on Guibert's affirmations allows us better to understand the aristocratic origins of the romantic movement, for those who no longer saw their reflection — even indirectly — in this mirror for princes would not be able to find it either in the language of a triumphant and oratorical classicism.

For Guibert, Frederick's heroic accomplishments were a source of inspiration and amazement. In fact, this author provides us with a perfect illustration of the secular marvelous. Nothing illustrates better the essential qualities of the king of Prussia than his spectacular victory in the battle of Leuthen:

> Considering all these circumstances, the imagination remains astounded by the dangers of Frederick's position, and by the grandeur of the resolution that he made. It is here, indeed, that the entire extent of his genius and his character is measured, and that the hero shows himself with proportions that are more on the scale of Divinity than on that of human nature.

En considérant toutes ces circonstances, l'imagination reste étonnée des dangers de la position de Frédéric, et de la grandeur de la résolution qu'il prit. C'est bien alors que se mesure toute l'étendue du génie et du caractère, et que le héros se montre avec des proportions qui tiennent plutôt de la Divinité que de la nature humaine.[68]

Grandeur, audacity, and genius that go beyond our comprehension have their own solidity. What Guibert calls "that consistency of glory and renown"[69] serves as a foundation for the construction of a peace enabling a vast range of initiatives for the good of society. For "the prestige of glory, like a divine vapor, was spread over his Person and surrounded him completely."[70] The prestige he developed for himself played a constitutive role and proved to be a source of dynamism for a society that, like the army, was characterized by its motivation, its unanimity, and its spirit of emulation. Defying those who would oppose power and glory, Guibert exclaims:

> Now analyze that life, you who are annoyed by praise, and who cannot endure the weight of admiration! You who seek to downplay everything and render everything obscure, who call that loving the truth, and claim to be freeing us from the blindness of enthusiasm, and who in the end have only the criminal intent to degrade glory.

> Maintenant analysez cette vie, ô vous, que la louange importune, & qui ne pouvez supporter le poids de l'admiration! Ô vous, qui cherchez à tout atténuer & à tout obscurcir, qui appelez cela aimer la vérité, et se dégager de l'aveuglement de l'enthousiasme, & qui n'avez, dans le fond, que le but criminel de dégrader la gloire.[71]

A curious formulation, which sets up a contrast between the brilliance of glory and a certain obscurity that the Enlightenment was creating, between the creative and exalting power of admiration and enthusiasm on the one hand, and the stifling and reductive power of critical reason on the other. The hero enables man to re-enchant his own world through acts of will, audacity, and energy. Guibert points out that "this prodigious man was indeed more of his own making than a product of nature."[72] The discipline Frederick has imposed on himself, the motivation he has given himself in overcoming ill health and a natural propensity for pleasure, are qualities that he impresses on his army and on his entire people. Freeing himself from all obstacles, Frederick makes himself into a hero by his own strength, and this spectacle of the heroic man serves to demonstrate to others their potential for greatness. As far as glory is concerned, this Modern would triumph over all the Ancients, even Caesar.

In the *Essai général sur la tactique*, however, Guibert explicitly claims he is no "blind admirer of the Ancients," describing himself rather as a "philosopher" contemplating the situation of "political Europe."[73] In a sense, he suggests the specificity of modern glory. For him, the key is to be found in the idea of scientific mastery. As in mathematics, where, having risen to the very top of their fields, thinkers like Newton, Leibniz, and d'Alembert "set opinions, spread their method and their genius over all knowledge,"[74] the goal Guibert sets himself, as a true child of the Enlightenment, is to set forth the "complete tactics," that "vast and sublime science," that would subsume military and political sciences.[75] Frederick's importance, then, would be in illustrating the effects of a mastery of that knowledge. Yet even Frederick's extraordinary exemplarity, Guibert cautions, has its shortcomings. The king of Prussia had not traveled enough and could not make informed comparisons between different countries, political systems, and customs. More important, in our own perspective,

> he had not benefited from the new knowledge that had spread across the field of political economy; in this area he had remained behind his time.
>
> il n'avoit pas profité des nouvelles lumières qui se sont répandues sur l'économie politique; il était sur ce point resté en arrière de son siècle.[76]

And for good reason, we might be tempted to say. Because the evolution of what used to be termed "political economy" seems to have taken a radically different, indeed incompatible, path: that of the free market, of the legitimation of profit and even luxury, the will not to die for one's nation but to help it live in prosperity.

While the incompatibility between the heavy, controlling hand of a Frederick II and the invisible hand of an Adam Smith seems obvious to us, it was not so to eighteenth-century eyes. Certainly not for Montesquieu, who saw the *doux commerce* and the call for glory each functioning on its own level. In a different vein, among the various attempts to redefine glory, the abbé Coyer attempted to "ennoble trade" by suggesting that the French nobility, following the example of the English nobility, should also engage in trade. According to Coyer, it was not a matter of abandoning glory but of conceiving of it in another way:

Glory, that passion of great souls, that motivation for great actions, is not always well understood. The nobility is made for glory. It is a lesson they learn
in the cradle. Prejudice cleaves to that opinion and disdainfully asks whether
there is any glory in trade.

La gloire, cette passion des belles âmes, ce ressort des grandes actions, n'est
pas toujours bien entendue. La Noblesse est faite pour la gloire. C'est une
leçon qu'on lui donne au berceau. Le Préjugé se tient à ce point de vue, & il
demande avec dédain s'il y a de la gloire dans le Commerce.[77]

Clearly, the abbé is defending the thesis that there is glory in trade because it
augments both the well-being and the power of the nation. But in France, the
same dynamics that constitute the notion of glory as a "third way," overcoming the opposition between virtue and personal interests, prevent the fusion
of glory and commerce. For even in materialist thinking, in which everything
is done through self-interest, the individual interest manifest in the desire
for recognition implies a certain grandeur and opens a realm of freedom far
from the petty calculations of the profit motive, which, however useful it may
be to society, remains bogged down in the immediacy of personal enrichment
and the limited confines of contractual timeframes. Yet it is quite possible to
conceive of a parallel, even complementary, functioning of both economies —
the commercial economy on the one hand, and the economy of glory on the
other — within the same society.

Shortly before the outbreak of the Revolution, the abbé Sieyès provided
the most coherent description of a society that not only would accept the
incompatibility of an interest in profit and the appeal of glory, but would
exploit that very incompatibility. In his *Essai sur les privilèges* (1788), Sieyès
identifies two fundamental human passions: the desire for money on the one
hand, and the desire for glory, honor, and recognition on the other: "The desire to deserve public esteem is [. . .] a necessary impediment to the passion
for wealth."[78] Granted, a passion for money has its beneficial effects, not the
least of which is to draw society out of an unhealthy preoccupation with the
past. To a nobility transfixed by a past that absorbs all its attention, Sieyès
contrasts the image of "city dwellers," *bourgeois*, endowed with a coherence
that we might call a "class mentality":

What is a *bourgeois* next to a man of privilege? The latter constantly has his
eyes fixed on the noble time of the *past*. He sees all his titles there, all his
strength, he lives off his ancestors. The bourgeois, on the contrary, with his

eyes always fixed on the ignoble *present*, on the indifferent *future*, prepares for the one and supports the other with the fruit of his work. He is, rather than having been; he endures hardship and, what is worse, the shame of employing all his intelligence, all his strength, to serve us today, and to live from his work, which is necessary to all.

Qu'est-ce qu'un *bourgeois* près d'un bon privilégié? Celui-ci a sans cesse les yeux sur le noble temps *passé*. Il y voit tous ses titres, toute sa force, il vit de ses ancêtres. Le bourgeois, au contraire, les yeux toujours fixés sur l'ignoble *présent*, sur l'indifférent *avenir*, prépare l'un, et soutient l'autre par les ressources de son industrie. Il est, au lieu d'avoir été; il essuie la peine, et qui pis est, la honte d'employer toute son intelligence, toute sa force à notre service actuel, et de vivre de son travail nécessaire à tous.[79]

Motivated by a passion for wealth, by the profit motive, the bourgeois fulfills the material needs of society. But Sieyès also describes another economy, that of honor defined as the freely granted esteem of the public:

Ah! Let the prize of public consideration flow freely within the nation to pay its debt to genius and virtue. Let us not violate the sublime relationships of humanity that nature has been careful to etch in the depths of our hearts. Let us applaud this admirable commerce of benefits and praise that is established, for the consolation of the whole world, between the needs of appreciative peoples and the great men handsomely paid for all their services by a simple tribute of recognition. All is pure in this exchange: it is rich in virtue and powerful in happiness, as long as it is not disturbed in its natural and free progress.

Ah! Laissez le prix de la considération publique couler librement au sein de la nation pour acquitter sa dette envers le génie et la vertu. Gardons-nous de violer les sublimes rapports d'humanité que la nature a été attentive à graver dans le fond de nos cœurs. Applaudissons à cet admirable commerce de bienfaits et d'hommages qui s'établit, pour la consolation de la terre, entre les besoins des peuples reconnaissans, et les grands hommes surabondamment payés de tous leurs services par un simple tribut de reconnaissance. Tout est pur dans cet échange: il est fécond en vertu, puissant en bonheur, tant qu'il n'est point troublé dans sa marche naturelle et libre.[80]

In this context, public esteem becomes a sort of "moral currency."[81] Sieyès thus describes a politico-moral economy conceived on the model of the commercial economy of free exchange. Nothing must impede its free and natural progress. Great men and geniuses are paid "abundantly" with esteem. Closely linked to an ever-growing emphasis on the legitimizing function of public opinion, the "free" market of esteem remunerates in accordance with the value of the action, and encourages emulation. This vision of the workings of recognition and emulation would acquire even more strength after the abolition of the nobility's privileges.

Thus Sieyès describes a society organized on two parallel levels. Both may call upon *amour-propre*, self-interest, and a concern with self. But the economic level is that of abstract calculation and contractual relations. On the political level, contractualist thinking favors the will of the collectivity at the expense of the will of the individual. Glory, however, is profoundly personal and favors the individual as such in his relationship with society. Not only does the desire for recognition impede the desire for profit, but it confers dignity on man as a social being. In this vision of a society, a happy medium must be found between the centrifugal force of a desire for money, and the centripetal force of glory. If desire for money produces a system capable of satisfying material needs, desire for recognition enables society to establish distinctions based on something other than financial calculations, too closely linked to the idea of luxury. Each level has its utility and encourages individual initiative, one through contract and the profit motive, the other through emulation and the need for recognition — hence a bi-level society, both levels being sites of competition and merit, and each having its own rules. But the "noble" level is destined for great men, geniuses, virtuous persons recognized by public opinion.

In 1792, Marat announced the forthcoming French version of *Chains of Slavery*. Published in 1793, a few months before the assassination of the revolutionary journalist by Charlotte Corday, *Les Chaînes de l'esclavage* retained the same argument as in the English version of 1772.[82] But in the context of a French Revolution becoming ever more radicalized, the author chose to reinforce his description of the workings of glory as a regulating principle in society, and to flesh out his denunciation of commerce. Once again, we hear echoes of Montesquieu as Marat asserts that the mercantile spirit renders everything venal, because "by constantly and rigorously calculating his personal interest, each person adopts a position of strict equity [. . .] hostile to any noble behavior and to any elevation of the soul."[83] As for glory, "that sublime incentive," it nourishes grandeur of the soul and heroism; it is "the prize of merit in all things, the reward for all services rendered to one's country".[84] Central to this thinking is the quest for dignity and the grandeur of man as *an individual in society*, qualities that society as a collectivity, the "public," as Marat would say, recognizes in various symbolic ways.

The Measure of a Man

By making the economy of glory a sort of self-regulating market — provided it is allowed to function freely — these visions seem to ignore a danger integral to the pursuit of glory, a danger consisting in one of glory's basic components: that of individual excess, so well incarnated in the figure of Achilles. The other components, one might say, have obscured the risks posed by glory's excess. The association with the idea of merit, the crucial role played by public opinion, the inciting to emulation as a motor for moral reform, all these aspects of the economy of glory were certainly enough to be seductive. But it was perhaps in its assertion of the potential for grandeur and freedom that this model made such an impact in the French Revolution. Thinkers as profoundly different as Montesquieu and Marat readily agreed that glory is never the companion of servitude. The ideal of glory could appear as a means of immediate, even marvelous, liberation, in transcending the opposition between virtue and interest and between the individual and the collectivity, precisely because emulation was presented as a form of disinterestedness. Here we are in a world not of contracts but of exuberance and enthusiasm, joining the individual to the collectivity. In this world there was no longer a need to think about the Revolution in rational, contractual terms; what mattered was to accomplish it by acting in accordance with man's fundamental nature, at the heart of which were freedom and the potential for grandeur.

The Revolution, in fact, continued to explore the connection between freedom and disinterestedness with a view to inserting them into its own logic. That relationship was probably nowhere better developed and "revolutionized," to borrow Barère's expression, than by Jean-Baptiste Salaville, who, in *L'Homme et la Société, ou nouvelle théorie de la nature humaine et de l'état social* (1798), puts it, so to speak, at the ontological center of a regenerated man. This text is of particular interest in that Salaville, a fairly moderate revolutionary, deeply influenced by the thinking of Diderot, attempts to detach the notion of freedom from that of the social contract, which, by definition, implies reciprocity as an essential condition, man imposing on himself obligations toward others because they impose the same toward him. For this theoretician of the social connection, the love of self that characterizes the human condition is in the end only a love of freedom, that is, the freedom to act beyond or in spite of the constraints of the material and tangible world:[85]

"Freedom in man is the principle of disinterestedness and generosity, consequently, of all sociability, of all human morality."[86] A man truly exists as a man only insofar as he asserts his own freedom:

> This is why the sacrifices of virtue, duty, and heroism are eminently free acts, because they prove that the determinations of moral will have prevailed over the more energetic determinations of physical will.

> Voilà pourquoi les sacrifices de la vertu, du devoir, de l'héroïsme, sont des actes éminemment libres, parce qu'ils supposent que les déterminations de la volonté morale ont prévalu sur les déterminations les plus énergiques de la volonté physique.[87]

And the desire for freedom triumphs even over the instinct for survival. Thus we arrive at a sort of democratization of the soul's grandeur and of transcendence in immanence. In each one of us there is "a supernatural being, so to speak, or one that is beyond the natural laws of the world and inhabits this world without being subjected to the order of necessity that rules and directs it; from which it follows that this being is free by its nature."[88] Significantly, we find in Salaville's thinking an element that once characterized certain strains of aristocratic thinking, a particularly strong expression of which we saw in the seventeenth century in Lartigue: the imperative of war beyond all teleology, with no other finality than itself. In Salaville's perspective, perpetual peace would constitute a threat because it would deprive every individual of the opportunity to assert his fundamental freedom in the ultimate act of generous disinterestedness, sacrificing himself for the collectivity:

> If a perfect and unalterable peace could be established among nations; if they had neither foreign nor internal wars to fear, their security would be absolute, and henceforth, nothing would create in their citizens the obligation to risk their lives or to die for their nations: by suppressing all opportunities for war, one would also suppress that obligation, and since man is unable to be free except through that obligation, by depriving him of it one would take away his freedom: his nature thus demands that he be maintained in the duty to risk his life and to die, if necessary, for his nation.

> Si une paix parfaite et inaltérable pouvoit s'établir entre les nations; si elles n'avoient à craindre ni guerres étrangères ni guerres intestines, leur sécurité seroit absolue, et dès lors, rien ne motiveroit de la part des citoyens,

l'obligation de s'exposer et de mourir pour elles: en supprimant toutes les chances de la guerre, on supprimeroit aussi cette obligation, et l'homme ne pouvant être libre que par elle, en l'en dépouillant, on le dépouilleroit de sa liberté: sa nature exige donc qu'il soit maintenu dans le devoir de s'exposer et de mourir s'il le faut, pour sa patrie.[89]

Whether we're talking about Telemachus, Charlemagne, or an ordinary citizen, heroic disinterestedness, closely linked to the generous nature of man and the possibility of pure love, often appears against a backdrop of confrontation and armed conflict.

▲ △ ▲

Charles Lemire, the Elder, *Bonaparte Disembarking in Egypt* (early nineteenth century?). Drawing (Inv.Pl.1526). Palais des Beaux Arts, Lille, France. Photograph by René-Gabriel Ojéda. Photograph © RMN-Grand Palais / Art Resource, New York.

CHAPTER 4

An Economy of Glory

Ancients and Moderns: The Final Battle

As it developed over the course of the eighteenth century, the ideology of glory acquired a discursive force that offered a way out of the impasse of contractualism and past the problem raised by the abstraction of the general will. The emotion and enthusiasm kindled by glory were seen as generators of social bonds, even of fraternity. This ideology had the ability to combine devotion and disinterest with a concern for oneself, to appear a simultaneous affirmation of both individual and collective grandeur, to play—cannily—on the esteem of public opinion and on an appeal to posterity. The ideology of glory became operational, so to speak, in a context in which a regimen of virtue led to the impasse of the Terror and in which financiers, motivated explicitly by profit, found themselves doubly discredited—first under the Ancien Régime, then under the Directoire. The ideology was bolstered by war, which, from the first campaign in Italy, enabled Bonaparte to develop a series of practices tending to blur the distinctions between the love of glory and the love of profit, between recognition and remuneration, between devotion to the nation and a concern for oneself.

A purveyor of both glory and riches, Napoleon sought throughout his reign to exalt the former while recognizing that it could flourish only within relative prosperity. This dualist vision reserved an important place for economic liberalism, which, however, would always be sacrificed on the altar of national greatness. One need only look at the disastrous effects of the continental system or the way France's allies modified their budgets in deference to French needs.[1] In the context of the Revolution, the entire ideology of glory was anchored in a patriotism formulated in terms of universal values.[2] Insofar as there existed a set of perfect connections extending from the individual to the nation and from the nation to humanity, the ideal of glory remained coherent. Early on, Robespierre expressed very concisely the imperative of this concentric arrangement:

> There are two types of egotism: one is vile, cruel, it isolates man from his peers, seeks an exclusive well-being, paid for by the misfortunes of others; the other is generous, benevolent, it combines our happiness with the happiness of all, it connects our glory to that of the nation. The former breeds oppressors and tyrants; the latter, defenders of humanity. Let us follow these healthy impulses; let us cherish the peace achieved through glorious works: let us not fear the death that crowns those achievements, and we will ensure the happiness of our nation, and even our own.
>
> Vice and virtue create earthly destinies: they are two opposing spirits locked in struggle over the earth. The source of each lies in the passions of man: depending on the direction he gives to his passions, man rises to the heavens or sinks to murky depths; but the goal of all social institutions is to direct him toward justice, which is both public happiness and private happiness.

> Il y a deux sortes d'égoïsmes: l'un vil, cruel, qui isole l'homme de ses semblables, qui cherche un bien-être exclusif, acheté par la misère d'autrui; l'autre, généreux, bienfaisant, qui confond notre bonheur dans le bonheur de tous, qui attache notre gloire à celle de la patrie. Le premier fait les oppresseurs et les tyrans; le second, les défenseurs de l'humanité. Suivons son impulsion salutaire; chérissons le repos acheté par de glorieux travaux: ne craignons point la mort qui les couronne, et nous consoliderons le bonheur de notre patrie, et même le nôtre.
>
> Le vice et la vertu font les destins de la terre: ce sont les deux génies opposés qui se la disputent. La source de l'un et de l'autre est dans les passions de l'homme: selon la direction qui est donnée à ses passions, l'homme s'élève jusqu'aux cieux ou s'enfonce dans des abîmes fangeux; or le but de toutes les institutions sociales, c'est de le diriger vers la justice, qui est à la fois le bonheur public et le bonheur privé.[3]

For Robespierre, glory and happiness can be established only on the moral foundations of virtue and justice. Individual, nation, and humanity are concentric spheres that develop in relation to universal values. The French, taken individually and collectively as a people, have become bearers of these values. But the load proves very heavy indeed. In a sense, it could not be otherwise, for as soon as the spheres fail to coincide, the tensions inherent in the model intensify. In this new era of a modernity imposing itself by force, the mythic power of the Napoleonic epic entailed both the aspiration to that concentric harmony and the impossibility of maintaining it. Indeed, circumstances constantly pushed Bonaparte to choose between humanity and the nation, between the nation and the individual. Liberal universalism, as we know, does not need to force this kind of coincidence because, from its point of view, harmony is achieved without needing to be consciously sought as an objective. The Napoleonic project for establishing a political legitimacy grounded in glory grew out of Enlightenment optimism and a profound belief in the grandeur of man, whose modern origins go back to a humanism inherited from the Counter-Reformation. In the case of France, this project led to the reformulation of certain warrior values of the nobility in such a way as to democraticize and "nationalize" them. In its appeal to posterity, it meant turning resolutely to the future while claiming to have definitively surpassed the Ancients.

It is precisely because the notion of glory had always been at the heart of French identity — penetrating it while constantly being transformed throughout its history — that Napoleon would turn to that notion when pursuing his politics of fusion. We have seen the degree to which the eighteenth century developed the idea of a veritable economy of glory, in which glory would constitute an effective mechanism to manage society, and through which society would manage itself. It was in the space of this fundamental ambiguity that Napoleonic politics would evolve. The glorious self that Napoleon strove to incarnate was imbued with all the force and contradictions of an idealized vision of will, in a society that sought to rule itself through the mechanisms of glory. This vision is far from antimodern; on the contrary, it is the vision of a modernity that man was fighting to impose, of a liberty that, by becoming absolute, was transformed into its opposite and perhaps for that very reason could never flourish without armed conflict. In the Revolution, the ideology of glory offered the promise of reconciling personal ambition with submission to the collective cause, distinction with equality, the logic of reason with the energy of imagination. Relying on the mechanisms of emulation, it invited comparison with the greatest: the heroes of antiquity. By confronting myth on its favored terrain—that of war—and asserting the superiority of the Moderns over the Ancients in terms of epic grandeur, the ideology of glory furnished a spectacular demonstration of the power of equality while nevertheless enabling the establishment of distinctions. The heroization of Republican armies, the rising cult of martyrs of the Revolution, the creation of the Pantheon, and the celebration of great generals provide ample illustration.[4]

By competing with the Ancients, and surpassing them, the French were able to rediscover a national tradition of glory, and to integrate it. It was thus by way of myth that France was able to return to history. This movement took off with the establishment of the Consulat. The victory at Marengo unleashed a series of public reflections on the mechanisms of glory. As we shall see, there was a shift from a politics of glory based on virtue and pure love— a politics that demanded an alignment of humanity-nation-individual—to a politics that allowed for a concern with both the individual and the collective self and therefore accepted a certain *amour-propre de vanité* as a means of regulation and even of transcendence in immanence.

The Marengo Moment

The "Marengo moment" marks the transition toward a politics of legitimation through glory.[5] The poem on death that François de Neufchateau read before the Institut de France on 15 Messidor year VII (3 July 1800) illustrates the phenomenon while throwing light on Napoleon's role in it after the establishment of the Consulat.[6] This long meditation on death includes an elegy for Desaix, killed at Marengo on 14 June. Neufchateau evokes all the components of the *locus classicus*: the inevitability of death, the fear of suffering, the despair of the bereaved, the illusory nature of any happiness on earth, the need to benefit from life (*carpe diem*) and to learn to die, the value of friendship and wisdom. Invoking his illustrious predecessors—Ancients from Athens and Rome, as well as Moderns—Despréaux (Boileau), La Fontaine, and Molière—the poet chooses to seek inspiration in the silence and cool of the woods. Meditating "on the banks of a pure stream," he allows his thoughts to wander; in a deep reverie he sees himself beyond the grave facing Death, who attempts to convince him of the vanity of life:

> You seek rest; you will find none on earth.
> On earth, from the beginning, one finds only hell.
> You will know exile, shipwreck, and irons.
> In vain you will bear to the point of idolatry,

The primary virtue, a love of country.
O unfortunate martyr, what fruit do you hope to reap
From this passion, this obstinate zeal?

Tu cherches du repos; il n'en est pas sur la terre.
Sur la terre, d'avance, on trouve les enfers.
Tu connaîtras l'exil, le naufrage et ses fers.
Tu porteras en vain, jusqu'à l'idolâtrie,
La première vertu, l'amour de la patrie.
De cette passion, martyr infortuné,
Quel fruit espères-tu de ton zèle obstiné?[7]

Love of one's nation is only obstinate zeal for someone in search of true and eternal rest — which is found only beyond the grave — but the poet ends by rejecting Death's contention that living is merely learning how to die. As a counter-argument, and better than any reasoning, the poet cites the example of French soldiers:

To defy death's treacherous terrors,
Let us follow the generous example of our warriors:
Existence is nothing, for them glory is all.
O source of admirable and fecund heroism!
Those who defy death are the masters of the world. [. . .]
Thebes once had only one Epaminondas
The Republic has as many as it has soldiers.
Each one is a hero full of the noble desire
To extend his memory beyond his life;
And his gaze piercing through the darkness of the grave,
From immortality sees the glow of the flame.

Pour braver de la mort les terreurs infidèles,
Suivons de nos guerriers l'exemple généreux:
L'existence n'est rien, la gloire est tout pour eux.
O source d'héroïsme admirable et féconde!
Ceux qui bravent la mort sont les maîtres du monde. [. . .]
Thèbes n'eut autrefois qu'un Épaminondas:
La république en nombre autant que de soldats.
Chacun est un héros plein de la noble envie
D'étendre sa mémoire au-delà de sa vie;

Et son regard perçant dans la nuit du tombeau,
De l'immortalité voit luire le flambeau.[8]

Here we find, in an effective coincidence, the mastery of self, of death, and of the world. The key to the superiority of modern heroism? Equality. Heroes are as numerous as the nation's soldiers; *every person* is motivated by a "noble desire." The ideal of glory is collective.

Just a few days after the battle of Marengo (25 Prairial year VIII / 14 June 1800), Pierre Daunou delivered a speech before the Tribunat in which, from the last words that Desaix had allegedly spoken — "Tell the First Consul that I am dying with the regret of not having done enough to live in posterity'"[9] — he develops a reflection on glory:

> The love of glory, the motive for all truly great actions, is refined within republics; it assumes a more noble character because it distinguishes itself from all other ambitions [. . .]. Through a love of glory, through the need to live in posterity, all strengths and talents do all that is possible for them to do for the happiness of society. May republican institutions inspire and cultivate in us that beneficial feeling which commands the most widely recognized and healthiest practice among types of power, which discourages all cowardly, unjust, oppressive, immoral acts; inspiring in soldiers a steadfast devotion, counseling moderation to the victorious, and peace to the conquerors.

> L'amour de la gloire, mobile de toute action véritablement grande, s'épure au sein des républiques; il y prend un caractère plus noble, parce qu'il s'y détache mieux de toutes les autres ambitions [. . .]. C'est par l'amour de la gloire, par ce besoin de vivre dans la postérité, que les forces et les talents quelconques font pour le bonheur de la société tout ce qu'il leur est possible de faire. Puissent parmi nous les institutions républicaines susciter et cultiver ce sentiment bienfaiteur qui commande l'usage à la fois le plus entendu et le plus salutaire de tous les genres de puissances, qui détourne de toute action lâche, injuste, oppressive, immorale; inspire aux guerriers un dévouement sans réserve, conseille aux victorieux la modération, et la paix aux conquérants.[10]

For Daunou the quest for glory frees one from other passions such as the simple "desire for power" or "instant renown" ("renommée contemporaine") and promotes a full development of "the faculties of the superior man." It is up to each person to find that which is best in himself. Thus Daunou emphasizes that, during battle, each "Republican phalanx and, so to speak, each handful of men" distinguished itself through "specific feats" ("prodiges particuliers") and shone "by its own brilliance." At the center of the Marengo battle stood Bonaparte, the first magistrate of the Republic, distributing crowns and instructing the soldiers in how to deserve them. For Neufchateau, the final words attributed to Desaix allow the poet to stress the essential role that Bonaparte would henceforth play on the stage of glory and that would continue to be exploited over the course of the Empire. The "magnanimous Desaix" was marked by his modesty and his sense of his own inadequacies: he fully believed that he had not done enough to survive in posterity. But such a formulation of his devotion, which also expresses a concern with himself, becomes in itself a source of individual distinction. Recognition passes through the mediation of the First Consul, who, in taking care of Desaix, nourishes his own glory:

> A single thought concerns you: O too modest warrior!
> You alone are not satisfied with yourself;
> You fear to have done too little for posterity.
> Desaix! May your great shadow today be consoled!
> Among our last nephews your final word
> Will ring without end, and your memory
> Will speak to centuries to come.
> The first of all heroes fully understands glory;
> And it is he who inscribes you in the temple of memory.
> Bonaparte honors himself in honoring you.

> Un seul penser t'occupe: ô guerrier trop modeste!
> De toi-même toi seul tu n'es point satisfait;
> Pour la postérité, tu crains d'avoir peu fait.
> Desaix! Que ta grande ombre aujourd'hui se console!
> Chez nos derniers neveux ta dernière parole
> Retentira sans cesse, et de ton souvenir
> Sans cesse entretiendra les siècles à venir.
> Le premier des héros doit se connaître en gloire;
> Et c'est lui qui t'inscrit au temple de mémoire.
> Bonaparte s'honore, en sachant t'honorer.

Little by little, a discourse emerges in which the conflict between equality and distinction diminishes. On 16 Messidor, Louis-Alexandre Jard-Panvilliers, president of the Tribunat, on the occasion of the memorial for Desaix, expresses the strong emotions of the assembly following the triumph of the Republican armies at Marengo. In his eulogy, he shows how Desaix sought to distinguish himself as compared to the heroes of antiquity: nothing attracted him more

> than the study of the history of those republics of Greece and Rome. His spirit was moved upon reading of the great deeds and traits of virtue that had graced so many great men, on whom those republics could pride themselves. Steeped, too, in admiration for the conqueror of the Persians at Marathon, he vowed, rather than flattering himself, to be one day capable of walking in the footsteps of his heroes.

> que l'étude de l'histoire de ces républiques de la Grèce et de Rome. Son esprit s'échauffait à la lecture des hauts faits et des traits de vertu qui avaient illustré tant de grands hommes, dont ces républiques avaient à s'honorer. Également pénétré d'admiration pour le vainqueur des Perses à Marathon, il formait le vœu, plutôt qu'il n'osait se flatter, d'être un jour à même de marcher sur les traces de ses héros.[11]

In this perspective, the final words of the dying soldier translate a sentiment of failure compared to the Ancients. Only Bonaparte, "the first hero," assures the measure of Desaix's heroic grandeur relative to the Ancients and, at the same time, the legitimacy of self-assertion within the framework of a Republican devotion channeled through the First Consul. At the dawn of the nineteenth century, the first "Napoleon effect" would be his acting as both operator and guarantor of the grandeur of modern heroes in their face-off with the Ancients. It is only from this position that the reconquest of French history could begin: the fusion of pre- and post-Revolutionary France.

In his speech before the Tribunat, Jard-Panvilliers had already pointed out that French and enemy soldiers alike in 1792 had described Desaix, borrowing the motto of the renowned sixteenth-century French knight Pierre Terrail de Bayard, as a "fearless warrior beyond reproach."[12] The initiative appeared to have come from below, from the soldiers, even enemy soldiers. For collectively — spontaneously, it would seem — they could recognize a new Bayard and connect Desaix's "noble desire" to the the chivalrous history of France.

Turenne at the Temple de Mars

The transfer of Turenne's remains to the Temple de Mars symbolizes the beginning of what would become the politics of fusion. In 1791, the heroization of the Republican armies led the Revolution to rebaptize Les Invalides as the Temple de Mars — yet another sign that the deeds of its soldiers were to be evaluated in relation to those of the Ancients. Such a gesture was perfectly in keeping with the logic of revolutionary rupture. But in his speech delivered on 22 September 1800, which corresponded to the fifth complementary day of year VIII — a day designated the *Fête de la récompense* (day of national reward) — on the occasion of the transfer ceremony, Carnot, the very Republican minister of war, enlarges upon the duty to remember that falls to the republican armies. He emphasizes that this duty obeys a logic of continuity rather than rupture:

> To the brave belong the ashes of the brave; they are their natural guardians; they must be their jealous depositaries. After death the soldier has a right acquired on the battlefield; that of remaining under the protection of the soldiers who survive him, to share with them the refuge devoted to glory; for glory is an acquisition that death cannot take away.

> Aux braves appartient la cendre du brave; ils en sont les gardiens naturels; ils doivent en être les dépositaires jaloux. Un droit reste après la mort au guerrier qui fut moissonné sur le champ des combats; celui de demeurer sous la sauvegarde des guerriers qui lui survivent, de partager avec eux l'asile consacré à la gloire; car la gloire est une propriété que la mort n'enlève pas.[13]

To respect the right to memory thus becomes the duty of the soldier-citizen. Preserving memory, keeping it alive, is in itself an act of courage.

> The greatness of every hero is seen in the greatness of the heroes he has surpassed; he increases his own glory by causing to shine ever more brilliantly that of the greatest men without the fear he will be overshadowed by them.

> La grandeur de tout héros est attestée par la grandeur des héros qu'il a surpassés; il rehausse sa propre gloire en faisant briller de tout son éclat celle des plus grands hommes sans craindre d'être effacé par eux.[14]

The economy of glory described by Carnot implies the competition that goes with emulation. It is not a zero-sum game; on the contrary, it is in continual expansion. Provided that the right to memory is respected, the glory achieved by men increases in splendor over time. Our modern heroes are great in the light of the Ancients; they are great for the good of the French and of all of humanity.[15] Rather than illustrating the values of the nobility, Turenne "made the brilliance of his rank disappear through that of his victories, and one saw only the great man in him."[16] Turenne's heroism comes from the greatness of an individual and not from the splendor of a class. It is not a nobleman who is being honored, but a man. Turenne did not sacrifice himself for the monarchy, but for France:

> It was not to maintain the then dominant political system that he devoted his efforts, that he sacrificed his life, but for the defense of his country, *independent of any system*. The love of the nation was his motive, as it is today for those such as Dampierre, Dugommier, Marceau, Joubert, Desaix, La Tour d'Auvergne.

> Ce ne fut point au maintien du système politique alors dominant qu'il consacra ses travaux, qu'il sacrifia sa vie, mais à la défense de son pays, *indépendante de tout système*. L'amour de la patrie fut son mobile, comme il fut de nos jours celui des Dampierre, des Dugommier, des Marceau, des Joubert, des Desaix, des La Tour d'Auvergne.[17]

Thus France, *regardless of its political regime*, is envisaged as a fundamental value. As for Turenne, "his glory must not be separated from that of these Republican heroes."[18] This fusion of the glory of the pre- and post-Revolutionary France results in detaching a love of France from any perceived need for love of the Republic. For the first time, the heroes of the Republic are assembled in the Temple de Mars not only with the heroes of antiquity but also with those of the monarchy. The continuity of national recognition, respect for the duty of memory, in turn enable us to appeal to posterity and to expect that it will remember us as well. The recognition of past heroes depends on our mediation; at the same time, by taking care of them, we nourish our own glory, we become agents of transcendence, including our own. In such a context a concern with self finds its raison d'être. The very universality of the duty to remember — every individual showing greatness has the right to be remembered — prevents the exclusion of great Frenchmen of the past. To recognize the magnanimous men of that earlier France is an act of courage, generosity, and self-interest. It is the best way to fulfill a contract totally different from the one Rousseau had proposed.

The social contract of the philosopher from Geneva is unique in that the process by which it is carried out is marked by a strange temporal discontinuity. For each person contracts not only with everyone else *but also with himself as he will become from the moment the contract is enacted.* Before the contract, the individual is, so to speak, morally incapable of entering into a true contract with others, and it is only with the institution of the social contract that "a moral and collective body" arises, which, paradoxically, constitutes the very condition of possibility for the contract.[19] This temporal discontinuity, prioritizing the contractual moment, continued to haunt the Revolution, which never seemed to get beyond it. It was at the heart of the dynamics of the revolutionary rupture with history. That the ideal of glory is imbued with a kind of ahistoricity has often been noted. From that point of view, Plutarch's *Parallel Lives* serves to illustrate this absence of continuity in time,[20] and the enormous influence this text had on Bonaparte is evoked to illustrate the degree to which on some level he extracted himself from the historical moment to settle in the timeless republic of heroes. In many respects, Napoleon was merely carrying on a process begun in the Revolution that turned to the heroes of antiquity the better to break out of monarchical history. The revolutionary heroes demonstrated that they could match ancient heroes and even surpass them. It was from the perspective of the timeless city of heroes and great men that undertaking a return to history became possible. The ideology of glory had the advantage of encompassing the duty of remembering, while being perfectly compatible with the notion of progress. And Carnot's reflections are based on those elements, developing the idea that the men born of the Revolution are the posterity of their ancestors; so it is the nation's duty to recognize the greatness of a Turenne, for example, regardless of the political regime. If there is a contract, it is between past generations and generations to come. Seen this way, the present is no longer a flight forward, so to speak, but a moment between the past and the future; it is part of a long continuity.[21] One can now think in terms of a national history and develop a political view that takes into account the specificity of that history.

The *Fête de la République* of Year IX

Carnot delivered his speech on the last day of year VIII, an important moment in the Republican calendar, as was also the following day, the first day of year IX and the *Fête de la fondation de la République.* On that day François

Andrieux spoke before the Tribunat—which he describes as the sanctuary of "noble disinterestedness," of "heroic devotion," in sum, of "all Republican virtues"[22]—to celebrate the Republic and its heroes, of course, but also to reflect on the pros and cons of the parallels between the French Republic and the great models of antiquity. He begins by emphasizing the difference between the monarchy and the Republic. The driving principle of the monarchy is a love of distinctions and preferences, and its institutions only "exalt egotism, greed, the ambition for frivolous honors, and a stupid predilection for itself [. . .], a profound indifference for the general good."[23] In these preliminary observations, Andrieux develops an argument worthy of Robespierre, asserting that the principle of the Republic is virtue and all that is associated with it: benevolence, reciprocal esteem, disinterestedness, simplicity. Virtue assures that even the love of glory comes *after* a love of the nation in the hearts of citizens. He insists on the direction that the Republic gives to a concentric arrangement:

> In the monarchy, each person is concerned first with himself, then with his family, then with his friends, then with those who are of interest to him; the good of the State comes last. In the Republic, the opposite must be true; one must begin with the nation, and end with oneself.

> Dans la monarchie chacun s'occupe d'abord de soi, puis de sa famille, puis de ses amis, puis de ceux qui l'intéressent; le bien de l'État vient le dernier. Dans la République, ce doit être tout le contraire; il faut commencer par la patrie, et finir par soi-même.[24]

Up to this point, he has said nothing surprising; it is a standard celebration of the universal Republic. But immediately following that dose of Republican rhetoric, the president of the Tribunat makes a turn that leads him to nuance his words greatly.

The former friend of the Girondins begins by softening his condemnation of the monarchy. One mustn't believe, according to Andrieux, that under a monarchical government there can be no virtue, no happiness for the people. Love of country can be found there, as well as "a certain degree of freedom," especially if the monarch himself proves to be a friend of Enlightenment.[25] But then comes an attempt to disengage France from a harmful parallel with the Ancients and to formulate the specificity of the modern Republic. Andrieux maintains that the French must not seek to establish an absolute democracy; nor, above all, should their democracy resemble that of Sparta,

Athens, or Rome. "An admiration for beautiful Greek and Latin literature" inspired great talents of the previous century in their struggles against the crimes of despotism. But their enthusiasm was too exalted; "everything threw us into exaggerations,"[26] which alienated us from ourselves and incited us to identify too much with the Ancients:

> All the essential differences that exist between those ancient societies and a nation of twenty-five to thirty million individuals spread over a surface of twenty thousand square lieues, surrounded by monarchic and powerful States, connected among themselves and with it through a political system that covered all of Europe, have been rendered abstract; so, too, the old habits of this nation, its many prejudices, and its long-lived corruption. Those who claimed suddenly to transform the French into Greeks and Romans even seemed ignorant or unaware of the institutions of those ancient peoples; they forgot that in Sparta and Athens each citizen possessed a herd of slaves; that in Rome not only was horrible slavery common practice, but there were five different classes of citizens.

> [L']on fit abstraction de toutes les différences essentielles qui se trouvaient entre ces anciennes sociétés et une nation de vingt-cinq à trente millions d'individus répandus sur une surface de vingt mille lieues carrées, environnée d'États monarchiques et puissans, liés entre eux et avec elle par un système politique qui embrassait l'Europe entière; on fit abstraction et des vieilles habitudes de cette nation, et de ses nombreux préjugés, et de sa longue corruption. Ceux qui prétendaient transformer tout à coup les Français en Grecs et en Romains semblaient même ignorer ou méconnaître les institutions de ces anciens peuples; ils oubliaient qu'à Sparte et dans Athènes chaque citoyen possédait un troupeau d'esclaves; qu'à Rome non seulement l'horrible esclavage était aussi usité, mais qu'il y avait cinq classes différentes de citoyens.[27]

By rendering history abstract, by turning its back on an entire heritage of customs, prejudices, and habits, and by having idealized the Ancients, the French Republic fell into the criminal excesses of the Terror. And Andrieux goes on to affirm that the roots of the current administrative reforms are to be found in the pre-Revolutionary past, that the département councils "are retracing the former *provincial administrations*, whose patriotic idea is owed to Turgot, that citizen minister and true friend of the people."[28] As for the exploits of Republican soldiers,

what words can, I won't say eulogize, but do justice to the French soldiers
who died in defense of the nation! Who can recount the true value of their
magnanimity and their heroic devotion! The eight years of revolutionary
war offer more glorious feats of arms, more military triumphs, than any of
the most brilliant centuries in our history."

[q]uel discours peut, je ne dis pas offrir des éloges, mais rendre justice aux
guerriers français morts pour la défense de la patrie! Qui pourrait raconter
dignement leur magnanimité et leur héroïque dévouement! Les huit années
de guerre de la révolution offrent plus de glorieux faits d'armes, plus de
triomphes militaires qu'aucun des siècles les plus brillans de notre histoire."

Andrieux then asserts the grandeur of the French soldiers, not in relation to
an ancient ideal, but with regard to *"our"* own history, that of France.

In a speech delivered the same day at the Temple de Mars, the minister of
the interior, Lucien Bonaparte, rather than making a parallel with times and
places that are not those of France, invites the French to look into their own
history find a comparison—one that would become ever more common as
France evolves toward Empire. "One must go back to Charlemagne to find a
France as vast in territory, as powerful through the strength of its armies."[29]
Gradually, the legitimizing image of Napoleon as a new Charlemagne takes
shape. But here Lucien Bonaparte insists that the glory of the soldiers of the
Republic is to be measured in comparison with their own French ancestors.
In this perspective, the significance of the transfer of Turenne's remains be-
comes clear:

Yes, today I invoke the memory of that great master of the military arts, to
whom the monarchy owed such brilliant days [. . .]. Turenne expected from
the French people the justice he has just now obtained [. . .]. For a long time
his tomb was among the tombs of the kings [. . .]; here he is in the temple of
Victory, under the flags conquered by the heirs to his renown. Might we not
say that at this moment the two centuries have come together and clasped
hands above this august tomb? That which was great in the past, that which
is great today, the living heroes, the illustrious dead, gather together in the
same place to celebrate the great day when France changed laws *without
interrupting the course of its great destinies. This union of our ancient glory and
our present glory must strengthen the union of the citizens*; it is above all an example for our descendants. May they respect the memory of heroes far into
the distant future!

Oui, j'invoque dans ce jour la mémoire de ce grand maître de l'art militaire, à qui la monarchie dut des jours si brillans [. . .]. Turenne attendait du peuple français la justice qu'il vient d'obtenir. [. . .] Son tombeau fut longtemps au milieu des tombeaux des rois [. . .]; le voilà dans le temple de la Victoire, sous les drapeaux conquis par les héritiers de sa renommée. Ne dirait-on pas que les deux siècles en ce moment se rencontrent, et se donnent la main sur cette tombe auguste? Ce qui fut grand autrefois, ce qui l'est aujourd'hui, les héros vivants, les morts illustres, se rassemblent dans le même lieu pour célébrer le grand jour où la France a changé de lois *sans interrompre le cours de ses grandes destinées. Cette réunion de notre ancienne gloire et de notre gloire présente doit redoubler l'union des citoyens;* elle est surtout un exemple pour nos descendans. Qu'ils respectent le souvenir des héros jusqu'à la postérité la plus reculée![30]

By means of glory, according to Lucien Bonaparte, France could overcome the revolutionary fracture, find its past, reestablish its history as a continuity. Even if customs, habits, and laws have varied, asserts the minister of the interior, heroism and virtue endure. France, as an entity, retains its fundamental identity in a continuous chain that extends from Charlemagne through the monarchy up to the Republic. Because the French fulfill their duty of memory, they can turn with confidence toward their descendants. National recognition reflects a public opinion informed by the national history and sustained by a controlled momentum of enthusiasm. It is less a matter of erasing the Ancients than of relativizing their position in relation to a modernity that has its own specificity.

Constructing the Self as a Self-Regulating Model

The Marengo moment represented an opportunity not only to celebrate military heroism but also to develop a way of thinking about glory in terms of the renewal that the Consulat proposed to carry out. Fate had it that on the very day of Desaix's death in Italy, Jean-Baptiste Kléber also died, in Egypt. Andrieux and Lucien Bonaparte spoke of these men at the Tribunat and the Temple de Mars on the occasion of the *Fête de la fondation de la République*. But it was the senator Dominique-Joseph Garat who, on the same afternoon on the place des Victoires and in the presence of Bonaparte, delivered the eulogy to the two heroes, who died under such different circumstances. Experienced in the genre, Garat had been recognized by the French Academy well before the Revolution for his eulogies to Suger, Montlausier, and Fontenelle.[31]

A member of the Ideologues, as was Daunou, he had been named professor
of "analysis of human understanding" at the École normale, when it was
founded in 1794. In his classes, he invoked Bacon, Locke, and especially Con-
dillac, who, as Garat explained, became "tired of listening to ramblings" in
an obscure language on the "principles of political economy that must govern
and enrich nations," and decided to apply what he considered a truly scientific method to clarify the "universal principles of political economy."[32] In his
speech on the place des Victoires, Garat presents a diptych of the two heroes
that makes each of them a model connected to the other by "a common goal,"
that is, love and defense of the nation on the one hand, and pursuit of glory
on the other. He concentrates his efforts on the latter element. In that period
of transition and consolidation, the Marengo moment thus provides Garat
with an opportunity to develop his thinking on the mechanisms of glory, in
which he sees the means to overcome two fundamental problems plaguing
post-Revolutionary France: instability and usurpation.

It is of course no coincidence that, with the general erosion of faith in
politics, military glory clearly appears to be a means capable of pulling the
country out of the impasse of interminable constitutional maneuverings, sul-
lied as they are both with self-interested calculations and with abstractions
lacking any basis in reality.[33] There remained the problem of conceiving
glory such that it could serve as a model generalizable to all of society and
as a remedy for the ills that continued to endanger the accomplishments of
the Revolution. In his speech the day after the battle of Marengo, Pierre Daunou had made "the love of glory" the "motive for all truly great action [. . .],"
which deflects any cowardly, unjust, oppressive, immoral act."[34] And we
have seen how that motive established a bond of continuity between pre- and
post-Revolutionary France. Garat attempts to develop Daunou's thinking by
deepening and enlarging that motivation; he stresses the interaction of the
temporal, psychological, and collective aspects of motivation. The portrait
of two very different personalities reinforces the idea of the real power of a
love of glory and its general significance. Garat takes pains to show how the
pursuit of that ideal leads the individual to fashion himself into a model for
his own behavior, to develop, cultivate, and exercise *self*-emulation. Through
this process he comes — naturally as it were — to internalize, embody, and en-
act in his person guarantees against usurpation and excessive use of power.
In a sense, then, Garat aims to describe the self-regulation, the workings of
"the invisible hand" of the economy of glory. In so doing, he sketches the
broad outlines of the politics of glory that would be pursued throughout the
Consulat and the Empire.

The Kléber/Desaix duo in itself represents a sort of fusion of classes and temperaments: one was the son of a mason, the other a former nobleman; one was emotional, the other contemplative; one died in Egypt, the other in Italy. This triple comparison — social, psychological, and geographical — provides some universality to Garat's explanation of their motivations. Desaix was a sweet, sensitive, and strong soul who loved to contemplate nature, studied war "as a science," and was able to cultivate "that severe integrity and those generous virtues that so embellished heroism and victory throughout the history of ancient republics."[35] Kléber, for his part, "had received from nature the stature of the demi-gods of Homer." United as mind to body in their heroic deaths, both were victims of a Revolution that had lost its bearings and had forgotten that "fanaticism can only disfigure and endanger a freedom based on reason, and to be sustained only by talent."[36] Desaix knew that one must not deny "feelings for nature in order to have the virtues of a citizen;" he never abandoned his mother, who was imprisoned, "whose ancestors could have been pardoned on behalf of her son."[37] Similarly Kléber, in his victorious campaign in the Vendée, recalled that the "first law of the Republic based on reason" was above the bloodthirsty law imposed by violent men in the throes of the "delirium of freedom."[38]

> Among so many generals of the Republic too magnanimous to sully victory in this manner, none had disobeyed with less mystery than Kléber; none had been more intrepidly human.

> Parmi tant de généraux de la République trop magnanimes pour souiller ainsi la victoire, aucun n'avait désobéi avec moins de mystère que Kléber; aucun n'avait été humain avec plus d'intrépidité.[39]

As a reward for his victory, Kléber received from the Republic only disgrace, and was denied recognition. Garat exclaims: "What! Even in republics disgrace often closely follows glory."[40] Kléber chose to obey a law above that of the Republic, the law of humanity, which even despotism, "softened by general customs, by the arts and by philosophy, had adopted and respected."[41] Recalled to duty for the Rhine campaign, the great general carried out feats that one day history would place "alongside the campaigns of Turenne and Luxembourg."

A republic turned executioner; a despotism nonetheless humanitarian; two men, "neither with set opinions on different social systems"[42] but whose courage was on the level of the greatest warriors of the Ancien Régime: such

are the elements that allow Garat to shuffle the cards with a view to erasing
the revolutionary rupture and to showing the history of France in its continuity as comparable to the greatness of antiquity. On the Rhine, surrounded
by consternation and despair, Kléber mobilized his soldiers, gave orders,
and, "upon hearing that leader's voice which the soldier was used to calling
the god Mars, the soldier thinks he is hearing the master of Fortune and the
sovereign arbiter of battles."[43] He then redoubles his efforts and finally pulls
victory from the arms of defeat.

At this point in the speech Garat develops a reflection on the psychological and collective motivations and mechanisms that enabled such actions on
the part of Kléber or Desaix. Senatorial eloquence had already placed Kléber
above the law; the hero's disobedience proved to be a source of glory. But the
essential question remained: to what voice was he listening, he who opposed
the laws of a misguided Revolution? If Garat's response may retrospectively
be classified among attempts to square the circle, it nonetheless suggests a
way of understanding the legitimizing dynamics at work in glory. Indeed, his
description lays out the whole logic of the movement leading to Empire. It is
possible, he says, that those who fix their eyes on such a soul "believe that it
can have neither the need nor the means to rise any further,"[44] that the grandeur of the names consecrated by history could give pause to even the most
ardent "desire to surpass them"? But glory as a motivation, Garat maintains,
implies a strong moment of self-constitution, a psychology in which one
obeys oneself, that is, the self *one has forged*. Of course, recognition can play
an important role in making it possible for the great man to discover himself
as such, but then he becomes autonomous and rises to correspond to his own
vision of himself:

> When one has heard one's name proclaimed in the triumphs of a great
> people, one becomes in some way a model for oneself, so to speak, and one
> emulates this very model; this type of emulation is extremely tormenting;
> it no longer allows fate to surprise you either in faults or in negligence,
> so greatly do the talents that one receives from nature endlessly grow in
> their compelling and constant need to add further illustriousness to a name
> already illustrious. If one were to stop, at whatever height one has reached,
> one would think one was descending; and that feeling, which allows no rest
> for the soul, also removes any boundaries to one's greatness.

> Lorsqu'on a entendu proclamer son nom dans les triomphes d'un grand
> peuple, on devient pour soi-même un modèle en quelque sorte et un émule,

et ce genre d'émulation tourmente de plus près; il ne permet plus à la fortune de vous surprendre ni en faute ni en négligence; tant ce qu'on a reçu de talens de la nature croît sans cesse dans le besoin impérieux d'ajouter incessamment à l'illustration d'un nom devenu illustre. Si on s'arrêtait, à quelque hauteur que ce fût, on croirait descendre; et ce sentiment, qui ne laisse aucun repos à l'âme, ôte aussi toutes les bornes à sa grandeur.[45]

In the end, it is no longer in relation to the great models of antiquity that one acts, *but in relation to oneself*, to a need to show oneself always worthy of the example one has set up for oneself. If there is indeed a dialectics of self and the other, the concern with self has a primordial place in this dynamics. It is only after defining it as primordial that Garat associates this personal ambition with love for one's nation. He speaks of a passion

> before which all others are silent or are purged, [and] as long as the nation needs efforts and sacrifices, there can be no end to the ambition to add to its prosperity and its glory.

> devant laquelle toutes les autres se taisent ou s'épurent, [et] tant que la patrie a besoin d'efforts et de sacrifices, il ne peut y avoir aucun terme à l'ambition d'ajouter à ses prospérités et à sa gloire.[46]

But after emphasizing the compelling needs of a grandeur "without any boundaries," Garat, in the abundant notes he adds to his text, raises the very question of limits. In his opinion, society must know how "to create for glory ceremonials and representations whose brilliance erases the petty, tedious pomp of power." Hence, when "a great man who is great because of his genius" finds himself next to a man occupying a powerful position, one has to make sure that the latter disappears before the former, that "all the eyes of this nation become fixed on the one who attracts them only by his name and his glory."[47] Ultimately, all legitimacy based on rank or position should pale before the recognition granted to the superior man, who, through his very genius and superiority, arouses neither jealousy nor hatred on the part of the people. On the contrary, the risk may lie in an excess of enthusiasm and recognition. Moreover, it is this excess that creates a danger, for how can one distinguish between the luster of power and the luster of glory in those instances when both are apparent in the same man? But such a danger usually comes from outside. As Carnot had done the day before, Garat contends that the psychology of the ambition for glory encompasses its own limits, its own decency, and that even if it is not pure disinterestedness, it leads to the same results:

> One of the best means to turn sensitive and lofty souls away from the ambition for illegitimate power is to inspire in them the ambition for glory.

> [L]'un des meilleurs moyens de détourner les âmes sensibles et élevées de l'ambition d'un pouvoir illégal, c'est de les enflammer de l'ambition de la gloire.

To that end, society needs to develop appropriate means for recognition:

> We have to know how to award glory: we must be careful not to lavish it, but even more careful not to deny it to those who have deserved it and to grant it to them freely and without pettiness.

> [I]l faut savoir décerner la gloire: il faut se garder de la prodiguer, mais il faut se garder encore davantage de la refuser à ceux qui l'ont méritée ou de la leur accorder avec défiance et mesquinerie.[48]

A society will be judged—judged, that is, by posterity—by its ability to distinguish and recognize its great men. It is again a matter of a dialectics: between the pole of individuals and the pole of the collectivity. On the one hand, the ability of the individual is exalted; on the other, there is always the problem of knowing in what instance to award glory. Garat notes that although, in principle, it should be possible to distinguish between power and glory, most of the time the two end up being conflated. From this admission, which would seem to doom any attempt to establish effective checks on power, Garat concludes that glory itself fulfills that function:

> I know well that one may want to unite the two powers: I assume both are united in the highest degree. When the power of a position is legitimate, far from fearing the power of glory, we must see it *as a guarantee and as a barrier*. The one who unites the two, unless his head is turned and he becomes a fool or a madman and no longer a great man, will certainly always prefer the latter power, and he will not be able to ignore that in a free nation, that is, one attentive to its rights and its interests, every encroachment, every usurpation in political power, will be a loss and a destruction for the power of glory.

Je sais bien qu'on peut vouloir réunir l'une et l'autre puissance: je les suppose réunies l'une et l'autre dans le plus haut degré. Quand celle d'une place est légitime, loin de redouter celle de la gloire, il faut la regarder *comme une garantie et comme une barrière*. Celui qui les réunira, à moins que la tête ne lui tourne, et que d'un grand homme il ne devienne un sot ou un fou, préférera à coup sûr toujours la dernière, et il ne pourra ignorer que chez une nation libre, et par conséquent attentive à ses droits et à ses intérêts, chaque empiètement, chaque usurpation dans la puissance d'une place sera pour la puissance de la gloire une perte et une destruction.[49]

As we see, controls are inherent in the psychology of the individual moved by an ambition for glory. If the enthusiasm of recognition can occasionally be excessive, the man who unites power and glory combines the legitimacy and wisdom acquired in the acts of his self-constitution into a model for himself, as well as for others. In forging himself, he erects internal barriers against the abuses of usurpation. Thus Garat depicts a society of distinction that is characterized by three elements:

- It is a society that, through recognition, offers incentives while discouraging corruption; the duty to remember is an essential component;
- The individual constitutes himself through his own actions into a model of emulation for himself;
- The very same mechanisms that prompt the pursuit of glory function such that the individual, in realizing his goal, learns to self-regulate, to reject temptations for abuse and usurpation.

Here, then, are the basic traits of this new political economy of glory that was laid out during the Marengo moment. Public tributes and monuments, like schools, are, so to speak, concrete applications of the vectors of progress, leading to a modern use of parallels, for which Plutarch was for so long recognized as a master:

At the moment when an enlightened nation accords recognition through public praise, it opens to those who receive it what might be called the temple of memory, a Pantheon of all peoples and of all centuries, which exists wherever that which is sensitive honors that which was great [. . .]. Kléber and Desaix, both so worthy of being assimilated into those parallels which teach nations to appreciate virtues, to distribute glory, are thus natu-

rally brought together, and compared to each other in this solemn homage
that they are receiving jointly.

> À l'instant où la reconnaissance d'une nation éclairée décerne des éloges
> publics, elle ouvre à ceux qui les reçoivent cette espèce de temple de
> mémoire, ce Panthéon de tous les peuples et de tous les siècles, qui existe
> partout où ce qui est sensible honore ce qui a été grand [. . .]. Kléber et
> Desaix, si dignes tous les deux d'entrer dans ces parallèles qui enseignent
> aux nations à apprécier les vertus, à distribuer la gloire, sont appelés bien
> plus naturellement à être rapprochés, à être comparés l'un à l'autre dans cet
> hommage solonnel qu'ils reçoivent ensemble.[50]

Drawn by an enlightened nation, the parallel of those two Moderns testifies
to the establishment of an economy of glory. If Garat seeks to reflect on a
new political economy inherited from the Enlightenment, while at the same
time demonstrating by example the functioning of that new society, in many
respects he is only reworking, in the context of the Revolution, the logic of the
immemorial ideology of glory. By delving so deeply, however, Garat is forced
to deal—in the notes that accompany his text—with another side of history than that of a happy continuity of glory. The flipside of the coin reveals
the dark face of history, the abuses of the many tyrants who have risen up
throughout the ages. Garat's response is to highlight the emblematic value of
military glory on the one hand, and the specificity of modernity on the other.

Focusing on Rome, he notes that among the emperors characterized
by their despotism and evildoings, not one was a "great man of war." And
Caesar? Garat believes that if you read Suetonius carefully, you can distinguish a lofty and generous soul:

> I remain convinced that if his mind or that of his century had presented him
> with a plan for a free government, for a constitution based on our principles,
> prepared by a happy and wise system of public instruction and institutions,
> that great man [. . .] would have devoted his life to carrying it out.

> [Je] reste convaincu que si son esprit ou celui de son siècle lui avait pré-
> senté le plan d'un gouvernement libre, d'une constitution fondée sur nos
> principes, préparée par un heureux et sage système d'instruction publique
> et d'institutions, ce grand homme [. . .] n'eût plus voulu vivre que pour
> l'exécuter.[51]

After Caesar, Augustus ruined everything, but there were, nevertheless, some emperors "democratic in all their thinking, in all their actions": Trajan, Marcus Aurelius, Julian, alone among Caesar's successors whose military acts and heroism could, according to Garat, be compared to those of Caesar or Alexander. "More true democracy still breathes in the genius of those absolute princes than in the turbulent harangues of the tribunes of the Republic."[52] In the speeches of the orators, in the deliberations and debates in the senate and in the councils, under the reign of those great leaders, everything breathed freedom. For Garat, the only reason they had not fully realized that "magnanimous goal" was that

> a true social theory did not yet exist, and it was impossible to execute anything similar or even close with the worn out remains of a tyrannical aristocracy, a wild democracy, and an imperial power forced to rule over twenty or thirty nations.

> [. . .] la vraie théorie sociale n'existait pas encore, et qu'il était impossible d'exécuter rien de semblable ou d'approchant avec les débris usés d'une aristocratie tyrannique, d'une démocratie insensée, et d'un pouvoir impérial obligé de s'étendre sur vingt ou trente nations.[53]

In short, modernity is superior to antiquity in that it has established "a true social theory" that clearly owes much to the philosophers of the eighteenth century and, in particular, to that current extending from the Sensualists to the Ideologues. Glory is an immemorial value. But while the Ancients can still serve as examples, and the duty of remembering them is still to be fulfilled; glory can do for the modern French what it could not do for the Ancients, or for the great French forefathers: Charlemagne, Saint Louis, Louis XII, François I, and Henry IV. Of these kings, all warriors, the two greatest were Charlemagne and Henry IV because they "had the most legislative and most popular conceptions."[54] The Consulat, unburdened of the remains of a tyrannical aristocracy and establishing itself as a remedy to a wild and fanatic democracy, manifests the fundamental link between the military hero, the absolute prince, and "true" democracy. After this review of history, Garat claims he is unable to name a single true hero who was "the destroyer of the laws and the rights of his country";[55] he posits,

> as a general truth of the human heart and of the entire body of history, that *usurpations are never the work of heroes, that heroes are never usurpers,* and that

one of the surest guarantees against military tyranny was great military glory connected to the name of the one who in a free country occupies the highest magistrature.

[. . .] comme une vérité générale du cœur humain et de tout le corps de l'his-toire, que *les usurpations ne sont jamais des héros, que les héros ne sont jamais usurpateurs*, et qu'une des plus sûres garanties contre la tyrannie militaire est une grande gloire militaire attachée au nom de celui qui dans un pays libre est revêtu de la première magistrature. [56]

Here, then, the legitimizing quality of glory resulting from military heroism is asserted. Referring to the hero occupying the highest office, Garat contends:

When one looks into his soul, one sees that it feels, thinks, and always wants to act in the presence of nations, of posterity and of the historian; that it knows perfectly well that its grandeur is attached not to titles and valets who flatter it, but to the grandeur of the human race, and it understands what it can do for freedom and for the happiness of so many peoples by the means vested in the office it occupies — the most legitimate authority on earth — by its mind and, by the greatest of all powers, its own strength.

Quand on s'approche de son âme on s'assure qu'elle sent, qu'elle pense, et qu'elle veut toujours agir en présence des nations, de la postérité et de l'historien; qu'elle comprend à merveille que sa grandeur est attachée non à des titres et aux valets qui les encensent, mais à la grandeur de l'espèce humaine, et ce qu'il peut faire pour la liberté et pour le bonheur de tant de peuples par les moyens que lui confie sa magistrature, l'autorité la plus légi-time de la terre, par sa tête, et, par la plus grande de toutes les puissances, par ses forces.[57]

While the eighteenth century, as Voltaire incarnates it, has a tendency to denounce history as a long series of atrocities and abuses, Garat's "fusional" vision portrays it differently, focusing on something else: history appears, on the one hand, as a source of examples confirming an anthropology of human grandeur and heroism, and, on the other hand, as the origin of a French iden-tity that is the product of modernity. This modern history is seen as a forward movement culminating in a new configuration of legitimacy, combining will, power, and knowledge in a society based on a political economy of recognition. This new vision contains the seed of the entire politics of fusion that Napoleon would put in place. But also, unwittingly, it describes what was to become its principal stumbling block: the difficulty of generalizing the model of glory beyond the military realm.

Anne-Louis Girodet de Roussy-Trioson, *The Apotheosis of French Heroes
Who Died for Their Country* (homage presented to Napoleon I) (1800).
Oil on canvas. 192.5 × 184 cm. (MM.40.47.6955). Châteaux de Malmaison
et Bois-Preau, Rueil-Malmaison, France. Photograph by Franck Raux.
Photograph © RMN-Grand Palais / Art Resource, New York.

CHAPTER 5

New Sensibility, New Knowledge,
New Institutions

Madame de Staël and Girodet

In a work that, like Garat's *Éloge,* appeared in 1800, Madame de Staël voices her appreciation for Garat's teaching at the École normale.[1] Profoundly influenced by notions of perfectibility and progress interited from the Enlightenment, *De la littérature considérée dans ses rapports avec les institutions sociales* clearly asserts the superiority of the Moderns over the Ancients. But this work by Necker's daughter was a milestone in that it fully integrates the Middle Ages into the progressive current under way. For Madame de Staël, the fusion of the peoples of the South with those of the North, like the rise of Christianity, constitutes an essential step in the emergence of modernity, a step that should in no way be ignored, for to do so would mean risking a failure of self-recognition, or an inability to manage either the complex relationships between the past, the present, and the future, or the relationships between the individual and the collectivity:

> Nothing is less philosophical, that is, nothing would lead less to happiness, than the jealous system that seeks to strip nations of their rank in history by leveling the reputation of men. We must tirelessly propagate general education; but alongside a deep interest in the advancement of learning, we must preserve the goal of individual glory. The Republic must give more encouragement than any other government; it is enriched by the increased work

that [glory] inspires. A small number reach the goal, but all hope for it; and if renown crowns only success, even attempts to gain it may have some kind of utility. We must not strip great souls of their devotion to glory; we must not strip peoples of the sentiment of admiration. From that sentiment come all the degrees of affection between the magistrates and the governed.

Rien n'est moins philosophique, c'est-à-dire, rien ne conduirait moins au bonheur, que ce système jaloux qui voudrait ôter aux nations leur rang dans l'histoire, en nivelant la réputation des hommes. On doit propager de tous ses efforts l'instruction générale; mais à côté du grand intérêt de l'avancement des lumières, il faut laisser le but de la gloire individuelle. La république doit donner beaucoup plus d'essor que tout autre gouvernement; elle s'enrichit des travaux multipliés qu'il inspire. Un petit nombre d'hommes arrivent au terme: mais tous l'espèrent; et si la renommée ne couronne que le succès, les essais mêmes ont souvent une obscure utilité. Il ne faut pas ôter aux grandes âmes leur dévotion à la gloire; il ne faut pas ôter aux peuples le sentiment de l'admiration. De ce sentiment dérivent tous les degrés d'affection entre les magistrats et les gouvernés.[2]

Clearly, we are still in the same model of a political economy of recognition. But what interests us in particular is that the arguments Madame de Staël develops here would eventually serve to fuel a liberal opposition to Napoleon's politics.[3] Glory is a legitimate and profoundly individual aspiration; it should, de Staël believes, play a key role in the new French republic. In fact, she had already written a long reflection on glory in *De l'influence des passions* (1796), in which she focuses on the implicit contract inherent in glory:

The worthy and sincere lover of glory proposes a fine pact to humanity; he tells it: "I will devote my talents to serve you, my dominant passion will excite me constantly to make a greater number of men enjoy the happy results of my efforts; [. . .] as a price for this devotion, I ask only that you celebrate it; consider renown to be the payment for your recognition."

Le digne et sincère amant de la gloire propose un beau traité au genre humain; il lui dit: "Je consacrerai mes talents à vous servir, ma passion dominante m'excitera sans cesse à faire jouir un plus grand nombre d'hommes des résultats heureux de mes efforts; [. . .] pour prix de ce dévouement, je ne vous demande que de le célébrer, chargez la renommée d'acquitter votre reconnaissance."[4]

In this rather classic description, the one who seeks glory as a reward admits that although the enjoyment of virtue ought to suffice in itself, it is actually not fulfilling, and so he seeks to be paid in moral currency. Whence the need for others to tie the glory of his name to the merit of his actions.

The glory of the Moderns, however, as Madame de Staël describes it in *De la littérature*, no longer functions like that of the Ancients, because we are endowed with a profoundly different sensibility — richer than theirs — and we better understand its impetus, because we Moderns have acquired an entirely new and deeper understanding of our passions and the role they play. The Ancients had neither the means nor the need to know the secrets of the heart or the value of domestic happiness. For them, virtue consisted "in control over oneself and the love of reputation."[5] Rather than proceeding from observation, moral philosophy of that time developed through precepts. It was a question of mastering oneself rather than of knowing oneself as an individual. Even Cicero — in whom, alone among the Ancients, according to Madame de Staël, we could perceive a bit of individuality — struggled systematically against that which his *amour-propre* allowed to escape. And yet, de Staël insists, the Ancients were certainly not hypocrites *"but trained themselves inwardly for outward appearance."*[6] *Decorum*, an exterior form of virtue, was assimilated to virtue itself:

> It taught, as a moral duty, the various means of imposing respect, through purity of language, through elegance of pronunciation. All that can add to the dignity of man: such was virtue for the Romans. Philosophical enjoyments, and not the sweet ideas of a lofty religion, were proposed as rewards for sacrifice. They did not call upon consolations of the heart to support men, but upon pride; so majestic was their nature, so hard did they try to keep their distance from anything that could pertain to motives of sensibility, even such motives that might support of the strictest morality.

> [I]l enseigne, comme un devoir de morale, les divers moyens d'imposer le respect, par la pureté du langage, par l'élégance de prononciation. Tout ce qui peut ajouter à la dignité de l'homme, était la vertu des Romains. Ce sont les jouissances philosophiques, et non les idées douces d'une religion élevée, qu'ils proposent pour récompenses des sacrifices. Ce ne sont point aux consolations du cœur qu'ils appellent pour soutenir les hommes, c'est à la fierté; tant leur nature est majestueuse, tant ils s'efforcent d'éloigner d'eux tout ce qui pourrait appartenir à des mouvements sensibles, ces mouvements fussent-ils même à l'appui de la plus sévère morale.[7]

Gradually, however, general corruption took hold in Italy, unbridled egotism: "the southerner lost himself completely in the enjoyments of the flesh"; he lost all taste for glory. The invasion of the barbarians certainly put an end to a culture of arts and letters, but it restored new strength and energy. The northerners had "imagination, melancholy, a penchant for mysticism."[8] Their only happiness was independence:

> A certain pride of the soul, a detachment from life, born of both the harshness of the land and the sadness of the sky, made servitude intolerable. [. . .] The warrior spirit that Erse and Scandinavian poetry lauded with so much enthusiasm gave man a prodigious idea of his individual strength and of the power of his will. Independence existed for everyone, until freedom was constituted for all.

> Une certaine fierté d'âme, un détachement de la vie, que font naître, et l'âpreté du sol, et la tristesse du ciel, devaient rendre la servitude insupportable. [. . . L]'esprit guerrier que les poésies Erses et Scandinaves chantent avec tant d'enthousiasme, donnait à l'homme une idée prodigieuse de sa force individuelle et de la puissance de sa volonté. L'indépendance existait pour chacun, avant que la liberté fût constituée pour tous.[9]

Thus Madame de Staël takes up theories of climate inherited from Aristotle and Montesquieu to paint a portrait of those peoples from the North worthy of Tacitus. The invasion of the barbarians put an end to the degradation of the waning Roman civilization. These warriors brought not only energy and courage, but also a practice of freedom, *individual* independence. Christianity took advantage of their penchant for melancholy; it favored "the empassioned sadness of the inhabitants of an overcast climate" but redirected it and, "without altering the nature of their courage, managed to give it a different object:"[10]

> The Christian religion was the bond linking the peoples of the North and the South; it blended, so to speak, contrasting customs into a common opinion; and bringing enemies together, it created nations in which energetic men fortified the characters of enlightened men, and the enlightened men developed the minds of energetic men.

> [L]a religion chrétienne a été le lien des peuples du nord et du midi; elle a fondu, pour ainsi dire, dans une opinion commune des mœurs opposées;

et rapprochant des ennemis, elle en a fait des nations, dans lesquelles les hommes énergiques fortifiaient le caractère des hommes éclairés, et les hommes éclairés développaient l'esprit des hommes énergiques.[11]

From that fusion, history marched forward to the Renaissance and the Enlightenment.

The invasion of the barbarians provides Madame de Staël with more than just one stage in a very long history; it also gives her a paradigm for interpreting the French Revolution. For in French society as it had developed, the nobles, who occupied the highest class and enjoyed the advantages of a distinguished education, were mellowed and softened by prosperity itself:

> The common people, on the contrary, had only a rudimentary civilization and customs that were contained by laws, but, once free to act, they returned to their natural ferocity. They invaded, so to speak, the upper classes of society, and all that we suffered, all that we condemn in the Revolution, came from the fatal necessity that has often conferred leadership to such conquerors of the civil order. They have a philosophical idea as a goal and a standard; but their education is several centuries behind that of the people they have conquered.

> Les hommes de la classe du peuple, au contraire, n'avaient encore qu'une civilisation grossière, et des mœurs que les lois contenaient, mais que la licence devait rendre à leur férocité naturelle. Ils ont fait, pour ainsi dire, une invasion dans les classes supérieures de la société, et tout ce que nous avons souffert, et tout ce que nous condamnons dans la révolution, tient à la nécessité fatale qui a fait souvent confier la direction des affaires à ces conquérants de l'ordre civil. Ils ont pour but et pour bannière une idée philosophique; mais leur éducation est à plusieurs siècles en arrière de celle des hommes qu'ils ont vaincus.[12]

If well led, the Revolution could enlighten a larger number of men. But just as the "vulgarity of language, manners, opinions" caused taste and reason to regress during the barbarian invasions, France has—temporarily, Madame de Staël hopes—lost "the urbanity of customs and that of emulation."[13] The new barbarians are armed with a philosophical idea but have no knowledge of the human heart. In a sense, they err in trying to do as the Ancients did, that is, to encourage action through precepts and laws as if only people and the City existed, without taking into account the entire inner space that char-

acterizes modern man, which was being explored in greater depth starting
with the seventeenth-century moralists and continuing throughout the eighteenth century. The mechanisms of modern man's sensibilities must be put
in the service of the new Republic, and to that end Madame de Staël proposes
a new configuration, integrating "freedom, virtue, glory, knowledge, those
impressive elements of man in his dignity."[14]

But emulation implies distinction, for one has to recognize merit and, if
necessary, arouse enthusiasm in a moral republic in which esteem, approba-
tion, and respect compete with public utility. According to Madame de Staël,
the new barbarians, with their absence of subtlety and taste, are wrong in
wanting to level everything, in seeking to blend "through a gross and jealous
equality that which natural inequality distinguishes."[15] Whence a state of
chaotic indistinction that prevents the healthy comparison upon which all
judgment must be based:

> Where is the dignity, if nothing is in its place? What difficulties do we have
> to overcome if no barriers exist? But also, what monuments can we build, if
> we have no foundation? One can throw insults and praise around indiscrimi-
> nately without inspiring either enthusiasm or hatred.

> Où est la dignité, si rien n'est à sa place? Quelles difficultés a-t-on à vaincre,
> s'il n'existe aucune barrière? Mais aussi quels monuments peut-on fonder si
> l'on n'a point de base? On peut parcourir en tout sens l'injure et l'éloge, sans
> faire naître l'enthousiasme ni la haine.[16]

Because speaking the truth requires finding the right words, eloquence
informed by philosophy ought to play a major role. To escape the chaos of
indistinction—a free-for-all—propriety must be respected and taste re-
developed. And for modern man, *decorum*, that is, the exterior forms of virtue, is no longer enough. The new legislator has to know how "to contain
freedom through virtue, ambition through glory. [For] what one admires in
great men is never anything but virtue in the form of glory."[17] Above all, this
new legislator must understand the sensibility of a modern man profoundly
marked by "the painful sense of the incomplete nature of his destiny."[18]

> The heroism of morality, the enthusiasm of eloquence, the ambition for glory
> provide supernatural enjoyments needed only by souls that are exalted and
> melancholy, tired of all that is measured, of all that is passing, of any term or
> limit, at whatever distance it is placed.

L'héroïsme de la morale, l'enthousiasme de l'éloquence, l'ambition de la gloire donnent des jouissances surnaturelles qui ne sont nécessaires qu'aux âmes à la fois exaltées et mélancoliques, fatiguées de tout ce qui se mesure, de tout ce qui est passager, d'un terme enfin, à quelque distance qu'on le place.[19]

As Madame de Staël explains, this blend of exaltation and melancholy is the fruit of the first barbarian invasion. The poetry of the North, that of Ossian, is especially conducive to this state of the soul, "the source of all generous passions as well as all philosophical ideas."[20] It is easy to understand the role that Madame de Staël reserves for literature in this new society, marked as it is by emulation and the quest for glory. In De l'influence des passions, she establishes a distinction between glory derived from writing and glory derived from actions: the genius of actions does not have to wait long for rewards, whereas that of writing is betting on the long term, and that implies patience, which, by definition, plays a moderating role.[21] In 1800, Madame de Staël was focusing on the status of literature, so as to make it an essential element in the governing of the collectivity.

Pre-Revolutionary French society certainly developed taste. But in the absence of freedom, and living in a regime in which the king was seen as the "dispenser of glory"—though he merely dispensed an imitation of glory— writers could find satisfaction in wild exaggeration as well as in subtleties of reasoning where words no longer really meant anything. Rousseau could dream of absolute equality apparently *without any consequences*. Others— d'Holbach comes to mind, although Madame de Staël does not refer to him specifically—managed, "through subtle reasoning, to represent the most generous devotion as obvious egotism."[22] For these men,

> everything comes back to self-interest because everything comes back to the self; but just as we would not say, *Glory is in my interest, heroism is in my interest, sacrifice is in my interest*, we would totally degrade virtue by telling man merely that virtue is in his interest.

> [t]out revient à l'intérêt parce que tout revient à soi; mais de même qu'on ne dirait pas: *La gloire est de mon intérêt, l'héroïsme est de mon intérêt, le sacrifice est de mon intérêt*, c'est tout à fait dégrader la vertu que de dire seulement à l'homme qu'elle est de son intérêt.[23]

For Madame de Staël, the moral and political sciences must emanate from virtue, but if the effectiveness, the utility, of all measures can be evaluated by

a statistical demonstration—the calculation of probabilities on a vast scale—
then motivation, encouragement, and recognition must be filtered through the
eloquence of truth. "This style of the soul, if I may express myself thus, is one
of the primary means of authority in a free government."[24] And so she arrives
at a conclusion that is striking in its resemblance to Garat's economy of glory:

> when the nature of the government promises a man of genius power and
> glory, victors worthy of winning such a prize quickly appear. Emulation
> develops talents that would have remained unknown in states in which one
> could not offer a proud soul any goal worthy of it.

> [. . .] lorsque la nature du gouvernement promet à l'homme de génie la
> puissance et la gloire, des vainqueurs dignes de remporter un tel prix ne
> tardent point à se présenter. L'émulation développe les talents, qui seraient
> demeurés inconnus, dans les états où l'on ne pourrait offrir à une âme fière
> aucun but qui fût digne d'elle.[25]

Madame de Staël notes that glory need not be contrasted to self-interest; she
affirms, however, that calling on self-interest is no way to encourage great
actions. It is not by appealing to some calculation of clear self-interest that
one can encourage man to go beyond himself; rather, it is by appealing to a
sense of incompleteness. And it is on the basis of that feeling, or sense, that
one can inspire the enthusiasm—the will to go beyond oneself—so essential
to any true politics of emulation.

Still, although one "must not devalue any type of exaltation,"[26] one type,
as Madame de Staël constantly stresses, can be dangerous: namely, military
heroism:

> The continual exercise of the total power of arms ultimately provokes scorn
> for the slow progress of persuasion. The enthusiasm aroused by victorious
> generals is quite independent of the justness of the cause they are supporting.

> L'exercice continuel de la toute-puissance des armes finit par inspirer du
> mépris pour les progrès lents de la persuasion. L'enthousiasme qu'inspirent
> des généraux vainqueurs, est tout à fait indépendant de la justice de la cause
> qu'ils soutiennent.[27]

An excessive influence of the military spirit, founded as it is on obedience
and discipline, harms the spirit of freedom. It is therefore essential to extend

the politics of recognition beyond military heroism, to all fields of human activity, especially, of course, to the realm of letters. Indeed, intellectuals should be placed "above any sort of power that compensates them."[28] For "the encouragement of great literature [. . .] is glory, the glory of Cicero, even of Caesar and Brutus." Through his eloquence, Cicero saved his nation; Caesar narrated his own deeds; Brutus was loved "for his enticing style" and the "philosophical elevation that imbued his writing."[29]

According to Madame de Staël, each nation must find its own way according to its particular history. In England, a mixture of commercial interests and love of freedom impeded a particular type of literature, characterized by irresponsibility, that could develop in France. The practices of commerce and freedom prevented the English from wandering off into abstractions unconnected to experience. In France, Madame de Staël seems to say, a certain practice of sociability, relayed and strengthened by literature, could lead to a proper balance, "to containing freedom through virtue, and ambition through glory."[30] If Garat sees genius as capable of self-regulation, Madame de Staël sees women, in the new French republic, as perhaps best suited to encourage and to arbitrate. "Indeed, men can always hide their pride and the desire they have to be applauded under the appearance or the reality of stronger and more noble passions."[31] Among men, ambition and a demand for freedom could be transformed into fierce passions hiding behind masks of glory and virtue. But if the Revolution stops trying to reduce women "to the most absurd mediocrity" and enables them again "as in the past, to have a useful ascendancy over opinion," they could exercise true moral authority over the practice of recognition.[32] For

> these are the only beings outside political interests and ambitious careers who heap scorn on all base actions, point out ingratitude, and know how to honor noble disgrace when noble sentiments have caused it.

> [i]l n'y a que ces êtres en dehors des intérêts politiques et de la carrière de l'ambition, qui versent le mépris sur toutes les actions basses, signalent l'ingratitude, et savent honorer la noble disgrâce quand de nobles sentiments l'ont causée.

Women's liminal position ensures them true disinterestedness, a blend of independence and pride; a long practice of sociability would give them the possibility to direct opinion toward "all that involves humanity, generosity, delicacy."[33] To deprive women of their minds, to reduce them to insipidity or frivolity, would deprive the republic "of the fame France enjoyed through the art of pleasing and of living in society,"[34] would rob France of one of the great means at its disposal to temper the raging passions of men, to develop the eloquence of truth, and to limit the dangerous military hold on glory and hence on the minds of men.

The economy of glory described by Madame de Staël echoes Republican ideology in that it demands an alignment extending from the individual to the nation and from the nation to humanity. But she renews it profoundly as she seeks to integrate it into the *longue durée* of French experience. It is no longer simply a matter of celebrating a few illustrious figures of the Ancien Régime, but of understanding a cultural system as it developed over the course of history. Madame de Staël thus attempts to conceive of a political economy of glory, which takes into consideration specifically French social and cultural practices. Only by taking those into account would the new Republic be able to break out of the trap of abstraction and anchor itself in society and its practices. The key, for Madame de Staël, is not only to reduce the revolutionary fracture but also to extend the model of glory to all of society. In a way, she too is seeking to reformulate certain values inherited from the nobility by democratizing them and "nationalizing" them, not the warlike values that went back to French origins, but those of civility and *politesse* out of which France and the nobility had created a very modern glory for themselves.

All the same, while military values might serve as a common ground between pre- and post-Revolutionary France, those of civility and *politesse*, far from being associated with virtue, recall hypocrisy and privilege too vividly to be put in the service of the Republic. The brilliant society of the *salonnières* had been too implicated in the weakness associated with excessive refinement and had therefore been reviled since the Seven Years' War; Madame de Staël herself is quick to denounce that weakness. In the end, if Necker's daughter establishes the basis for a liberal opposition to Napoleonic politics, she does so on the terrain of the ideology of glory, a consensual value par excellence. Even while opposing a hegemony of the military spirit, she reinforces the connections between glory and legitimacy. At the same time, Madame de Staël clearly announces the advent of a new aesthetics, which Chateaubriand would develop in his own work. Napoleon, however, would have no trouble recuperating this type of discourse, which grants glory a powerful legitimizing function. And the new aesthetics could harmonize very well with his politics of fusion.

Nothing better illustrates the turmoil of the era than Anne-Louis

Girodet's extraordinary painting *The Apotheosis of French Heroes Who Died for Their Country* (1801).[35] David, Girodet's very classical master, admitted he didn't understand anything of the strange luminosity of a painting swarming with figures of modernity. Profoundly unclassical in spirit, the work seems to announce a new alliance among power, poetry, and painting, all to the benefit of Napoleon, who, as in Neufchateau's poem, introduces new heroes into the Celtic Elysian Fields. But it is no longer Homer who is singing; it is now Ossian, and the figures that inhabit the painting evoke an entire medieval tradition unique to Europe. In his description of the work, Girodet explains that the old bard of Morven "is leaning to embrace Desaix. Kléber extends one hand to Fingal as a sign of alliance; with the other he is holding, along with Desaix, a war trophy taken from the mamelukes."[36] Then, among others, appear Dampierre, Dugommier, Hoche, Joubert, La Tour d'Auvergne, and a column of grenadiers and brigadeers, exactly as if Girodet had wanted to translate into painting all the magic of the Marengo moment. The work would not crown Girodet with the recognition he hoped for, but it is profoundly indicative of a movement valorizing a past liberated from the weight of Greco-Roman antiquity or, rather, capable of holding its own alongside it.[37] Such a movement was perfectly compatible with Napoleon's politics of fusion. In a similar vein, invoking the "religion of our fathers" in his *Génie du christianisme*,[38] Chateaubriand feels comfortable declaring his allegiance in the famous dedication to Napoleon in the second edition of his work.[39]

Honor Rediscovered and Institutionalized

Inscribed in Article 87 of the Constitution of Year VIII, the idea of establishing national rewards for soldiers fighting for the Republic would serve as constitutional grounds for the creation of the Legion of Honor. The same logic would govern the creation of the nobility of the Empire. It would be at the heart of a whole set of policies concerning monuments and artistic creation throughout the Napoleonic regimes. Bonaparte would have relatively little difficulty putting these policies in place, in that the eighteenth century had already established a theoretical basis for them. The development and implementation of a true political economy of glory offered the promise of bringing the Revolution to an end. In its formulations, such a goal was perfectly in keeping with the revolutionary demands of equality and freedom. We may recall Pierre-Louis Roederer's famous speech on 25 Floréal Year X (15 May 1802) before the legislative body on the creation of the Legion of Honor. Defining the Legion as a moral, political, and military institution, he asserts that it "erases noble distinctions that placed hereditary glory before acquired glory, and the descendants of great men before great men."[40] Borrowing the idea of moral currency, he sees in the Legion

> the creation of a new currency of a very different value than that which comes out of the public treasury; a currency whose value is unchangeable and whose source cannot be depleted, because it resides in every French person.

> la création d'une nouvelle monnaie d'une bien autre valeur que celle qui sort du trésor public; d'une monnaie dont le titre est inaltérable et dont la mine ne peut être épuisée, puisqu'elle réside dans l'homme français.

What matters is to extend the field of glory to civil society. The Legion "pays for military service, as well as for civil service, the price they deserve for their courage; *it binds them together in the same glory*, as does the Nation in its recognition of them."[41] The government has the ambition to blend civil and military servants in the same glory: merit and service are to be compensated with the same moral currency. If honor could be rehabilitated by the Revolution, it would be institutionalized through the workings of glory.

In fact, objections to the new institution during earlier discussions in the Conseil d'État were diverse and discussions lively. Théophile Berlier maintained that "crosses and ribbons are the baubles of the monarchy"; Antoine-Claire Thibaudeau denounced a "system diametrically opposed to the principles professed during the Revolution;"[42] while Mathieu Dumas wanted to limit the new institution only to the military. According to Thibaudeau's account, Napoleon told Mathieu Dumas that his way of conceiving things was perhaps fine for the feudal age, but that one must not "apply the reasoning of centuries of barbarism to the present time."[43] He continued:

> We are thirty million men joined by knowledge, ownership, and commerce. Three or four hundred thousand soldiers are nothing by comparison to this population [. . .]. It is characteristic of soldiers to want everything despotically; whereas for civilians everything should be subject to discussion, to considerations of truth and reason. This leads me to believe that preeminence belongs incontestably to the civilian sphere [. . .]. If we distinguish between military and civil honors, we would be establishing two orders, whereas there is only one nation. If we were to grant honors only to soldiers, that would be even worse, for henceforth the nation would no longer count for anything.

Nous sommes trente millions d'hommes réunis par les lumières, la propriété et le commerce. Trois ou quatre cent mille militaires ne sont rien auprès de cette masse." [. . . L]e propre du militaire est de tout vouloir despotiquement; celui de l'homme civil est de tout soumettre à la discussion, à la vérité, à la raison. Je n'hésite donc pas à penser en fait de prééminence, qu'elle appartient incontestablement au civil. [. . .] Si l'on distinguait les honneurs en militaires et civils, on établirait deux ordres, tandis qu'il n'y a qu'une nation. Si l'on ne discernait des honneurs qu'aux militaires, cela serait encore pire, car dès lors la nation ne serait plus rien.[44]

The opponents of the project saw it as the institution of an order, an undertaking that violated the spirit of equality, a first step toward the re-creation of an aristocracy. It is in this context that Berlier speaks of ribbons and trappings, and that the First Consul formulates his famous reply:

I challenge you to show me an ancient or modern republic in which there have been no distinctions. You call these *baubles*. Well, it is with such baubles that men are led. I would not express these thoughts in front of a tribune; but in a council of wise men and statesmen, one must not hold back. I do not believe that Frenchmen care for *liberty and equality*; the French have not been changed by ten years of revolution; they are what the Gauls were, proud and light-hearted. They care for one thing only: *honor*. This sentiment must be fed; they must be given distinctions. See how the people bow down before the medals of foreigners; they have been surprised by them; and so they wear them [. . .]. We have destroyed everything; we must rebuild. There is a government, powers; but what is all the rest of the nation? Grains of sand. We have in our midst the former privileged, organized by principles and interests, who know well what they want. I can count our enemies; but as for us, we are scattered, without a system, without unity, without contact. As long as I am here, I can answer for the Republic; but we must think of the future. Do you believe that the Republic is truly established? You are seriously mistaken. We are the people who can do it; but we do not and will not have it unless we lay masses of granite on French soil.

Je défie qu'on me montre une république ancienne ou moderne, dans laquelle il n'y ait pas eu des distinctions. On appelle cela des *hochets*; eh bien! C'est avec des hochets que l'on mène les hommes. Je ne dirais pas cela à une tribune; mais dans un conseil de sages et d'hommes d'État, on doit tout dire. Je ne crois pas que le peuple français aime *la liberté*, l'égalité; *les Français ne* *sont point chang*és par dix ans de révolution; ils sont ce qu'étaient les Gaulois, fiers et légers. Ils n'ont qu'un sentiment, *l'honneur*. Il faut donc donner de l'aliment à ce sentiment-là; il leur faut des distinctions. Voyez comme le peuple se prosterne devant les crachats des étrangers; ils en ont été surpris; aussi ne manquent-ils pas de les porter. [. . .] On a tout détruit; il s'agit de recréer. Il y a un gouvernement, des pouvoirs; mais tout le reste de la nation, qu'est-ce? Des grains de sable. Nous avons au milieu de nous les anciens privilégiés, organisés de principes et d'intérêts, et qui savent bien ce qu'ils veulent. Je peux compter nos ennemis; mais nous, nous sommes épars, sans système, sans réunion, sans contact. Tant que j'y serai, je réponds bien de la République; mais il faut prévoir l'avenir. Croyez-vous que la République soit définitivement assise? Vous vous tromperiez fort. Nous sommes maîtres de la faire; mais nous ne l'avons pas, et nous ne l'aurons pas, si nous ne jetons pas sur le sol de la France quelques masses de granit.[45]

In his work *Napoléon et la noblesse d'Empire*, Jean Tulard sees evidence of cynicism in the First Consul's positions.[46] He may be right, but one thing is certain: cynicism or not, for Napoleon the French could not escape their history, and the same sentiment that had motivated the nobility could be democratized to motivate the entire nation. Present glory, therefore, should cover the reestablishment of the old French connection of honor to honors and distinctions. The oppositions structuring this debate are those that cover the entire reign of Napoleon: Ancients versus Moderns, military men versus civilians, individualism versus collective cohesion. The evolution from the Legion of Honor to the nobility of the Empire recapitulates the movement from the Ancients to the Moderns. To avoid any link to the institutions of the former monarchy, Mathieu Dumas, according to Roederer, learned from the entry *"Honneur"* in the *Dictionnaire encyclopédique*, that "Marcellus, the sword of Rome, had erected a temple to Honor, to which one had access only by going through the temple of Virtue"; Dumas thus "created an oratory connection between Marcellus, *the sword of Rome*, and Napoleon Bonaparte, *the sword of France*, encountering each other in the same idea. Enthusiasm took hold of the assembly; they applauded for ten minutes."[47] If Jean Tulard was right to emphasize that the vote demonstrated the skepticism of the legislative Body (166 for, 110 against), we can safely assume that Mathieu Dumas's eloquence played a role in the defense and legitimation of the project during the session. Indeed, all the symbolism of the new institution refers back to Roman antiquity: the cohorts, the eagles, the very name (inspired from the *Legio honoratorum conscripta*). By way of antiquity, national history returns;

and the Legion paves the way for the nobility of the Empire. The imperative
to extend the economy of glory was especially urgent for Napoleon, as has
often been noted, because of his insurmountable distrust of the idea (so dear
to Sieyès and Roederer) of a notability based on wealth. "One cannot create a
title from wealth," he declares to Roederer:

> Even a rich merchant is rich only through the art of selling high, or of theft
> [. . .]. I do not see in wealth any entitlement to consideration or political
> distinction; and in the present time such distinction would be more badly
> received than in any other; wealth is today the fruit of theft.

> Un riche négociant même, ne l'est souvent que par l'art de vendre cher, ou de
> voler. [. . .] Je ne vois pas de titre à la considération dans la richesse, ni à une
> distinction politique; et dans le temps présent, une telle distinction serait
> plus mal reçue encore que dans tout autre; la richesse est aujourd'hui le fruit
> du vol.[48]

For these very reasons, under the Consulat as well as under the Empire, Napoleon always strove to ensure a material superiority for those who had been
recognized for their service and their merit. For he knew that it was essential
to reconcile self-interest and glory. But Bonaparte, as Roederer stresses, believed that his own power, as well as the society of emulation that he sought
to establish, were founded "on the imagination of the French." In this, he was
closer to Madame de Staël than to Roederer, who attempted to persuade him
that citizens "behave only through reason or a sense of personal interest."[49]
This was because, for Napoleon, the imagination of the French was the fruit
of a long history, whereas reason or a sense of personal interest could, at least
in principle, do without history:

> My policy is to govern men as the greatest number of them wish to be gov-
> erned. This, I believe, is the way to recognize the sovereignty of the people.

> Ma politique est de gouverner les hommes comme le plus grand nombre veut
> l'être. C'est là, je crois, la manière de reconnaître la souveraineté du peuple.[50]

These words may be cynical, but they reflect a reading of history, an accep-
tance of the gap between things as they are and things as they should be,
the profound relativity of values. For Napoleon, the governing of customs
and mores could not emerge from universalism. Roederer well understood

that this belief implied a power that can perform extraordinary actions. But Bonaparte was convinced of what Sieyès had already asserted in 1795 during the constitutional debate regarding the sovereignty of the people:

> [That] word appeared so huge before the imagination only because the minds of the French, still full of royal superstitions, felt compelled to endow it with the entire heritage of pompous attributes and absolute powers [. . .]. They seemed to be saying, with a sort of patriotic pride, that if the sovereignty of great kings is so powerful, so terrible, the sovereignty of a great people must be something else entirely.

> [Ce] mot ne s'est présenté si colossal devant l'imagination que parce que l'esprit des Français, encore plein des superstitions royales, s'est fait un devoir de le doter de tout l'héritage de pompeux attributs et de pouvoirs absolus [. . .]. On semblait se dire, avec une sorte de fierté patriotique, que si la souveraineté des grands rois est si puissante, si terrible, la souveraineté d'un grand peuple devait être bien autre chose encore.[51]

None of Sieyès's meticulously crafted constitutional mechanisms producing political reason could belie the fundamental truth of his observation of 1795.[52] Issued from a very long history, the French imaginary envisaged sovereignty in a particular light: this is the lesson that Bonaparte retains.

History certainly has its lessons, but so does military experience. Questioned by Roederer on the transformed behavior of soldiers who have become "more disciplined, more peaceful, more the friends of the citizen," the First Consul replies:

> It is because they are other men." Indeed they are other men also because war, glory, the respect for oneself, the hope for advancement and for retirement, have rendered them other than what they were before.

> "C'est que ce sont d'autres hommes." En effet ce sont d'autres hommes aussi, parce que la guerre, la gloire, le respect de soi-même, l'espoir de l'avancement, celui d'une retraite, les ont rendus autres que ce qu'ils étaient eux-mêmes auparavant.[53]

We know how all his proclamations and bulletins resound with words of glory, and how his policies always aim to ensure that army salaries be *paid in cash*. In *Lendemains d'Empire*, Natalie Petiteau stresses the depth of this transformation and how long its impact was felt;[54] and Jean-Paul Bertaud, in *Quand les enfants parlaient de gloire,* has explored with a great deal of finesse the repercussions of glory and the role of the army in Napoleon's France.[55] If the words "freedom" and "equality" had meaning for Napoleon, it was to be found, it seems, in the idea of self-respect, in the sense each person could have of his own dignity; individual recognition was cut from the same cloth as national recognition.

Thibaudeau describes the metamorphosis that took place on 18 Brumaire as a "revolution." Previously, he observes, there were symptoms of dissolution everywhere. Afterwards, everywhere there were signs of a renovating vigor. I cite the following passage at length because it describes not only the effectiveness of Bonaparte's vision but also the fundamental weakness inherent in the economy of glory within the French context:

> Everywhere we saw a noble emulation of all that was good, beautiful, and great. To provide a foundation for the new regime, there was true enthusiasm, just as there was at the beginning of the Revolution to overthrow the old regime. We no longer marched toward our goal in tumult and disorder: a firm hand directed the movement, showed us the way, and warned of diversions.
>
> The First Counsul wanted to govern nationally, and consequently to do away with factions. His great principle was that of fusion, that is, hatred and discord no more, reconciliation, and the support of all the French for the glory and prosperity of the nation and for the maintenance of the new government. He wanted to make the French forget the emigration of the aristocrats, royalists forget the Bourbons, republicans forget political freedom, all patriots forget the Revolution. According to him, the Revolution was fixed in the principles that had inspired it; it was over; he had founded a new era from which everything should be dated, and behind which no eyes should be cast.

> Partout on voyait une noble émulation pour tout ce qui était bon, beau et grand. Il y avait, pour fonder le nouveau régime, un véritable enthousiasme, comme au commencement de la révolution pour renverser l'ancien. On ne marchait plus au but en tumulte et en désordre: une main ferme dirigeait le mouvement, lui traçait sa route et prévenait ses écarts.
>
> Le Premier consul voulait gouverner nationalement, et par conséquent éteindre les partis. Son grand principe était la fusion, c'est-à-dire l'oubli des haines et des discordes, la réconciliation et le concours de tous les Français

> à la gloire et à la prospérité de la patrie, au maintien du nouveau gouverne-
> ment. Il voulait faire oublier aux Français l'émigration, aux royalistes les
> Bourbons, aux républicains la liberté politique, à tous les patriotes la révolu-
> tion. Suivant lui, elle était fixée aux principes qui l'avaient commencée; elle
> était finie; il avait fondé une ère nouvelle dont tout devait dater, et derrière
> laquelle il ne fallait plus porter ses regards.[56]

Enthusiasm, order, a will to terminate the Revolution through the politics of fusion, the support of all French for the glory and prosperity of the nation: all the elements for a moral transformation of the country are in place. And it is clear that Thibaudeau, his reservations concerning political freedom notwithstanding, truly supported the new order.

While this passage helps explain the enthusiasm generated by the events of 18 Brumaire, it also reveals the basic contradiction that would continue to sap the regime of glory established by Bonaparte. It is to be found in the need to make people forget—"faire oublier," in Thibaudeau's words. While a liberal economy can probably do without memory, that is certainly not true of an economy of glory. Napoleon's entire politics are based on a judgment of what the French have become; for him, there is a basic historical condition that has to be taken into account. In a sense, the depth of his aspiration as well as the extent of his failure can be seen in the paradoxical demand for forgetting and for remembering. In Napoleon's view, transcendence in imma-nence must function in the national context, and that implies fulfilling one's obligations as a descendant of one's own ancestors: "For you must understand that I do not separate myself from my predecessors and that, from Clovis to the *Comité de Salut publique*, I feel solidarity with them all," he asserts in a famous letter to his brother Louis, then king of Holland;[57] or, in a phrase that he would recall in the *Mémorial de Sainte-Hélène*: "I am the guardian of their glory [. . .]. I will not let their names perish."[58] Wanting to espouse such a guardianship of memory in a context where forgetting is the order of the day is like espousing the logic of forward flight that characterized the Revolution. For it was even more important to produce glory than to remem-ber that of others, or at least it was important to produce enough of it finally to get beyond the need to forget. Napoleon's policies fostering national splen-dor in the arts, in architecture, in public works—policies so well described by Annie Jourdan in *Napoléon: Héros, imperator, mécène*[59]—bear witness to his attempt to act on all fronts, from the beautiful to the useful, from the true (the Institute, the University) to the good.

In the meantime, fleeing forward to ever greater exploits serves to initiate an entire population into the practice of glory. "Of course," declares General Pelleport, "I would be proud and happy to descend from the generous citizens who were able to maintain their titles nationally, just as we have gained ours on the battlefields, but no such luck: *I date only from myself.*"[60] General Lefebvre, duke of Dantzig, also asserts: "Ancestors, who cares? I am an ancestor."[61] This constant pursuit of glory is essential for rallying the former nobility. But this new glory is erected on the irreducible contradiction between the duty of remembering and the need to forget. Such a tension did, however, bear fruit, as evidenced by the massive production of memoirs that the Napoleonic era produced: in some way, the duty to remember begins with oneself.

In many respects, Napoleon succeeded in his politics of fusion. The nobility of the Empire assimilated a strong dose of the old nobility into the new, and elevated elements of the petty and middle bourgeoisies, even of the lower classes; two-thirds of those who received titles during the Empire had not belonged to the old nobility. Although there was certainly a strong military presence in the upper ranks, State civil servants were also making their presence known: they constituted 70 percent of the barons of the Empire.[62] The Emperor tells Cambacérès explicitly: "Supporting to the present dynasty, *letting the (former) nobility be forgotten*; this is the goal we wished to achieve."[63] But how can one foster forgetfulness while respecting the duty to remember? The response is already inscribed in the reflections on the Marengo moment: essentially by celebrating the exploits of individuals. This is why the economy of glory established by the Empire marks the triumph of a certain individualism—of which Napoleon himself is at once an example, the emblem, and the guarantor. In making hereditary the titles accompanied by the patrimony linked to them, the "present dynasty" resolutely directs itself toward the future so as to assure its posterity without fully assuming its duty to remember. The imperative to forget undermines the will to found a political economy of glory.

We can now better appreciate the reference to Charlemagne and his reign; it was an attempt to overcome the memory/forgetfulness contradiction by establishing the great emperor as the ancestor of the figure of Napoleon and the founding father—or rather, the refounding father—of imperial and liberal France. There is here a double correspondence: man to man, and regime to regime. Fontane, in his speech of 21 Nivôse year IX (13 January), spoke of the glory of the conqueror-legislator so often evoked in the eighteenth century:

Thus, the greatest man in our history, at once conqueror and founder like the man who governs us, wrote, in the tumult of the camps, laws that were to maintain the peace of families, and mediated new victories by opening peaceful assemblies on the Champ de Mars [. . .]. But the current head of State, in an endeavor perhaps more difficult, is using all the knowledge of our century to discover what is most instructive and most secure in the examples of ages past.

Ainsi, le plus grand homme de notre histoire, conquérant et fondateur à la fois comme celui qui nous gouverne, écrivait dans le tumulte des camps les lois qui devaient maintenir la paix des familles, et méditait de nouvelles victoires en ouvrant les paisibles assemblées du Champ de Mars. [. . .] mais le chef de l'État aujourd'hui, par un effort plus difficile peut-être, emploie toutes les lumières de son siècle à découvrir ce qu'il y a de plus instructif et de plus sûr dans les exemples des siècles passés.[64]

Charlemagne had the advantage of reigning before feudal times, before the Capetians, and of having become the object, in the eighteenth century, of an intense work of mythification, which made him a prodigy in a history interpreted as a process of corruption, usurpation, and degradation. In these narratives, the great emperor rises above the chaos that has engulfed the country to reverse the course of history and restore the nation in its rights and liberties. He shows himself capable of reforming government and establishing the happiness of his people. From 1750 on, the figure of Charlemagne is constantly evoked by adversaries of absolutism proposing ever more radical reforms. The association of Charlemagne with republicanism developed and strengthened as the century advanced. In these evocations of the medieval past, the figure of the great emperor is touted as that of an ideal monarch.

Gabriel Bonnot de Mably's portrait of him in his *Observations sur l'histoire de France* (1765) sums up and republicanizes the an entire current of representations. The picture seems tailor-made for the Napoleonic context, because it outlines a perfect reciprocity between the will of the nation and that of the monarch, between the collectivity and the exceptional man, between democracy and empire. Mably's Charlemagne restores the "inalienable rights" of the people by inviting them to participate in the Champ de Mars, "thus making of it the assembly of the nation once again."[65] Philosopher, legislator, patriot, and conqueror, this providential man rises up and imposes himself as supreme mediator in a divided nation and incites the three orders ravaged by hatred to "agree to have only the same interests" and to "form a single body."[66] For Mably and many others, the identification between the great man and France is complete:

> Charlemagne wanted, ordered, commanded, because the nation wanted, ordered, and commanded, and charged him to publish his laws, to observe them, and to be their protector and avenger.

> Charlemagne vouloit, ordonnoit, commandoit, parce que la nation avoit voulu, ordonné et commandé, et le chargeoit de publier ses lois, de les observer et d'en être le protecteur et le vengeur.[67]

To the political idyll, Mably adds the epic conquest: united and liberated, the French nation set off to conquer the world.

> Finally acting with the zeal that comes from freedom, and with a union that makes for ever greater strengths, nothing could resist the French. They subdued part of Spain, Italy, all those vast lands that extend as far as the Vistula and the Baltic Sea; and the glory of the French name, like that of the ancient Romans, went as far as Africa and Asia.

> Agissant enfin avec ce zèle que donne la liberté, et avec cette union qui multiplie les forces, rien ne put résister aux Français. Ils soumirent une partie de l'Espagne, l'Italie, toutes ces vastes contrées qui s'étendent jusqu'à la Vistule et à la mer Baltique; et la gloire du nom Français, pareille à celle des anciens Romains, passa jusqu'en Afrique et en Asie.[68]

For Mably, the passion for freedom and unity are at the heart of the conquering strength of the nation. The return to democracy — for in the evocations of Charlemagne it is always a matter of *restoring* an originary constitution — leads naturally to conquest and empire, and by means of conquest the French can equal the ancient Romans in grandeur.

Such a figure was perfectly suited to both the ideology of glory and the politics of fusion promoted by Bonaparte. It was constantly evoked to justify the founding of the Empire, to "anchor" the new regime in French history and in the long tradition of the *translatio imperii,* now redeployed to the benefit of the new nation. It enabled the continued targeting of the "feudal hydra,"[69] while connecting "our former glory with our present glory," to promote a monarchy that was somehow at once Republican, national, and universal. By making a motion before the Tribunat that "the Government of the Republic be conferred to an emperor" and that the Empire be hereditary,[70] the senator Jean-François Curée lyrically evokes the great emperor Charlemagne, disinterested enemy of the privileged, indeed prince of liberal ideas:

> Charlemagne had governed France as a man who was far superior to his time; in the midst of universal ignorance, he had shown a universal genius, at once a wise legislator, a great man of State, and an indefatigable conqueror. Some time after this glorious era, one of the most powerful families in the feudal regime became sovereign. This odious system covered France with abuse, banished all national freedom, and seemed to destroy definitively the very principle of the liberal ideas that history still admires in the institutions of Charlemagne.

> Charlemagne avait gouverné la France en homme qui était supérieur de beaucoup à son siècle; au milieu de l'ignorance universelle, il avait montré un génie universel; tout à la fois profond législateur, grand homme d'État et conquérant infatigable. Quelque temps après cette époque glorieuse, une des familles les plus puissantes dans le régime féodal, fut appelée à la souveraineté. Cet odieux système couvrit la France d'abus, en bannit toute liberté nationale, et sembla anéantir sans retour jusqu'au principe de ces idées libérales que l'histoire admire encore dans les institutions de Charlemagne.[71]

These liberal ideas were to reemerge with the Revolution, a time when the French, "in a spontaneous movement and through a unanimous will [. . .], cried out: Let equality be established, let privileges disappear, and let the nation be all that it should be."[72] Thus, the Revolution cleared the path to fusion with an originary moment that preceded the distortions resulting from the feudal system. Curée's motion occasioned a set of responses characterized by almost lyrical grandiloquence. For his part, the senator Duvidal stressed the advantages of the hereditary transmission of the crown:

> The hereditary leader shares a common glory and power with the State; he arrives surrounded and supported by all of his ancestors; and at ease concerning the future when he settles the debt of nature, he leaves without fear his family and friends under the protection of his successor.

> Le chef héréditaire est en communauté de gloire et de puissance avec l'État; il arrive entouré de l'immense clientèle de ses ancêtres; et tranquille sur

l'avenir lorsqu'il acquitte la dette de la nature, il dépose sans crainte sa
famille et ses amis sous la protection de son successeur.

To become all that it should be, France is doing nothing more than "reclaim-
ing the place it had occupied among nations for fourteen centuries."[73]

> It is asking of you on behalf of a great man the rank and honors that once
> rendered its leaders respectable in the eyes of other sovereigns. The
> growth of its power and glory demands for the man it entrusts with all of
> its destinies a wreath of majesty worthy of himself and the people he shall
> represent. The eyes of the French will not be dazzled by foreign pomp; these
> honors are an ancient legacy whose return is fully legitimate. The crown of
> Charlemagne is the just inheritance of the one who has had the knowledge to
> imitate him.

> Elle vous redemande pour un grand homme le rang et les honneurs qui ont
> rendu ses chefs respectables aux yeux des autres souverains. L'accroisse-
> ment de sa puissance et de sa gloire, réclame pour celui qu'elle investit du
> dépôt de ses destinées, une auréole de majesté digne de lui-même et du
> peuple qu'il doit représenter. Les yeux des Français ne seront point éblouis
> d'une pompe étrangère; ces honneurs sont un antique patrimoine dans
> lequel tout les autorise à rentrer. La couronne de Charlemagne est le juste
> héritage de celui qui a su l'imiter.[74]

With the Empire, France finally reestablishes its ties to its own origins under the standard of freedom, power, and glory. This glory is both individual
and national. Seen in this light, the coronation represents a double act of
recognition: the nation's recognition of Napoleon, but also the nation's self-
recognition, that is, the collective self that it has fashioned — or refashioned —
on its own.

Moral Enrichment, Continual Growth

The glowing correspondence sprinkled throughout *Le Moniteur* bears witness to the collective exaltation that surrounded Napoleon. It was less the
manipulation of a passive population than a general adherence to the ideology of glory, that powerful amalgam of a series of currents that in many ways
were mutually incompatible: the legacy of antiquity, an immemorial ideal

of France, certain developments of eighteenth-century thought, and a set
of practices inaugurated under the Revolution. The ideology of glory constituted a common ground of understanding, even without full agreement
on the proper balance of the various constituent elements — the role of the
military as compared to the civil, for example, or the place of intellectuals as
compared to the more "productive" classes of society. As a political economy,
the ideology carried within itself a certain requirement for generalization.
And Napoleon felt compelled to pursue it in all realms of society; moral currency was to compensate all those who contributed to the well-being and
happiness of society. Emulation was seen as a general mechanism of encouragement and regulation. As Madame de Staël put it:

> A small number of men succeed [that is, in obtaining glory]; but all hope
> for it; and if renown crowns only success, attempts themselves are often of
> some use.

> [U]n petit nombre d'hommes arrivent au terme [c'est-à-dire à la gloire];
> mais tous l'espèrent; et si la renommée ne couronne que le succès, les essais
> mêmes ont souvent une obscure utilité.[75]

This ideology allows for diverse motivations, extending from "pure love" or
disinterestedness to a self-centered concern with returns on an investment.
One might count on posterity rather than on present renown, but renown
could also be a true sign of glory. Sometimes the investment is for the long
term; at other times there is greater liquidity and a quicker return on the
investment. To recall a passage by Cicero:

> But as there is a method not only of acquiring money but also of investing it
> so as to yield an income to meet our continuously recurring expenses — both
> for the necessities and for the more refined comforts of life — so there must
> be a method of gaining glory and turning it to account.[76]

Such an observation fits well into a utilitarian morality in which the well-
being of society is ultimately defined around two poles: that of the collectivity
and that of the individual.

The ideology of glory enabled men of very different ideas to rally around
what appeared to be a common project. It was not just that it offered possible
satisfaction to individuals; it also offered the perspective of a "moral enrichment" of all of society. As we have seen, Fénelon had already affirmed that

one must "never deprive a soul of the support of interested motives, when, following the attraction of its grace, one begins to show it pure love."[77] While the times were clearly not ripe for the politics of virtue, that didn't prevent one from aspiring to it. The ideology of glory allowed for a range of motivations and aimed at fostering moral and civic reform on both the individual and collective levels. As Garat says, by raising oneself up, "one becomes, in a sense, a model for oneself, and an emulator."[78] As we have seen, this elevation rested on a complex set of relationships between the individual and the collectivity, between the past of our ancestors, the present of our fellow citizens, and the future of our posterity. And Napoleon's attempt to resolve the contradiction between the duty to remember and the need to forget by a legitimizing identification with Chalemagne hardly modified the reality of the situation. If such a strategy had the advantage of asserting the value of a modern tradition as opposed to antiquity and, in doing so, of facilitating a transition from myth to history, it further delegitimized the "feudal hydra's" usurpation, that is, all of French history, extending from the first Capetian monarchy to the Revolution. In sum, the Emperor's legitimating acrobatics suppressed neither the need to forget nor the logic of fleeing forward. Rather than flowing from a historical continuity, the Napoleonic Empire remained suspended between the fragile pillars of a founding Carolingian moment and a heroic present. It is in order to have more solid foundations that Napoleon seeks to lay down "masses of granite," an image that in three words sums up the entire politics of fusion.

The figure of Charlemagne, despite its weaknesses, thus enables an evocation of the Napoleonic Empire as both a return to origins and an accomplishment of destiny. "The destinies of France will be carried out; [. . .] an immense future of success and glory is opening before it,"[79] exclaim the authors of a collective letter published in the *Moniteur*, addressed to the First Consul and signed by the "government of Paris, generals stationed there, and the troops of the first military division." The encomiastic letters that accompany the founding of the Empire thus elicit a continuity in the history of France, leading to what Thibaudeau describes as a "heterogeneous amalgam" of divine right and popular sovereignty.[80] As we saw at the beginning of this work, Thibaudeau considers most of these tributes spontaneous. But he considered them "a dangerous trend, where truth is indistinguishable from flattery, hypocrisy from good faith."[81] This kind of verbal inflation must be understood in relation to an economy of glory as it developed under the Consulat and the Empire. For it was of a piece with a general attitude allowing for a range of motivations in the service of nation, from disinterestedness to self-concern.

Up to a point, the distinction between truth and flattery, hypocrisy and good faith, was not essential or even relevant. This vision entertained the belief, or at least the hope, that hypocrisy could be transformed into good faith and self-interested love into a purer love. Through grandeur, it seemed, one could achieve self-regulation, be it under the vigilant watch of the self that one had forged, or under that of a posterity toward which one was turning ever more frequently. The ability to forget usurpations and betrayals was fostered by the promise of glory, of present and future recognition. The famous clemency of Napoleon, who so often pardoned those who betrayed him, fit perfectly into a logic that encouraged moderation, that envisioned the French—corrupted by their history—adopting a behavior marked by the strange intertwining of hypocrisy and good faith. Thanks to the mechanisms of emulation, this hybrid motivation could lead to true devotion in the best of cases, but also allowed for a whole range of less disinterested motivations.

The words of praise heaped upon Napoleon suggest another essential aspect of the economy of glory: the need for continuous growth. In this system, it was never a question of a zero-sum game; the glory of some should not be obtained at the expense of the glory others. The authors of the letter of 12 May assert that "our hopes know no limits under the auspices of the hero who knows no obstacles."[82] Dated 19 June 1804, the letter from the "soldiers of all ranks" with which we opened this study sums up the sense of exaltation at finally seeing past, present, and future joined together under the Empire:

> And so finally today we can say that the happiness of France is set forever! Today we can regard as imperishable the brilliant glory that surrounds this great Nation [. . .]

> In the past our ancestors raised their Emperor upon a shield! Your Empire relies on our hearts.

> Your glory is immense: the Universe can scarcely contain, and posterity will scarcely believe, the most authentic events of your illustrious career, if faithful history does not distort its features.

> C'est donc enfin aujourd'hui que l'on peut dire que le bonheur de la France est fixé pour toujours! C'est aujourd'hui que l'on peut regarder comme impérissable la gloire éclatante qui environne cette Grande Nation [. . .]

C'était autrefois sur un bouclier que nos ancêtres élevaient leur Empereur! C'est sur nos cœurs que repose votre Empire.

Votre gloire est immense: l'Univers a peine à contenir, et la postérité croirait difficilement, les événements les plus authentiques de votre illustre carriere, si l'histoire fidèle n'en burinait les traits.[83]

As noted at the beginning of this study, these same authors hasten to add: "We know not the language of flattery!" Through the inflated language of these texts we see the idea of an unlimited glory, one that knows no obstacles and that would benefit the entire nation. The ascent of some does not prevent that of others: everyone would be enriched by this moral currency as the whole nation rises on the waves of glory. To the images of spatial expansion are added those of a temporal transcendence. In a speech delivered on 28 July 1807 to celebrate Napoleon's return to Paris after the treaty of Tilsit, Séguier, then president of the court of appeals, exclaims:

Napoleon is beyond human history: he belongs to heroic times; he is above admiration; only love can rise to his height.

Napoléon est au-delà de l'histoire humaine: il appartient aux temps héroïques; il est au-dessus de l'admiration; il n'y a que l'amour qui puisse s'élever jusqu'à lui.

If such words seem familiar to us, it is because we are not far from the lines Boileau addressed to Louis XIV: "Great king, cease your conquering, or I will cease writing [. . .] / I am stopping now, I am admiring, and I am silent," or those of the anonymous poet who, in 1686, admitted that "to sing worthily of an invincible Hero / [. . .] there is no voice strong enough."[84]

However, and in spite of the resemblances, we should not too hastily assimilate Séguier's words to mere courtly flattery; rather, we should attempt to understand them by locating them within a popular movement in which the distinction between hypocrisy and good faith is blurred. In her *Mémoires*, the duchess of Abrantès cites Séguier's speech in order to emphasize that he "is a man whose noble character is neither fearful nor flattering. He would not have spoken thus had he not felt it."[85] We are once again on the terrain of the Moderns as described by Madame de Staël, those having a sensibility richer than that of the Ancients, a psychology that takes into account the profound ambiguity of feelings, a theory of emulation that enables the effective management of that ambiguity for the greater good of society. Social harmony depends on the glory of some not being acquired at the expense of that of others, and also on the assurance that the person at the head of the political hierarchy can regulate himself, that he knows how to find his own equilibrium as an emulator of himself. In many respects, the two demands are incompatible, because to assign oneself limits means setting limits to the growth of glory, which risks bringing it back to a zero-sum game.

The dazzle of a potentially boundless glory certainly encouraged forgetting and thus promoted the work of fusion. As Thibaudeau so rightly observes, "inner suffering was quiet or disappeared before glory. The absence of freedom was compensated for by the greatness and supremacy of the nation."[86] But the promise of continually growing glory, the very condition for that fusion required by national stability, was achieved, as we know, to the detriment of other peoples. The individual exercise of freedom was replaced by a collective fascination for the exercise of a certain national freedom, that of imposing one's will on others. In one sense, the state of the "law of nations"—the *jus gentium*—was closer to a Hobbesian state of nature, that of the rule of force, than to any kind of harmony emerging from a universal law. Forgetting usurpations by some and betrayals by others was made possible by the oppression of other nations. Account after account emphasized the humiliation of France's enemies, a humiliation vividly felt and transformed by those adversaries into an instrument for revolt and for the consolidation of national identity. If growth enabling social harmony was achieved on the national level, the opposite occurred for other nations. French glory was erected on the debasement and the shame of other peoples, who had to pay dearly for the humiliation of their princes. Corresponding to the motivating combination of glory and prosperity that seemed to triumph in France, an equally motivating combination of humiliation and poverty arose elsewhere. Forced to choose between humanity and his nation, Napoleon consistently chose his nation. Speaking of the conditions imposed on Prussia by the treaty of Tilsit, the duchess of Abrantès oserved: "I believe that modern history offers no other example of such humiliation."[87] Granted, Napoleon managed to surpass Frederick the Great and even took possession of his sword. But he couldn't understand the final gesture of Friedrich Stabs, a student who chose his own nation and cried *"Long live freedom and Germany!"* as he was being executed for attempting to assassinate Napoleon with a kitchen knife.[88] Disinterestedness and abnegation were becoming motives for the enemy, and a weapon like a kitchen knife was a far cry from weapons of glory on the battlefields.

The concentration of power in the person of Napoleon and the expansion of the Empire are two sides of the same coin. The logic of fleeing forward contained a temporal element in the race against the clock to achieve political fusion, and a spatial element in the seemingly unlimited expansion of the Empire. We may denounce Napoleon's motives, yet also conclude that he was the prisoner of a vision with a long history or, at least, that he had little room for maneuver, given the complex period in which he was living. One thing is certain, however: if the economy of glory collapsed under its own weight, Napoleon never changed systems, and this is what makes his epic a founding myth of modernity. While he may well be associated with Achilles, it is ultimately less for his prowess than for his brilliance in illustating the contradictory relationship that a hero maintains with society, and this at a time in history when the Revolution was violently asserting the autonomy of modern man. The hero is charged with defending society, but, through his very grandeur and the awareness of that grandeur, he ultimately endangers it. Compared to modernity, the figure of Napoleon represents the crucial point at which the psychology of the individual and the collective psychology meet in both fusion and contradiction. "Incapable of giving in to a threat," explains Thibaudeau, "the Emperor would never himself consent to back down, to descend; it was simply against his nature."[89] In other words — and this is no surprise — Napoleon's psychology was perfectly adapted to the demands of the ideology of glory. Concern with self ends up being regarded as a primary value. Having raised himself to the status of self-emulator, it is to that self that Napoleon will try to remain faithful. "You have taken away my past,'" the Emperor would say to Benjamin Constant, who, during negotiations on the *Acte additionnel*, proposed that he abandon the constitutional right of the Empire; "I want to preserve it. The new constitution must be connected to the old ones; it will have the sanction of several years of glory."[90] He could not better have formulated the entire ideology of glory in its connections with the politics of fusion. Napoleon used the same language with regard to himself that he always used with respect to the nation. The continuity of history, the idea that one is what one has become is applied both to the individual and to the nation; in his case, of course, biography and national history had been — at least for a time — melded.

It was precisely in order to separate the man from the nation and to topple the ascendancy of glory that the powers gathered in Vienna, upon learning of

Napoleon's return from the island of Elba, signed the famous declaration of
13 March, placing Napoleon outside the law of nations. In drafting it, Talley-
rand, who had lived through the entire Revolution, used the same language
that the members of the National Convention had used to circumvent the
inviolability of the king and to justify their prosecuting Louis XVI in spite
of the constitution. Denunciations of Louis XVI as a traitor, an enemy of the
human race, and an outlaw had prepared the ground for an extraordinary
response justified by natural law:[91] the Convention's contrivance of placing
the enemies of the Revolution outside the law was born of the universalism
of natural law as well as the tradition of the law of nations. It is not by chance
that in the declaration of 13 March 1815 we hear echoes of the decree of 27
March 1793 proclaiming aristocrats and enemies of the Revolution to be out-
laws:

> By thus breaking the agreement that had established him in the island of
> Elba, Bonaparte destroys the only legal title on which his existence de-
> pended, and by appearing again in France, with projects of confusion and
> disorder, *he has deprived himself of the protection of the law, and has manifested
> to the universe* that there can be neither peace nor truce with him. *The powers
> consequently declare that Napoleon Bonaparte has placed himself beyond the pale
> of civil and social relations*; and that, as an enemy and disturber of the tran-
> quillity of the world, he has rendered himself liable to public vengeance.

> En rompant ainsi la convention qui l'a établi à l'île d'Elbe, Bonaparte détruit
> le seul titre légal auquel son existence se trouvait attachée. En reparaissant
> en France avec des projets de trouble et de bouleversement, *il s'est privé lui-
> même de la protection des lois, et a manifesté à la face de l'univers* qu'il ne saurait
> y avoir ni paix, ni trêve, avec lui. *Les puissances déclarent en conséquence, que
> Napoléon Bonaparte s'est placé hors des relations civiles et sociales*, que comme
> ennemi et perturbateur du repos du monde, il s'est livré à la vindicte
> publique.[92]

It is one of the ironies of history that the act of expelling Napoleon was formulated in terms echoing those used for the first time in France during the
trial of Louis XVI. For the *outlaw*, the moral currency of glory is worthless.
The punishment of exiling the fallen emperor to the island of Saint Helena
was a demonstration of his new status; as an enemy of the human race, Napoleon would be banished from the world of rights and legality. The resulting
drama, however, took on a primordial dimension. In theory, the collapse of

the Empire should have discredited the general economy of glory as it was conceived by Napoleon. But the *Mémorial de Sainte-Hélène*, as we will see, would enable the Emperor to redefine himself—and glory—in terms that would resonate throughout the nineteenth century. The polyphonic *Mémorial* would again sing of glory, but in a minor key, asserting that greatness could also be realized in the realm of the infinitely small. This reformulation was to play a major role in maintaining the ideal of glory as an essential element for the nation as well as for the individual.

Antoine-Jean Gros (Baron), *Napoleon Visiting the Battlefield of Eylau, 9 February 1807* (1833). 71 × 89.5 cm. (MM.58.3.60). Châteaux de Malmaison et Bois-Preau, Rueil-Malmaison, France. Photograph by Yann Martin. Photograph © RMN-Grand Palais / Art Resource, New York.

CHAPTER 6

Toward a Poetics of Fusion

The Mémorial de Sainte-Hélène

A Successful Publication

"What a novel my life has been!" ("Quel roman pourtant que ma vie"), exclaimed the former master of France and Europe, exiled to Saint Helena.[1] Vanquished by the combined forces of Europe, he was no longer either Napoleon or Bonaparte, but a living memory who was attempting to ensure his legacy, to accomplish with the pen — or that of his confidant — what he now desperately feared he had not accomplished with the sword. How close this final challenge was to that which Balzac defined for himself in the ambitious phrase he had inscribed on the statuette of Napoleon that he kept in his office: "What he began with the sword, I will complete with the pen." Discussing with Las Cases one of the most persistent criticisms of his reign, Napoleon stresses the burden that weighed upon him, observing that "the nation, its destinies, its doctrines, its future relied on [him] alone!" Las Cases — whose aristocratic rank and royalist origins make the *Mémorial* into a sustained illustration of national reconciliation that overcomes the fundamental contradictions at work in the Revolution, the Ancien Régime, and the Empire — responds that this was precisely the issue: "But sire, [. . .] this is just what everyone used to say, and people holding a range of different opinions reproached you for it and asked, with some bitterness, 'But why did he insist on relating everything to himself?'" "A banal, vulgar accusation," replies the Emperor:

This situation was not of my making, it was not my fault; it was entirely in the nature and the force of circumstances, in the struggle between two opposed orders of things. [. . .] I was the keystone of an entirely new edifice built upon such fragile foundations! Its very existence depended on every one of my battles! [. . .] The vulgar didn't hesitate to denounce my ambition in all these wars; but were they of my choosing? Were they not always in the nature and the force of things, always in that struggle between the past and the future?

Cette situation n'était pas de mon choix, elle ne venait pas de ma faute; elle était toute dans la nature et la force des circonstances, dans la lutte de deux ordres opposés. [. . .] J'étais, moi, toute la clef d'un édifice tout neuf et à de si légers fondements! Sa durée dépendait de chacune de mes batailles! [. . .] Le vulgaire n'a pas manqué d'accuser mon ambition de toutes ces guerres; mais étaient-elles de mon choix; n'étaient-elles pas toujours dans la nature et la force des choses, toujours dans cette lutte du passé et de l'avenir?[2]

In recognizing that the very existence of his regime depended on his battles, Napoleon is admitting that, in the final analysis, the legitimacy of his reign resided in military victories and in the glory that came from them. Such an observation could only highlight the bankruptcy of the ideology of glory as well as Napoleon's attempts to extend it beyond the domain of military exploits. As if to respond to this obvious fact, Las Cases observes elsewhere that it wasn't the glory of his countless victories that saved Napoleon, but his very downfall. By abdicating and turning himself over to the enemy, he clearly demonstrated that he had the good of the country at heart. He thus destroyed any idea that he was motivated by personal interest and ambition, and he regained the moral high ground that he seemed to have abandoned. Through a final act of generosity and sacrifice, he proved his disinterestedness: he "left as the hero of a cause for which he remains the messiah."[3] The Emperor as we see him in the *Mémorial de Sainte-Hélène* becomes a man who "refused to mix personal interests with the greater interests that were constantly on his mind."[4]

The success and influence of Las Cases's work were enormous. The themes of personal interest, glory, honor, and emulation recur frequently throughout the text. But the status of the work has always posed a problem. It is often seen mainly as a work of propaganda, or as a document from which one need only extract the pith to glean the Emperor's true political and philosophical doctrine. Our conception of romanticism continues to make the individual author a cult object; the "consecration of the writer"—to borrow Paul Benichou's famous phrase —took place during a time when the individual, the self, was being intensely asserted, and literature was being triumphantly upheld—notably in the face of politics—as the disinterested conscience of society.[5] Seen in this perspective, the *Mémorial* does appear to be a strange amalgam; it is a labyrinthine accumulation of styles, texts, and voices—a monster in form. In the many editions published in his lifetime, Las Cases continues to intervene, to add some elements and to remove others, responding to new information, criticisms, or events. The obvious instability of the text only increased the suspicion cast on a work whose author was neither Napoleon nor someone else. Banished from a literary canon inhabited largely by writers easily identified as the new clerics of modernity, this work appeared alternately as a final diabolical manipulation or as the ultimate word on true Napoleonic doctrine. Aside from merely reproducing all too well-known elements of the Napoleonic legend, be it black or golden, such interpretations do little to explain the effectiveness of a work that surveys all the elements of a life and an era marked by the pursuit of individual and national glory. The *Mémorial* was one of the vectors of romantic literature, and it played an important role in various practices of writing in nineteenth-century France. It certainly constitutes one of the foundations of the Napoleonic legend, but, more important for our perspective, it also occupies an essential place in the construction of a founding myth of post-Revolutionary modernity in France and, for that alone, deserves to be looked at more carefully, both as a text and for its workings.

In *The Red and the Black*, Stendhal expresses a profound intuition regarding the *Mémorial*. Julien Sorel's meager reading list—what Stendhal calls his *Coran*—is made up of three works: Napoleon's military bulletins from the Grande Armée, Rousseau's *Confessions*, and the *Mémorial de Sainte-Hélène*. The narrator informs us that Julien "would have died" for those three texts; but, of the three, the *Mémorial* was the young man's favorite. Using another voice, that of the old surgeon-major who has befriended Julien, Stendhal tells us that his young hero, who strangely resembles the young Bonaparte—a "short young man [. . .], weak in appearance, with uneven, but delicate, features and an aquiline nose"—"regarded all the other books in the world as liars, and written by rogues seeking advancement."[6] In this textual triad the *Mémorial* represents a kind of synthesis of the two other works. The epic material characteristic of the bulletins of Napoleon's Grande Armée and the

intimate self-representation of Rousseau's *Confessions* are fused to form a curiously seductive hybrid operating along an axis with glory at one end and
authenticity at the other. This technique of accumulating voices, themes, and
styles exemplifies what one might call a poetics of fusion or amalgamation,
which, as we will see, would continue to be developed over the course of the
nineteenth century.

A true appreciation of how this poetics works in the *Mémorial* requires
choosing among the various editions. Between the first edition, published in
1823, and his death in 1842, Las Cases brought out four major editions — 1824,
1830-32, 1835, and 1840 — each containing numerous additions, deletions,
and corrections. The editions of 1835 and, more particularly, 1840 are characterized by a "Bonapartist" emphasis, which led Las Cases to suppress many
details concerning daily life. The best critical edition of the *Mémorial*, by Marcel Dunan (1951), is based on the 1823 edition but incorporates many of the
stylistic changes Las Cases made in 1824.[7] For anyone trying to understand
the *Mémorial*'s aesthetics of fusion, however, Dunan's edition suffers from
a major defect: a good portion of the "epic material" and many other documents have been removed from the text proper and relegated to a series of
appendixes at the end of each of the two volumes. By favoring a certain vision
of the "true" contents, this flattening of the *Mémorial* prevents the reader
from understanding the poetics through which it influenced Julien Sorel, and
many others as well. Hence, the 1830-32 edition is perhaps the best, since it
contains passages concerning the Bourbons, which Las Cases had omitted for
obvious reasons in 1823 and 1824. Furthermore, it pursues a policy of integrating documents and dialoguing with other works, which Las Cases had already
begun in the 1824 edition. For our purposes, the best modern version is that
of Joël Schmidt and Jean Tulard (1968).[8] To help the reader, these editors have
divided the work into chapters, whereas contemporary editions were divided
by date and volume (and volume numbers varied from edition to edition). But
the work can quite easily be imagined as an intimate journal, a long series of
dated passages telling of daily life in minute detail; integrating conversations,
observations, and dictations; and extending from Napoleon's abdication and
his departure for exile up to the eve of the publication of the *Mémorial* in 1823:

> Heaven has blessed my efforts, allowing me to go to the end, and to finish
> as best I could what I've had the good fortune of doing at this time. If I've
> succeeded in winning over some good and righteous hearts, if I've overcome
> some prejudices, or animosities, I have reached my most cherished goal, the
> sweetest: my mission is accomplished.

Le ciel a béni mes efforts, en me permettant d'aller jusqu'au bout, et de terminer tant bien que mal ce que j'ai le bonheur de faire en cet instant. Si j'ai réussi à ramener des cœurs justes et droits, si j'ai détruit des préjugés, vaincu des préventions, j'ai atteint mon but le plus cher, le plus doux: ma mission est accomplie.[9]

Thus ends, in a decidedly Rousseauist tone, the strange work that sought to make Napoleon known as he was, and to that end combined narration, proclamations, administrative documents, summaries, and refutations of some of the most virulent criticisms.

The Amalgamated Voice of Las Cases / Napoleon

In many respects, and in spite of the incorporation of so many disparate elements, the *Mémorial* tells a rather simple tale: the story of two individuals bound together by destiny and forced by circumstances to abandon their homeland and all that was dear to them, two individuals who struggle valiantly with all the courage of their convictions yet succumb to the forces of isolation, the elements, and the inhumanities inflicted upon them. In the end, Napoleon dies, and while Las Cases survives to tell his tale, his own health is seriously compromised. All other figures in the story pale before the depth and presence of the two principals, who together create a dialogical voice that comes across as the confederated union of self and other. A complex interplay of formal elements underlies the creation of this amalgamated voice: a constant intertwining of direct discourse, indirect discourse, and free indirect discourse; shifts between the first and third person; the insertion of notes, then notes within notes; flash-forwards to anticipate and flash-backs to evoke the familial, educational, and affective past. All this movement is deployed in a text that highlights both its spontaneity and its immediacy, the better to affirm its authenticity. In many ways, the work is squarely in the aristocratic tradition of memoirs. As affirmations of self, memoirs are free of institutional and scholarly constraints.[10] In contrast to historians, who record rigorously, memorialists parade their individuality, their freedom to interpret or to criticize the events they have experienced and of which they are witnesses. But even as memoir, the *Mémorial de Sainte-Hélène* proves to be a hybrid work because it seeks to be the voice of both Las Cases and Napoleon. The commemorative nature of the book finds its legitimacy and justification in the duty to remember, so essential to any ideology of glory. But it is through the poetics of fusion that the work succeeds both in transcending simple commemoration and in preserving and transforming an ideology which, however one might regard it, had led to a national disaster: the *Mémorial* in effect achieves a literary transposition of the politics of fusion and the projection of glory onto the everyday.

Very early on, Las Cases recalls, when they were still aboard the *Northumberland* en route to the island of Saint-Helena,[11] it was clear that despite the orders given by the English ministers to address Napoleon by no other title than "General," the natural dominance of the man made itself felt, particularly among the young sailors and the most innocent, the children. Las Cases's gaze lingers on a group of children who have made a circle around the Emperor and are looking at him. Napoleon, seeing Las Cases, notes that "the hearts of children were always most disposed to enthusiasm."[12] As if by mental association, Las Cases then turns to Bonaparte's birth, while at the same time asserting his own role as narrator, who has assembled what has been provided him by "various moments" concerning the Emperor's earliest days:

> Napoleon was born on August 15, 1769, feast of the Assumption, around noon. His mother, a strong woman in both morals and physique, who was active in the revolt when pregnant with him, wanted to go to mass because of the solemnity of the day; she was forced to return home quickly, could not reach her bedroom, and gave birth to the child on one of those antique carpets depicting great figures, heroes of fables, or of the *Iliad*, perhaps: it was Napoleon.

> Napoléon est né le 15 août 1769, jour de l'Assomption vers midi. Sa mère, femme forte au moral et au physique, qui avait fait la guerre grosse de lui, voulut aller à la messe à cause de la solennité du jour; elle fut obligée de revenir en toute hâte, ne put atteindre sa chambre à coucher, et déposa son enfant sur un de ces vieux tapis antiques à grandes figures, de ces héros de la fable ou de l'*Iliade* peut-être: c'était Napoléon.[13]

This collection of "moments" begins in the third person like a classic factual account: "Napoleon was born." But immediately the narration is interrupted by a footnote containing an official and impersonal document: an excerpt from the birth certificate in Italian followed by its translation into French, as well as a short account of the history of the document and the way in which Las Cases—here, the memorialist refers to himself in the third person—came to possess the document, but only in 1824, *after* the publication of the first editions of the *Mémorial*:

This text was found in Ajaccio, in 1822, by Edouard Favand d'Alais, and offered to M. le compte de Las Cases, on 6 September 1824, by his uncle, the colonel Boyer Peyreleau.

Cet extrait a été pris à Ajaccio, en 1822, par Édouard Favand d'Alais, et offert à M. le compte de Las Cases, le 6 septembre 1824, par son oncle, le colonel Boyer Peyreleau.

A little further on, we arrive at the beginning of Napoleon's adolescence, still narrated in the third person: "At puberty, Napoleon became morose, dark."[14] Once again Las Cases adds a note, this time specifying that he is taking "direct dictation from the Emperor." In this particular case, then, it is Napoleon who is speaking about himself in the third person. But with the following paragraph, quotation marks—classic markers of direct discourse—are introduced: Napoleon is telling his own story, explaining that his trainer at the École militaire de Bienne was Pichegru and providing many details on the family of the man who was to become his archenemy. He even ends up quoting Pichegru, who, after crossing over to the royalist party, reminisced about the young Bonaparte, evoked his "inflexible" character, and declared that it was useless to try to win him over, because once "he has taken a position, he will not change it." Even in the direct discourse where he himself is supposedly speaking, Napoleon refers to himself as "Napoleon," as if Las Cases were continuing to narrate the story. The two voices blend together to the point of being confused in a dialogical unity made possible by a dizzying series of alternating points of view, a subtle gliding between discursive registers, and a balance between text and paratext.

Even the scene of Napoleon's birth on a carpet manages to fuse elements that would seem mutually exclusive. The precipitous birth is confusingly linked both to a Christian religiosity—his mother's wish to attend mass—and to the epic grandeur of antiquity, of the "heroes of fable or the *Iliad*." His appearance—"it was Napoleon"—recalls the "*ecce homo*" of the New Testament. Victor Hugo would remember this for the character in *Les Misérables* who represents anti-glory and anti-Napoleon: "it was Jean Valjean." The birth of baby Bonaparte occurs in a context that is both familiar and familial. Implicitly calling upon a common experience, Las Cases evokes "one of those antique carpets depicting great figures," an object we all recognize and that he doesn't even need to describe, since it is so much a part of the everyday life of most of his readers. And so Napoleon's birth occurs against a background of ancient glory. But all these "mythologizing" anecdotes about the hero's childhood are quickly relativized, encompassed in the Emperor's amusement at such legends: he "admits to almost none of them."[15] The inflated language of grandeur is then deflated, suddenly reduced by the healthily skeptical glance of Napoleon himself.

As for the tale of Napoleon's childhood and adolescence, Las Cases marks the beginning of the Emperor's dictation not with quotation marks but in a note, and without additional details: "the Emperor's own dictation; we will see later when and how."[16] Thus he arouses the reader's curiosity, with respect less to the subject matter—in this case, the childhood and youth of Bonaparte—than to the text in itself, that is, to the very writing of the *Mémorial*. This expectation, which dates from the passage of 27–31 August 1815, will be satisfied only a year and a thousand pages later, in the passage dated 5 October 1816. There, Las Cases points out that Napoleon knew he was keeping a journal recording "everything that Your Majesty does from morning to night every day." Often, moreover, the Emperor notices "the faithful Ali" recopying, glances over his work, and "after going over two or three lines, that is, after having recognized it, he walked away or spoke of something else without having touched upon the subject."[17]

But the morning of 5 October 1816 was different. We read that Napoleon asked to see "that famous scribbling" ("ce fameux fatras"), and when Las Cases's son brought him the first notebook, he read and approved the preamble (the opening narrative Las Cases writes about him), introduced a few corrections himself on his family and childhood, and then, having Las Cases's son take the pen, "he began to dictate details on Brienne, old Patrault, etc." Thus Napoleon corrected and supplemented the text by dictating details of his childhood. Las Cases then moved those passages, integrating them into the narrative that is dated 27 to 31 August 1815, and added the note that we have seen. It would have been simple and clear to change the punctuation to show that the text was directly citing Napoleon's dictation. But Las Cases chose to intervene in a more personal way, in a note, to add his voice to that of Napoleon, which, without a textual marker, becomes indistinct from Las Cases's own. This process enabled Las Cases to highlight his adherence to the authenticity of the text. We find the same strategy at work in the note containing Napoleon's birth certificate. Las Cases doesn't just provide the document but intervenes, while speaking of himself in the third person, to tell of an event that occurred in 1824, well after the publication of the first edition. His quest for the truth and, hence, the confines of the text extend in time. These interventions also serve to reassert a major aspect of the *Mémorial*: its spontaneity and authenticity.

Indeed, these multiple registers of voice and perspectives, this constant variation of narrative strategies, are so many ways of telling a story that is constantly threatened by immobility and *ennui*. Warning the reader about the dryness of the text, Las Cases begs his indulgence for

> the petty monotony of our complaints. Doubtless it's always the same thing; but believe me, it was more tedious for us to repeat them than it will be for the reader to read them.

> l'insipide monotonie de nos plaintes: on les trouvera toujours les mêmes, dans doute; mais qu'on se dise bien qu'elles ont dû nous causer beaucoup plus d'ennui à répéter qu'on n'en aura à les lire.[18]

Las Cases's challenge, then, is to give the reader a text that will rise above the very *ennui* and pettiness of the existence it is relating. He responds to the challenge by creating an open, polyphonic work in which the adventure of the text plays a role as important as that of any of the actors it represents in it. This amalgamated voice, the union of the same and the other, is thus created by means of a set of techniques that tend to blur those elements that would allow the reader to distinguish clearly one voice from the other. The weaving of direct, indirect, and free indirect discourse, the ostensible inclusion of documents are so many various writerly means to suggest a spontaneous construction, to highlight the *drama* of the text as such, and to establish a truth that is continually reinforced as the text progresses.

At times it is by portraying a romantic sensibility through themes of transparency, proximity, and intimacy that Las Cases seeks to reveal authenticity:

> Who on earth today could pretend to know the private man in the Emperor more than I? [. . .] Who benefited from those long walks in the moonlight, those many hours spent with him?

> Qui aujourd'hui sur la terre pourrait se flatter de connaître dans l'Empereur l'homme privé plus que moi? [. . .] Qui a joui de ces longues promenades au clair de lune, de ces heures nombreuses écoulées avec lui?[19]

Napoleon's truth is the simple and spontaneous truth of Las Cases:

> It is doubtless surprising to see me sketching Napoleon's character traits with such simplicity. Everything that is usually written about him is in such

a highfalutin style; writers believe they need to use antitheses and to be brilliant; they are trying to create an effect and end up torturing their minds; as for me, I write what I see and express what I feel.

On sera surpris sans doute de me voir esquisser ces traits de caractère de Napoléon avec autant de simplicité. Tout ce qu'on en écrit ordinairement est si recherché; on se croit obligé à tant d'antithèses, à tant de brillant: c'est qu'en général les autres cherchent l'effet, ils se torturent l'esprit; moi j'écris ici ce que je vois, j'exprime ce que je sens.[20]

The *Mémorial* presents itself as a work of immediacy and presence, but also as a text confronting the world, engaging it in debates and even participating in its own way in events that are unfolding. Napoleon's words, like those of Las Cases, are simple and direct. But they are often confronted by those of his detractors — the abbé Pradt, for example, who enjoys describing Napoleon as "uniting in his strangeness all that is most elevated and most vile among mortals; [. . .] a sort of *Jupiter Scapin*."[21] And in this description of Napoleon as half god, half clown, Las Cases sees the very essence of brilliant antithesis and an *esprit recherché*.

Yet for all his decrying of these antitheses in the name of straightforward simplicity, it is hard to deny that the *Mémorial* itself is structured largely around a series of oppositions: Napoleon as son, preserver and tamer of the Revolution versus Las Cases the noble *émigré*; the glory versus the fall; the old order of things versus the new; the European alliance versus Napoleon's France. Napoleon famously described himself as unwittingly caught up in a binary struggle between the past and the future.[22] But his dream, he states over and over again in various ways, was to "reconcile France with Europe [. . .] and fully to amalgamate the new France with the old."[23] In many ways the *Mémorial* can best be understood as a *literary* enactment of the politics of fusion. The given, the real, of Napoleon is to be captured neither in the monolithic, single, Rousseauesque discourse of the self by the self, nor in unresolved antitheses. Rather, it is to be found in the living harmony of the poetics of fusion. The dialogical space of the *Mémorial* is one in which the hero of a moderate revolution and a nobleman steeped in the traditions of aristocratic heroism act out and textually display — that is, *in and through writing* — the ideal of a possible harmony created through mutual recognition. But this is not the self-contained harmony of a utopia; it is a harmony that is constantly listening to others, friends and foes alike, introducing them into the text for comment, discussion, or refutation. The fusion of the two voices and the themes of mutual trust and respect that underlie it create the possibility of introducing other, more oppositional voices.

One might object that this mutual recognition is far from egalitarian. After all, on several occasions, Las Cases likens his sentiments for Napoleon to those of a cult or a religion and describes Napoleon as "the hero of a cause to which he remains the messiah."[24] Seen in this way, the *Mémorial* is more devotional than dialogical, and contains more hierarchy than mutuality. Yet, it is important not to underestimate the role Las Cases plays in relation both to the text and to Napoleon himself. After all, not only does he open the text and define its parameters—he also ends it. The entire final part of the *Mémorial* is devoted to his tribulations after what he calls his "removal" from Longwood on 25 November 1816.[25] Las Cases formulates and delineates what it is that will give meaning to Napoleon's life in captivity and thus to the *Mémorial* itself. When Napoleon talks of suicide, Las Cases becomes the teacher and Napoleon the pupil:

> I violently objected to such thoughts. Poets and philosophers had said that, for them, seeing a man struggling with misfortune was a worthy spectacle; setbacks and constancy also had their glory; such a noble and great character could not sink to the level of the most vulgar souls; he who had governed us with such glory, who had held the admiration and the destinies of the world, could not end it all like a gambler in despair or a lover betrayed. What would become of those who believed, who hoped in him?

> Je me récriai sur de pareilles pensées. Le poète, le philosophe avaient dit que c'était un spectacle digne des dieux que de voir l'homme aux prises avec l'infortune; les revers et la constance avaient aussi leur gloire; un aussi noble et aussi grand caractère ne pouvait pas s'abaisser au niveau des âmes les plus vulgaires; celui qui nous avait gouvernés avec tant de gloire, qui avait fait et l'admiration et les destinées du monde, ne pouvait finir comme un joueur au désespoir ou un amant trompé. Que deviendraient donc tous ceux qui croyaient, qui espéraient en lui?[26]

While remarking that Las Cases's words were interesting, Napoleon wonders what they were going to do in such a godforsaken place as Saint Helena. Las Cases replies:

> Sire, we will live on the past; it has everything we need to satisfy us. Don't we take pleasure in the life of Cesar, in that of Alexander? Well, we have better

than that, we'll reread you, sire! "Right!" he said, "we will write our *Memoirs*. Yes, we need to work; work makes time pass. After all, one must fulfill one's destiny; that is also my belief."

Sire, nous vivrons du passé; il a de quoi nous satisfaire. Ne jouissons-nous pas de la vie de César, de celle d'Alexandre? Nous posséderons mieux, vous vous relirez, sire! —Eh bien! dit-il, nous "écrirons nos *Mémoires*. Oui, il faudra travailler; le travail aussi est la faux du temps. Après tout, on doit remplir des destinées; c'est aussi ma grande doctrine.[27]

In this passage and in others, Las Cases intervenes with words that help Napoleon overcome bouts of despair. Fusing the moral philosophy of the ancients — mainly the Stoics — and Christian doctrine, Las Cases holds up the ideal of glory in suffering, of heroism in defeat. The infusion of glory into defeat and into the boredom of captivity is an essential theme, perhaps *the* essential theme of the text, and is masterfully played out over the course of the work. It is in the way he accomplishes this, in his use of the techniques of polyphony, the poetics of fusion, that Las Cases creates a work that would have profound resonance throughout the nineteenth century; by these means he manages to depict the tedium and despair that accompany him, to delve into the banality of existence, and yet to project into his depiction the inner glory of the struggle both protagonists wage to exist, to be and to remain themselves.

A Struggle to the Death for Recognition

The Las Cases of the *Mémorial* is himself a living metaphor, an incarnation of the politics of fusion — politics which, as we have seen, borrow heavily from the ideology of glory. He describes his adherence to Napoleon's cause as having been first and foremost that of a noble, a member of a warrior class, and as such, particularly attuned to the appeal of glory. We have already referred to his exclamation:

After Ulm and the flash of Austerlitz, I was vanquished by glory: I admired, I recognized, I loved Napoleon, and from this moment on I became fanatically French.

Enfin, les prodiges d'Ulm et l'éclat d'Austerlitz vinrent me tirer d'embarras; je fus vaincu par la gloire: j'admirai, je reconnus, j'aimai Napoléon, et dès ce moment je devins Français jusqu'au fanatisme.[28]

The passage is interesting because it highlights the degree to which glory is no longer an aristocratic trait; it is a *national* one. Napoleon is saying the same thing when he declares: "I ennobled all Frenchmen: everyone can be proud."[29] Las Cases becomes "fanatically French" when the nation under Napoleon's impulsion aspires to the most immemorial of aristocratic values: heroic, military glory. According to the *Mémorial*, however, the effectiveness of glory is not limited to attracting refractory noblemen because, as Napoleon asserts, if the great truths of the Revolution have become immortal, it is because "we have intertwined them with brilliance, with monuments, with great deeds; we have washed away their earlier stains in the waves of glory."[30] The technique of intertwining is, as we have just seen, at the heart of the poetics at work in the *Mémorial*. And the idea of a glory that benefits all French people proves to be the essence of a movement of fusion: it is an economy of glory with constant growth. But while insisting on its value, Napoleon unwittingly reveals the weakness of the doctrine:

> I wish to raise the glory of the French name so high that it becomes the envy of nations; I wish that one day, with God's help, a Frenchman traveling in Europe will always feel he is at home.

> Je veux élever la gloire du nom français si haut qu'il devienne l'envie des nations; je veux un jour, Dieu aidant, qu'un Français voyageant en Europe croit se trouver toujours chez lui.[31]

For the nations of Europe, the elevation of the French provokes reactions of envy and resentment precisely because it is done at the expense of other peoples. And yet, on the national level, the waves of glory would have laundered the Revolution, and the entire nation would have risen on that tide. Wasn't it glory that brought Las Cases back into the fold? As Napoleon says: "I was amalgamating."[32]

If Las Cases incarnates and recapitulates the politics of fusion, Napoleon assimilates, repeats, and puts into practice the lessons of Las Cases. Responding to the reproach that he submitted to deportation to Saint Helena without defending himself, Napoleon observes:

> Dignity in misfortune and submission to necessity have their glory too; it is that of great men felled by the ills of fortune.

> La dignité dans le malheur, la soumission à la nécessité, ont aussi leur gloire; c'est celle des grands hommes que l'infortune terrasse.[33]

We see here the same mixture of stoic indifference and Christian submission to adversity that Las Cases praises and that explain the many references to Napoleon's calm and serenity. Yet this very display of moral fortitude threatens the *Mémorial* as a book, for the memoir risks becoming flatter and flatter, engulfed by the uniformity and sameness it is describing. Happily for the reader, however, as time passes and the story progresses, stoic indifference and calm equanimity turn out to constitute a position that Napoleon simply cannot hold. The Emperor is drawn into a conflict with his jailors, primarily one of the great villains of literary history, the infamous Sir Hudson Lowe, of whom we are told:

> Soon, he seems to have no other occupation, have no other job than to torment us and to make us suffer in all forms, for everything, in all ways.

> Bientôt, il ne semble plus avoir d'autre occupation, n'avoir reçu d'autre emploi que de nous tourmenter et de nous faire souffrir sous toutes les formes, sur tous les objets, de toutes les manières.[34]

Faced with and pursued by this fearsome adversary who, in the *Mémorial*, has no psychological consistency and no other purpose than to torment his victim, Napoleon is forced to abandon his equanimity: "The Emperor, who had promised himself to maintain a totally stoic attitude, nevertheless got very upset and expressed himself in the strongest of terms."[35] The struggle that ensues creates a dramatic tension that enables Las Cases to project the epic dimensions of Napoleon's exploits onto the events taking place on the tiny island where he is held prisoner.

As time passes, then, and the story continues to unfold, the original struggle against circumstance and an impersonal enemy that we might call *ennui* is augmented by a second struggle against an enemy personified by Hudson Lowe. And this changes everything. For if the first struggle is a classic one that can be fought with the weapons of moral philosophy and Christian submission, the struggle that begins with the arrival of Lowe proves to be much more modern and much more deadly: it is one that had been forcefully described a few years earlier by a young Hegel — himself profoundly influenced by the spectacular rise of Napoleon — as a struggle to the death for recognition.[36] In the *Mémorial*, this struggle acquires particular force because it is set in the double context of the most banal details of an isolated and barren existence, and the recounting of the grandiose events of the Napoleonic wars and the epic glory of the savior and tamer of the French Revolution.

The struggle is all the more primordial in that it occurs "outside the boundaries of human laws,"[37] in a strange zone, at the farthest edges of civilization, where the directives of distant allies — mainly England — appear both worrisome and absurd (Kafkian, we might say), and where Lowe's inexplicable obsession seems to develop endlessly. The symbolic metaphor of the struggle for recognition acquires a powerful reality here because, simply put, the Napoleon of the *Mémorial* chooses to succumb rather than to yield. It is thus a human enactment of what in Hegel remains an abstract metaphor. According to the Hegelian scenario, one party chooses to submit, whereas in the *Mémorial* Napoleon refuses to submit, and dies. The struggle to the death for recognition is no longer a metaphor: it really costs Napoleon his life. But this existential choice to succumb is made possible only by the poetics of fusion. In the struggle between Lowe and Napoleon, recognition can become more important than life itself, only because there is a surviving witness to the struggle: the amalgamated voice of the *Mémorial*.

While the struggle to the death begins with Hudson Lowe's arrival, it is with the theme of *ennui* that the *Mémorial* opens, and this motif resonates like a basso continuo from beginning to end. It is found in the frequent descriptions of the weather as well as in those of the desolate landscape, serving to reinforce the barrenness of the group's existence. At Longwood, there are no seasons, only "a long continuity of winds, clouds, humidity, a constant, moderate, monotonous temperature that is boring rather than unhealthy."[38] The monotony of their existence is also expressed in the subtitles listing the subject of each dated entry, and it is picked up again in the text. The subtitles constitute another element in the *Mémorial*'s polyphony. Las Cases reveals himself to be a past master of suggestive concision: *"The Emperor settles at Briars. Description. Miserable situation."*[39] An entry dated 11 February 1816 reads: *"Uniformity. Ennui. Solitude of the Emperor. Caricatures."*[40] In this world of non-events, anything and everything becomes worthy of mention: bad coffee, good coffee, no coffee, lists of household items, and of course all kinds of conversation and speculation on almost every subject imaginable, including the arrival of five oranges.[41] From one day to the next we go from an evocation of the battle of Hohenlinden, where the soldiers and the generals of the corps "had fought as heroes," to an infestation of rats in the kitchen: "More than once we had to do battle with them after dessert."[42] Out of this mixture emerges an image of daily life marked by an oscillation between the banal and the profound, minutiae and grandeur: Napoleon articulates his dreams, memories, and ideas, while anchored in the pitiful *ennui* of daily routines.

Like Candide and his tattered group, work is the only way to make life bearable on the island of Saint Helena. The brief subtitles for 7–10 September 1815 — "*Uniformity. Ennui. The Emperor decides to write his* Memoirs"[43] — suffice to sum up the non-events and connect them to Napoleon's decision. *Ennui* is seen both as a source of writing and the obstacle that the writing must overcome. On one of those days, the Emperor becomes aware of a few pages from the journal that Las Cases is already keeping. While approving the project, he expresses reservations: "such a journal would be more interesting than useful." Las Cases suggests that Napoleon himself dictate his Italian campaign. Napoleon's dictations constitute an important part of the epic material in the *Mémorial*. Upon their arrival at the Briars Pavilion, the Emperor continues dictating to Las Cases the narrative of the Italian campaigns, initiated aboard the *Northumberland*. In the entry for 28–31 October 1815, Las Cases indicates that they have almost finished the campaigns, but then intervenes, in a footnote he added after his return to Europe, to tell his story and that of the manuscripts, including the Emperor's first dictations; how they had been confiscated when he was removed from Longwood but how he had nonetheless managed to conserve a small number of them, which the reader would find scattered "pell-mell" in the *Mémorial* itself. In this note, Las Cases announces a strategy privileging the spontaneity and disorder of improvisation, but surprisingly he includes none of these dictations, no part of them, in the text at this point, choosing, rather, to wait for a "textually" more propitious moment, which would not occur until the little colony was installed at Longwood.

At Longwood, boredom, tedium, *ennui* intensify. It is high adventure when the horse on which the faithful servant Ali is riding gets stuck in the mud. Las Cases relates the Emperor's concern for Ali, who is late in joining the little band. He describes the Emperor waiting for Ali to be retrieved, standing on "a little knoll, as if on a pedestal, in the midst of ruins."[44] He aims to turn "this minute event" into a lesson for the reader, who, on reading of this touching scene of domestic solicitude, would have "trouble finding the insensitive, harsh, cruel monster, in a word, the tyrant he was often made out to be."[45] This lesson is confirmed in time and through other voices. Las Cases adds a passage in which he tells how, *after* the first publication of the *Mémorial*, he had the opportunity of reading an account by the doctor O'Meara of a fainting spell the doctor himself had had on Saint Helena during a private conversation with Napoleon. Las Cases integrates O'Meara's voice into the *Mémorial* by directly transcribing the Irish doctor's description of the Emperor's concern, proof, if need be, "of the heart and true sensitivity of Napoleon."[46] But these anecdotes scarcely go beyond the minuscule dimensions of a lonely island in the middle of nowhere. And it is probably for this very reason that Las Cases, after these scenes highlighting Napoleon's humanity in the intimacy of the most banal and monotonous everyday life, chooses to intersperse the first of several passages drawn from what he calls "Fragments from the Italian campaign":

> I said earlier that I would place fragments from the Italian campaigns somewhere in the text. Well, here I am at the end of a month [January 1816], so I am going to put in a few chapters. [. . .] I will include the little that I possess, seven chapters in all, either at the ends of months, or else right in the middle of the month when things get too uneventful.

> J'ai dit plus haut quelque part dans ce recueil, que je donnerais des fragments de la campagne d'Italie demeurés en mes mains. Me voilà à la fin d'un mois, j'en vais placer quelques chapitres. [. . .] J'insérerai donc le peu que je possède, sept chapitres sur vingt-deux, soit a la fin des mois, soit dans le cours même du journal quand il viendra à languir.⁴⁷

We are at the end of January 1816. The final passage of January, dated the 28th, begins:

> The days went by, as you might expect, in long insipid monotony. Tedium, memories, melancholy were our dangerous enemies.

> Nos jours se passaient, comme chacun le soupçonne, dans une grande et insipide monotonie. L'ennui, les souvenirs, la melancolie étaient nos dangereux ennemis.⁴⁸

The accounts of the Italian campaign thus save the text from its own deficiencies, shore it up where it is weakest. Las Cases points out that he is going to absorb this material into the *Mémorial* for essentially aesthetic reasons, but in such a way as to preserve, indeed to reinforce, a certain textual spontaneity.⁴⁹

So we now jump into a third-person narrative dictated by Napoleon. We see the young Republican general putting down the royalist uprising on 13 Vendémiaire. A long interior monologue, indicated by quotation marks, conveys his hesitations:

> *Was it wise to show one's hand?* [. . .] Who would dare to descend alone into the arena to become the champion of the Convention? The victory itself would seem odious [. . .]. How to resign oneself thus to being the scapegoat for so

many crimes of which one knows nothing? [. . .] And yet, if the Convention succumbs, what is to become of the great truths of our Revolution? [. . .] Thus the defeat of the Convention would crown our enemies, and would seal the shame and the enslavement of our nation.

Était-il sage de se déclarer? [. . .] Qui oserait descendre seul dans l'arène pour se faire le champion de la Convention? La victoire même aurait quelque chose d'odieux [. . .]. Comment se dévouer ainsi à être le bouc émissaire de tant de crimes auxquels on fut étranger? [. . .] Mais d'un autre côté, si la Convention succombe, que deviennent les grandes vérités de notre Révolution? [. . .] Ainsi, la défaite de la Convention ceindrait le front de l'étranger, et scellerait la honte et l'esclavage de la patrie.[50]

The young Bonaparte has confidence in his strengths and in his destiny. He decides; he engages; he acts. By contrast to the seeming eternity on the island of Saint Helena, in Paris on 13 Vendémiaire *"there was no time to lose."*[51] Then, with the royalist rebellion quelled, the Republic saved, we follow the general to Italy where he leads the republican army to victory in the battle of Montenotte. And here, in this third-person narrative, is inserted the proclamation of 26 April 1796, published in *Le Moniteur*:

Soldiers! In fifteen days you have won six victories, taken twenty-one standards [. . .]. Only Republican phalanxes, soldiers of liberty, could have endured what you have endured. Soldiers, you are to be acclaimed!

Soldats! Vous avez en quinze jours remporté six victoires, pris vingt et un drapeaux [. . .]. Les phalanges républicaines, les soldats de la liberté étaient seuls capables de souffrir ce que vous avez souffert! Grâces vous soient rendues, soldats![52]

The narrative of the Italian campaign, as well as some of the more famous proclamations by the young Bonaparte, are thus amalgamated into the journal of ordinary, mundane, daily activities of the captives on Saint Helena.

Thirty pages of epic tales later we are brought back to the island, where we once again take up the day-to-day, on 1 February 1816. It is surprising to see the Emperor praise Saint Helena, with its "monotonous, unhealthy climate; but the temperature, one had to admit, was mild."[53] The little island was perhaps not the worst place to be exiled. And the conversations resume, on Egypt, the Nile, the invasion of England. Napoleon attempts to come to terms with his past, to justify his politics, his actions; he expands on his dreams, on his magical return from the Island of Elba, as if transformed, having understood that the time of conquests had come to its end.

> I returned a new man [. . .]. I would unhesitatingly have been the monarch of the Constitution and of peace.

> Je revenais un homme nouveau [. . .]. J'aurais été franchement le monarque de la Constitution et de la paix.[54]

Benjamin Constant is summoned for the occasion. His account of the Hundred Days echoes the Emperor's reflections on the island of Saint Helena. Las Cases doesn't hide the pleasure he takes in assimilating that voice, in citing at length the liberal thinker's report of what Napoleon had said to him:

> I am not simply, as has been said, the Emperor of soldiers, I am the Emperor of peasants, of workers, of France [. . .]. I am a man of the people; if the people truly want freedom, I owe it to them: I have recognized their sovereignty, I must listen to their will [. . .]; fate has decided, I am no longer a conqueror, I can no longer be one.

> Je ne suis pas seulement, comme on l'a dit, l'Empereur des soldats, je suis celui des paysans, des plébéiens, de la France [. . .]. Je suis l'homme du peuple; si le peuple veut réellement la liberté, je la lui dois: j'ai reconnu sa souveraineté, il faut que je prête l'oreille à ses volontés [. . .]; le sort en a décidé, je ne suis plus un conquérant, je ne puis plus l'être.[55]

Thus opponents and partisans alike see Napoleon as the "prince of liberal ideas."

But whatever the grandeur of the ideas evoked, in the context of the *Mémorial* they are always threatened by the insipidness of the everyday. The passage dated Tuesday the 13th to Friday the 16th of February 1816 begins: "It would be difficult for me to use four words to describe it; during these four days, no deviation whatsoever from our usual life."[56] The text dated Sunday the 25th to Wednesday the 28th begins almost the same way: "Most of our days were the same; if they seemed long in detail, they were quickly lost in the past, and left us only with vague memories."[57] The similarity of the days threatens to engulf the *Mémorial* and its reader.

Well after what we might call the first epic pause incorporating the "Fragments from the Italian campaign," and almost at the midpoint of an uninterrupted set of journal entries extending from the first of February through the end of April 1816, Las Cases introduces another paratextual technique: the recapitulative summary. In the 1822 and 1824 editions this added register, which interrupts the steady unfolding of days, comes at the end of the second volume.[58] These summaries play a powerful role in focusing only on Napoleon's personal situation and his state of mind:

> Here I am nine months into my journal and I fear that with all these different pieces laid out in a disorderly fashion, Napoleon and all that characterizes him—my principal, my unique preoccupation—might all too often have disappeared from sight.

> Voilà déjà neuf mois que j'écris mon journal, et je crains bien qu'au travers des parties hétérogènes qui s'y succèdent sans ordre, on n'ait que trop souvent perdu de vue mon principal, mon unique objet, ce qui concerne Napoléon et peut servir à le caractériser.[59]

The summaries describe in a concentrated manner and in a solo narrative voice what is at stake in all that has happened to Napoleon and to those who have accompanied him since the beginning of the *Mémorial*; they clearly establish a story line. Succinctly, Las Cases traces the trajectory leading from France to England and on to Saint Helena; Napoleon's stoic, passive behavior in the face of setbacks; and the calm and peace of their stay at Briars, where every day is filled with work, with pauses for intimate conversations and moonlight walks. It is at Briars that Napoleon seems to forget, as he immerses himself in the details of his childhood, all he has endured; he even seems fairly cheerful. A moment of paradisiacal peace to be followed by the entry into a world of suffering. Thus Las Cases marks the arrival in Longwood as the turning point of the story:

> There our exile and our new destinies were really to begin; the gaze of the world would now be upon us in that place.

> Là allaient commencer réellement notre exil et nos destinées nouvelles; les regards de l'univers allaient nous y considérer.

Las Cases emphasizes the common nature of their collective destinies (*"our exile," "our destinies"*) before turning this observation into a conclusion shared by Napoleon:

The Emperor, seeming to have reached this conclusion, organizes everything that is around him and adopts an attitude of dignity oppressed by force. *He traces a moral barrier around himself, and from behind it he defends himself inch by inch against improprieties and insults;* he doesn't let his persecutors get away with anything, takes offense at the least occasion, and rejects almost any proposition. The English had not doubted that habit would finally produce familiarity. *The Emperor brings them back to the first day*, and the deepest respect is then shown.

L'Empereur, semblant faire ce calcul, régularise tout ce qui l'entoure, et prend l'attitude de la dignité qu'opprime la force; *il trace autour de lui une enceinte morale derrière laquelle il se defend à présent pouce à pouce contre les inconvenances et les outrages;* il ne passe plus rien à ses persécuteurs, il se montre susceptible sur les formes, hostile contre toute entreprise. Les Anglais n'avaient pas douté que l'habitude ne produisît enfin la familiarité. *L'Empereur les ramène au premier jour*, et le respect le plus profound se manifeste.[60]

It suddenly becomes evident that the English now believe the Emperor has risen higher than ever before. In private, too, within the little group, things are transformed; Napoleon picks up his rigorous examination of European affairs. In a curious turn of phrase, to which we will return, Las Cases declares: "in a word, we had recovered the Emperor, and all of Napoleon."[61] Although Napoleon is now on war footing with the enemy, he remains even-tempered, warm, and affectionate to those around him, and he even joins them in planning, quite cheerfully, "sorties against the common enemy."

In his brief summary, then, Las Cases recasts the entire series of events, infusing them with a clear story line and a strong symbolic meaning in which recognition and respect are the key elements. The reader sees the banal reality of everyday life as part of a struggle that has been prepared imperceptibly and is now being engaged in. The daily thus acquires new dignity and is infused with the possibility of heroic glory.[62] In a few lines, Las Cases gives meaning to all that has already happened and paves the way for what is to come. Until this point, any meaning to the story would be found in the exemplum of the fallen hero who accepts his fate, in the mixture of stoic indifference and Christian submission that Las Cases presents from the outset of the *Mémorial*. The importance of this initial position is that it provides a space in which the author can emphasize Napoleon's disinterestedness as an essential element of his glory. If Napoleon abdicates and submits, it is for the good of the nation. By continuing the struggle and rallying his forces, he would have divided the country and unleashed a civil war.[63] Las Cases explains that Napoleon might have been able to preserve his crown, but it would not have been in the nation's interest to do so. Thus Napoleon proves his magnanimity by sacrificing himself without resistance for the good of France, an entity with which, as he repeatedly states, he has totally identified himself. In short, what Christ did for humankind, Napoleon does for the nation.[64] Following this logic to its conclusion, Napoleon would have undergone all forms of degradation and humiliation with the same sense of sacrifice and abnegation. *But that is not what happens.* For now, in the continued unfolding of the *Mémorial*, the stakes have changed. Napoleon shifts from a model of passive submission to one of active, even passionate resistance.

What justifies this change in orientation? The answer is to be found in Las Cases's redefinition in the recapitulative summary. Henceforth, the *Mémorial* revolves around the question of recognition: it is from the moment when nothing else is left at stake but recognition that Napoleon engages in the struggle, goes from passive submission to active resistance.

At the heart of the struggle lies a question of language and protocol: how should Napoleon be addressed? The problem arises very early on, immediately upon their departure from England on the *Northumberland*. The British government had condemned the respect accorded Napoleon aboard HMS *Bellerophon* and had issued orders to the officers and crew not to doff their caps to him. "And it was strictly ordered that he not be addressed in any other way than *general*, and that he be treated accordingly."[65] Napoleon's response was "energetic" but simple and circumspect: "*Let them call me whatever they like, they cannot stop me from being myself.*"[66] With his installation at Longwood, however, our hero seems to have reached the conclusion that if he were not addressed as Emperor, it would indeed stop him from being *himself*. He comes to this conclusion (in the unified voices of Las Cases and Napoleon) because his exile and new destiny have *really* begun and because he begins to see himself as "under the gaze of the world." Here then is Napoleon as he becomes himself again.

This self-awareness probably began at the time of his installation at Longwood (10 December 1815). But Las Cases describes it more than three months and around two hundred pages later (at the end of 21 and 22 March 1816). So it is only retrospectively that the reader learns that Napoleon has been on a war footing for some time. Clearly, Las Cases chose to wait to tell us this, to wait for the theme of *ennui* to be exhausted before revealing the epic material showing us a triumphant young Bonaparte. It is easy to see why he delayed: if such words had been inserted into the description of a sterile life of isolation, they might have seemed overblown, even absurd, given the circumstances. But placed as they are, in the first edition, at the end of the volume, thus on the very edge of the text, they acquire a certain nobility, and this precisely because the testimony of the *Mémorial*—along with other testimonies—has survived. Napoleon displayed his audacity by acting *as if* the eyes of the world were on him and his cohorts, by betting on the survival of this literary monument. Thus, it is in fusional writing, in his "textual self," that Napoleon abandons an attitude of submission and puts himself on a war footing, becoming once again an actor, though on a stage saturated with *ennui* and insipidness. In this context, to struggle is to stress the importance of self-assertion in a context in which the field of action is reduced to the infinitely small.

It remains to be seen what being oneself meant in the context of the *Mémorial*; for this, let us return to the phrase in which Las Cases, describing Napoleon's decision and his subsequent change of behavior, states that the tiny colony recovered "the Emperor and all of Napoleon." A radical break with the world is now being put definitively in place: exile will "really begin." But Napoleon is aware that he will *at the same time* be cut off from others *and* under the gaze of the world. He thus acts both in relation to himself in the purity of imposed solitude, and also in relation to distant others. Unlike Jean-Jacques Rousseau on the island of Saint Peter in Lake Biel, Napoleon does not indulge in the passive enjoyment of reverie, quite the contrary. For had he done so, he would have become someone other than himself. In the phrase "the Emperor and all of Napoleon" Las Cases seeks to emphasize a dual identity: a symbol of sovereignty (Emperor) and a person (Napoleon). In his decision to put up a *moral barrier* around himself and to defend inch by inch his symbolic territory—to fight, in other words—his friends find their Napoleon being precisely who he is: a heroic warrior. But they find him defending an ideal whose meaning now is purely symbolic. Above all, it is a matter of being himself and of being recognized as such. And Napoleon's self is dual; it contains a purely individual aspect and another that is established in relation to the collectivity, France.

At issue, essentially, is the recognition of legitimacy. The *Mémorial* constantly returns to this question. The argument is almost invariably threefold, sometimes fourfold: Napoleon has the right to be called Emperor because he has been consecrated by the will of the people, by force of arms and victory, and by religion; he also has that right because he has been recognized by all the powers of Europe.[67] The *Mémorial* places Napoleon the individual at the crossroads of a legitimacy that is in itself multiple, fusional, and therefore *un*-

deniable. In this perspective, Napoleon is himself the incarnation of fusion as legitimacy. His struggle is to defend tooth and nail the ideal of what might be called fusional legitimacy. Having established himself on the solid throne of this fusional legitimacy, he wants it to be recognized — more in principle than in any real-world practice. And he defends himself against a jailer whose sole objective is to subjugate him. "What an ignoble and sinister figure is the governor!" exclaims Napoleon; "I will never in my life encounter anything like him!"[68]

Lowe's principal tactics will be systematically to refuse Napoleon recognition beyond that of an individual, and ultimately to defeat him by carrying the assault from a symbolic to a material level. So he sets about reducing his prisoner's budget and his allotment of wine; limiting his ability to move about; and harassing the Emperor's entourage. This treatment is inflicted for many months, and the "Summary of July, August, September, October 1816" well illustrates its systematic nature. Lowe

> imposes the most extravagant rules on the Emperor; he capriciously and ironically restricts his usual boundaries, prescribes where he can walk, and goes so far as to try to determine the nature of his conversations and the extent of his words; he digs ditches around us, surrounds us with walls, raises barriers; he forces each of us, in order to remain near the Emperor, to swear that we submit to all these things; he uses our own hands to degrade him by forcing us to call him simply *Bonaparte* or to risk being immediately separated from him and to be deported immediately! Etc.

> [. . .] signifie à l'Empereur les règlements les plus extravagants; il resserre capricieusement et ironiquement son enceinte habituelle, lui prescrit la trace de ses pas, et va jusqu'à lui vouloir fixer la nature de ses conversations et l'étendue de ses paroles; il creuse des fossés autour de nous, nous entoure de palissades, élève des redoutes; il nous oblige, pour pouvoir demeurer auprès de l'Empereur, à signer individuellement que nous nous soumettons à toutes ces choses; il se sert de nos propres mains pour le dégrader, en nous forçant de la qualifier simplement de *Bonaparte*, sous peine de nous arracher immédiatement d'auprès de lui, et de nous déporter sur-le-champ! Etc.[69]

Lowe conducts this assault with a mixture of caprice and cruelty. At the height of the restrictions and psychological torment, the physical suffering of the victim increases. On the material level, Lowe successfully imposes his will without difficulty. But Napoleon never confuses his material needs with the basic question of recognition. In the intertwining of direct and indirect discourse that characterizes the amalgamated voice of the *Mémorial*, Las Cases describes exactly what is at stake: Lowe "wants to force the Emperor to descend, Napoleon would say, into the morass of his needs in order to discuss them directly with him."[70] Napoleon resists by doing whatever is necessary to avoid recognizing Lowe: by becoming, in short, a recluse. Little by little his existence grows more circumscribed, his living space smaller, his doings of less consequence, his conversations less interesting. The first bout of voluntary reclusion begins on Monday, 29 April 1816. The Emperor is supposedly ill. But he tells Las Cases privately that he is fine, he "just wanted to be alone." "However," notes Las Cases, "he seemed sad, upset."[71] This is followed by a second day of reclusion. There is little to report; the governor comes, the usual altercation and standoff. The Emperor tells Las Cases of their conversation. Yet again the *Mémorial* finds a way to emphasize that the Emperor could have guaranteed himself a better personal fate if he had pursued the war after Waterloo, but that he had decided against it in the interests of France. The Emperor was indignant to see French leaders betray France and "compromise that holy independence, which, no less than honor, is also *a steep island without edges.*" Having established this parallel between the independence of France and his own personal independence, Napoleon asserts before the governor that he will not allow himself to die, that "it is noble and courageous to overcome misfortune." But the reader knows this only too well. The text begins to sink under the weight of repetition and monotony. "The island is too small for me" exclaims Napoleon. "Everything here exudes deadly *ennui.*"[72]

Heroism in the Everyday

Las Cases is well aware of the dead end toward which the *Mémorial* is headed. The narrative is on the verge of being smothered by tedium and monotony, which, however, must be recounted so that the reader can understand the dimensions of the struggle for recognition and the projection of glory onto the banality of the everyday. To free the work from this dead end, Las Cases breaks into the daily narrative and inserts the second series of "Fragments of the Italian Campaign,"[73] this time with the simple, assertive footnote: "We are going to place three more chapters of the Italian campaign here." The reader is whisked away from the routine of Saint Helena and plunged into the glorious battles of Castiglione, Arcola, and Rivoli. On the bridge of Arcola, we watch the spectacular action of Napoleon as he "seized a flag, ran to the bridge and *planted it there.*" Thrown off the bridge into a swamp, he is saved by his soldiers, who come running to pull him out. Lannes puts himself between the enemy and Napoleon, covering him with his body, and Muiron, "the general's aide-de-camp, was killed covering his general with his body — a heroic and touching death!"[74]

Immediately following this second epic interlude, we return to the island of Saint Helena to witness a third day of reclusion, then a fourth, and a fifth. Thus a narrative rhythm is established: the struggle for recognition unfolds in a context of various conversations and petty concerns of everyday life, punctuated by epic interludes. A third section will be drawn from the "Fragments from the Italian campaign," but in order to maintain the rhythm, Las Cases will turn to other sources and find a way to incorporate them into the text.

The entry for Monday, 12 August 1816, for example, begins with the Emperor spending the morning in his bathtub reading newspapers. In the course of the day, the subject of the battle of Eckmühl comes up, and Napoleon states that "his most remarkable maneuver" occurred there, "without specifying it further."[75] In the next paragraph we find ourselves transported to Paris "just as this volume is being printed." Las Cases is talking with a friend who has been allowed to read the manuscript. The friend (the baron Pelet) comments that Napoleon's remark could be applied not only to the whole battle but to the entire campaign of 1809. Las Cases reports, in direct discourse, several of Pelet's observations confirming the brilliance of Napoleon's actions in the field, and then goes on to say that his friend revealed a secret to him: that he himself had undertaken to write "a truly national work." The title of the work was to be the *Portrait of Napoleon's Campaigns on the Continent of Europe, recounted by an Eyewitness*.[76] Since Pelet had already finished the part about the campaign of 1809, he gives Las Cases permission to incorporate part of it into the *Mémorial*. Thus we find some forty pages — mostly direct quotation but with some commentary by Las Cases — devoted to the campaign. The two voices tend to be confused in the succession of battles: Eckmühl, Essling, Wagram. Here are some words attributed by Las Casas to Pelet:

> Our troops had seemed to forget their hunger and extreme fatigue in these two long days, when the heat was excessive, where they fought for forty hours. A splendid time of glory!!! [. . .] The soul of the leader had passed into those of all the soldiers.

> Nos troupes avaient comme oublié la faim et l'extrême fatigue dans ces deux longues journées, où elles soutinrent quarante heures de combat. Belle

époque de gloire!!! [. . .] L'âme du chef était passée dans celle de tous les soldats.[77]

A few lines down and in the same tone, Las Cases continues:

> Starting with that moment, everyone worked without stopping; the leader was everywhere, and the soldiers were indefatigable. Their constancy, their ardor were without equal [. . .]. Under a leader such as Napoleon, everything had ceased to be impossible; no one was concerned with his own well-being anymore; life was glory.

> À compter de cet instant, chacun travaille sans relâche; le chef se multiplie et les soldats sont infatigables. Leur constance, leur ardeur sont sans égales [. . .]. Sous un chef tel que Napoléon, tout avait cessé d'être impossible; per-sonne ne s'occupait plus de sa propre conservation; la vie, c'était la gloire.[78]

But then the voice of Napoleon is superimposed, in a proclamation to the soldiers cited by Pelet and added by Las Cases:

> "Soldiers!" said the Emperor, "you have justified my expectations, you have supplemented our numbers by your bravery!"

> "Soldats!" dit l'Empereur, "vous avez justifié mon attente, vous avez suppléé au nombre par votre bravoure!"[79]

And again, when he reviews the Italian army the day after the battle of Wagram:

> "You are brave men, you are all swathed in glory!"

> "Vous êtes de braves gens, vous vous êtes tous couverts de gloire!"[80]

Thus, through an agile mixture of times (the Saint Helena exile, a conversation in Paris with a friend who is reading the manuscript just before publication, the campaign of 1809), Las Cases assimilates yet another voice into the *Mémorial* to supplement Napoleon's dictation. He would do something similar for the campaign of Moscow, relying on of Baron Larrey's account, whereas the account of Waterloo was dictated by Napoleon himself and published separately in 1820 under the title of *Mémoires pour servir à l'Histoire de France en 1815.*[81] This back-and-forth between the epic and the intimate appears to be an essential element in the success of the *Mémorial*. It is a set of juxtapositions that sustains the reader in a text in which Napoleon's dignity could easily disappear behind the banality of disputes concerning protocol and daily grousing. The recapitulative summary for July through to September 1816 begins:

> The usual summary need not be long now; three sentences will suffice: Torments at their maximum. Absolute reclusion. Certain destruction. The remainder of Napoleon's life will be nothing more than a long, cruel agony.

> Le résumé habituel ne saurait être long désormais; trois phrases, à la rigueur, pourrait suffire: Tourments au comble. Réclusion absolue. Destruction infaillible. Le reste de la vie de Napoléon ne sera plus qu'une cruelle et longue agonie.[82]

The struggle for recognition grows in purity and intensity as Napoleon's health declines. There are intimate scenes of great pathos. Thursday, 19 September 1816, is entitled: "*Emperor changes and becomes weaker. Silverware smashed.*" Las Cases notes that Napoleon "is visibly weakening; his walk is heavy; one foot drags, his features are changing."[83] On that same day, they had to smash the imperial silverware and sell it in order to meet their material needs. The Emperor insisted that they "file away the stamp and break the pieces such that no vestige of them could indicate that they had belonged to him [. . .]. Some of us wept."[84] In the evening of this pitiful scene, Napoleon continues his reading—the *Odyssey*. On Tuesday, 8 October, he has reached canto XVIII, which tells of the battle of Irus against Odysseus on the threshold of the hero's own palace. Odysseus not having revealed his identity, the two are disguised as beggars. Napoleon doesn't like this episode, finding it "unsavory," inappropriate, unworthy of a king. Then he questions his own reaction: "I guess what affects me still—putting myself in his place—is the fear of being thrashed by a beggar." He notes that Homer resolves the problem by turning his heroes into colossuses, but modern civilization "does everything for the soul, and favors it entirely at the expense of the body."[85] It is as if, before succumbing, Napoleon wants to point out the modernity of his final battle. He becomes, so to speak, the incarnation of the ideal described by Salaville, that the love of self that characterizes the human condition is ultimately the love of freedom—freedom to act beyond or in spite of the constraints of the material world of the senses. The struggle for recognition is a test not of physical strength but of strength of soul. Deplorable circumstances only reinforce the purity of this modern epic contest, which unfolds on a lonely island but against the background of narratives of great battles — Moscow, Waterloo, and so on — which led to the fall of the Empire.

In the logic of the *Mémorial*, the one who survives to recount and thus give meaning to Napoleon's death must accede to the heroic dignity of being a worthy witness. He too must refuse to submit and must carry on the struggle for recognition. The last part of the work, accordingly, tells the story of Las Cases's refusal to submit to Lowe and others who wish to silence him. He himself takes on heroic status as he wanders in exile through Europe, rejected by country after country, telling and retelling the story of Saint Helena in appeals to various sovereigns and authorities: *Letter to the Prince of Metternich, Letter to S. M. the Emperor of Russia, Letter to Lord Bathurst, Petition to the Parliament of England, Letter from Madame Mère to the allied sovereigns in Aix-la-Chapelle, Note addressed to the allied sovereigns meeting in Aix-la-Chapelle, Letter to S. M. the Emperor of Austria, Letter to Castelreagh, Letter to Lord Liverpool,* and so on. The numerous documents assimilated into the *Mémorial* tell the same tale over and over, they constitute a series of *mises en abîme,* the tale within the tale being always the same story fashioned in another manner. Each time we have a slightly different view of Napoleon — a series of tableaux, each depicting the "illustrious captive" abandoned on his rock.

In and by means of of the *Mémorial,* Las Cases achieves the status of hero, for the story he tells is also his own:

> I have lost my wife, my children, my friends, although they are still alive, but their world is no longer my own; and henceforth deprived of communication with others, I can only grieve for the intimacies of friendship, the sweetness of family, the closeness, the charms of society.

> J'ai perdu ma femme, mes enfants, mes amis, bien qu'ils jouissent encore de la vie, mais leur univers n'est plus le mien; et privé désormais de la communication des hommes, il me reste à pleurer les épanchements de l'amitié, les douceurs de la famille, les intimités, les charmes de la société.[86]

It is a story of devotion and sacrifice, then, but also of courage in his personal confrontation with Hudson Lowe after his "removal" from Longwood: Lowe "demanded my submission pure and simple [. . .]. I resisted heroically."[87] Back in Europe, he wanders from country to country denouncing the captivity and persecution of Napoleon, of course, but in doing so he emphasizes his disinterested heroism, daily engaging in unequal battle, beyond human laws. Both an eyewitness account and a work of pure love, the *Mémorial* uses every means to make visible that unseen struggle, the grandeur of the conflict that was pursued tirelessly on a tiny island until its tragic end, "the inevitable announcement" of Napoleon's death that appeared in *Le Moniteur*.

The fusional polyphony of the *Mémorial* conveys what was at stake in this struggle to the death for recognition. Precisely because the framework of this struggle was not a battlefield but the most banal of everyday living, Napoleon symbolizes every man, and his struggle is that of all men who are confronted with snubs, humiliation, and common bullying. Just as the simple soldier, throughout the *Mémorial*, is depicted as capable of the greatest heroic devotion, so too the glory of Napoleon, who describes himself as having come from the ranks of the people, is achieved in a context infused with the ordinary. If the *Mémorial* illustrates that all glory needs a witness, it also makes Napoleon a witness of the situation of modern man—born of the Revolution *and* the politics of fusion.

In spite of the apparent clarity of this message, however, the *Mémorial* is built on a fundamental paradox that would be explored by writers throughout the nineteenth century. For, while it praises Napoleon's heroism, the work also describes the failure of that vast experiment aiming to create a society based on the ideology of glory. During his reflections, Napoleon often returns to the role of his institutions in the reward for merit:

> My national titles reestablished precisely the equality that feudal nobility had proscribed. Merits of all types were included: for titles of nobility I substituted great actions, and for private interests, the interests of the nation.

> Mes titres nationaux rétablissaient précisément cette égalité que la noblesse féodale avait proscrite. Tous les genres de mérites y parvenaient: aux parchemins je substituais les belles actions, et aux intérêts privés, les intérêts de la patrie.[88]

Yet the *Mémorial* proves pitiless toward those who profited most from this system. Despite its privileging the politics of fusion, the work frequently asserts that the men promoted by that politics all too often proved unworthy of it; with the possible exception of those who had the grace to die, almost all yielded to the lure of self-interest. Napoleon takes obvious pleasure in telling how Sieyès, the theoretician of the role wealthy notables were to play in government, pilfers the coffers the Directoire had put aside in case of need.

Bonaparte refuses the share Sieyès offers him and suggests that he divide up the money with Ducos; Sieyès finds a way to take six hundred thousand francs while giving only two hundred thousand to Ducos. Sieyès would become a senator, with enormous financial advantages and property, and finally *comte de l'Empire*. This story is emblematic. The highest spheres of the imperial nobility thus abandoned the path of glory:

> The truth is that, generally speaking, the high-ranking generals had lost their drive: it is because I had glutted them with too much consideration, too many honors, too much wealth. They had drunk from the cup of enjoyment, and henceforth they asked only for rest.

> Le vrai est qu'en général les hauts généraux n'en voulaient plus; c'est que je les avais gorgés de trop de considération, de trop d'honneurs, de trop de richesses. Ils avaient bu à la coupe des jouissances, et désormais ils ne demandaient que du repos.[89]

These criticisms are aimed as much at the old aristocrats as the new nobles — all those who were particularly targeted by the politics of fusion:

> M. de *** and Fouché had their turn; he [Napoleon] dwelled on the subject for some time and went on to attack vigorously the immorality of the administrators in France, and generally all the bureaucrats or men in high positions, on their lack of political religion or of national sentiment, which led them to administer indifferently, one day for one person, the next day for another: "This lightness, this inconsequence, has been with us forever," he said; "we will always remain Gauls: and we will only show our true worth when we have substituted principles for turbulence, pride for vanity, and above all the love of institutions for the love of positions."

> M. de *** et Fouché eurent leur tour; il [Napoléon] s'y arrêta longtemps et partit de là pour faire une vigoureuse sortie sur l'immoralité des administrateurs en France, et généralement de tous les fonctionnaires ou hommes à place; sur leur manque de religion politique ou de sentiment national, qui les portait à administrer indifféremment, un jour pour l'un, un jour pour l'autre: "Cette légèreté, cette inconséquence, nous venaient de loin, disait-il, nous demeurons toujours Gaulois: aussi nous ne vaudrions tout notre prix que lorsque nous substituerions les principes à la turbulence, l'orgueil à la vanité, et surtout l'amour des institutions à l'amour des places."[90]

The failings described here are historical and national—inherent in the French character. Seen in this perspective, overcoming the revolutionary fracture amounts to nothing more than a fusion of former vices and new ambitions. It is an interpretation based on a vision of France inherited from the age-old commonplace concerning the lightness and vanity of the French. Such an interpretation is significant here because it saps the very foundations of fusion, implying that the French, in attempting to renew *with* their history, have been recaptured *by* their history. The discursive power of the ideology of glory consists in its ability to offer glory as a credible, legitimate principle of society and a powerful means for overcoming the conflict between self-interest and virtue. The *Mémorial* bears witness to the collapse of this synthesis. While maintaining glory as a legitimizing value accessible to all, the *Mémorial* seems also to deny it to "all those in power," new notables as well as the nobility. In society as it has become, to succeed and to be recognized is to be corrupted; rising in status necessarily results in moral debasement.

To judge from the *Mémorial*, the true "Napoleon effect" is to have promoted the ideology of glory and also to have discredited those who had benefited from it, with the exception of those who had had the good taste to die early. Of course, glory remains an existential ideal. But the politics of glory—which developed from a vision of the power of will and the grandeur of man—proved to be impracticable because it was built on an ever-widening fault line between true merit and the vanity of positions. The *Mémorial* exploits this chasm to the benefit of Napoleon as well as to that of "the people" and "simple soldiers." As the only survivors of the Empire still capable of devotion and true disinterestedness, they alone escaped the double trap of vanity and weakening resolve, which results from rising wealth and social status. In the end, running throughout the work we find the same fault line, though democratized, that had undermined France in the Ancien Régime. But this time, those taken to task in the *Mémorial* are those who stayed in place, in the service of a restored monarchy that was seeking to forget the years of revolutionary and imperial glory.

Louis-Léopold Boilly, *The Reading of the Bulletin of the Grande Armée* (1807). Oil on canvas. 18 1/2 × 23 5/8 in. Saint Louis Art Museum. Funds given by Mr. and Mrs. R. Crosby Kemper through the Crosby Kemper Foundations (74:1989).

Napoleon Effects in Literature

A Modern Heroic Death

Despite all his efforts, Napoleon never succeeded in inspiring and mobilizing literature as he did the other fine arts. While the visual in painting, sculpture, and architecture triumphed under his reign, Calliope stubbornly refused to join in; the formula *ut pictura poesis*, which in this context might have appeared as an imperial command, essentially went unheeded. But the *Mémorial de Sainte-Hélène* provided, as we have seen, an aestheticized account of the entire Napoleonic adventure, which is in itself the story of the fusion of an individual with a nation. Thibaudeau's publisher affirms this fusion when he declares that "beginning on 18 Brumaire, when Napoleon arrived in power, his story is truly that of France in all its internal and external relationships."[1] In the *Mémorial*, Napoleon seeks to become his own Homer. The sacred song of the blind bard is replaced by the amalgamated voice of Las Cases / Napoleon. Indeed, the absence of a voice capable of singing the glory of the Emperor — both warrior and legislator — had been felt throughout the reign.

Let us return to the "Frenchman" who, in the *Ode sur les victoires de Napoléon-le-Grand* cited at the beginning of this work, meditates on Homer's tomb. After recalling the exploits in which he saw the disappearance of "the supernatural quality of the feats of antiquity," the Frenchman interrupts himself to address the poet:

But what am I, a mad poet, doing?
What I have just told,
It is to you, divine interpreter,
That it befalls to sing it,
You, alone, on your heroic lyre,
Can paint the most sublime traits
Of such a magnificent subject;
Speak, and may that other Alexander
No longer express the vain regrets
Of Achilles visiting the grave.

Mais que fais-je, insensé poète?
Ce que je viens de raconter,
C'est à toi, divin interprète,
Qu'il appartient de le chanter:
Tu peux sur ta lyre héroïque,
Seul, d'un sujet si magnifique,
Peindre les plus sublimes traits;
Parle, et que cet autre Alexandre,
D'Achille visitant la cendre,
N'exprime plus de vains regrets.

Homer responds by advising patience; he must, in short, allow time to take
its course before the epic can be sung:

It is in vain that your zeal
Has troubled the repose of my remains.
What voice could utter
Songs worthy of this hero?
Feeble poets that we are,
Oh! What can the pomp and splendor of our verses
Do for great men
While their present virtue
Still fills the whole Universe
With its resplendent clarity?

When with a religious shadow
The venerable hand of Time
Veils the brilliant traits
Of his marvelous story,

The World, idolater of fables,
Will read unbelievable tales
Of his prodigious work;
It is then that, bearing my lyre,
I will come back to life to tell them again
For all time, in all places.

C'est vainement que de ma cendre
Ton zèle a troublé le repos.
Quelle voix pourrait faire entendre
Des chants dignes de ce héros?
Faibles poètes que nous sommes,
Eh! Que peuvent pour les grands hommes
La pompe et l'éclat de nos vers,
Tandis que leur vertu présente
De sa clarté resplendissante
Remplit encore tout l'Univers?

Quand d'une ombre religieuse
La vénérable main du Temps
De son histoire merveilleuse
Voilera les traits éclatants,
Le Monde, idolâtre des fables,
Lira les récits incroyables
De ses travaux prodigieux;
C'est alors que montrant ma lyre
Je renaîtrai pour les redire
A tous les tems, à tous les lieux.[2]

In the normal order of things, the response to the question "What voice" could sing "songs worthy of this hero?" should not be "Why, he himself!" To become the author of one's own epic would be an act of unheard-of audacity — indeed, the ultimate usurpation. But when, as in the world depicted by the *Mémorial*, an entire economy of glory crumbles and a restored monarchy tries to act as if nothing had happened in the years since the fall of Louis XVI, being silenced becomes a true threat. Despite its resplendence, the recent past seemed to have fallen into a chasm that all the monarchies in Europe were trying to fill in and cover over.

When it appeared in 1823, the *Mémorial* allowed Napoleon — in an act that would inspire Chateaubriand to do the same — to speak from "beyond the grave." Between the moment of his fall and that of his death this modern Achilles had time to take on the characteristics of Odysseus, a hero authorized by his misfortunes to tell his own story of glory and suffering.[3] Indeed, it is within the besieged little colony on a desolate island that Napoleon opens himself up to a chosen friend, and that the fusion capable of producing a new type of epic is made possible. Like the *Odyssey*, it is an epic that tells of the trials of a victim who resists and of the exploits of a great warrior. Unlike the *Odyssey*, however, the *Mémorial* describes the progressive weakening of its hero, the slow decline that leads to his death. The recapitulative summary of 16 June 1816 highlights the pathos:

> The Emperor's health is visibly changing, and we can see him change before our eyes [. . .]. A secret melancholy that is hidden from all eyes, perhaps even from his own, a concentrated decline, begins to seize him; each day he shrinks the already shrunken circle of his movements and his distractions; he has given up riding; he no longer invites the English to dinner; he has even abandoned his daily work [. . .].Yet the serenity of his soul, his even-tempered character, evince no change toward us in these circumstances; on the contrary, we seem all the closer as a family; he is more one of us, and we belong more to him; his conversations show more abandon, exuberance, and interest.

> La santé de l'Empereur s'altère visiblement, et nous le voyons changer à vue d'œil. [. . . U]ne mélancolie secrète qui se déguise à tous les yeux, peut-être aux siens propres, un mal concentré, commencent à le saisir; il rétrécit chaque jour le cercle déjà si resserré de son mouvement et de ses distractions; il renonce au cheval; il n'invite plus d'Anglais à dîner; il abandonne même son travail régulier. [. . .] Toutefois la sérénité de son âme, son égalité de caractère n'éprouvent par ces circonstances nulle altération vis-à-vis de nous; au contraire, nous n'en semblons que plus resserrés en famille; il est plus à nous, et nous lui appartenons davantage; ses conversations présentent plus d'abandon, d'épanchement et d'intérêt.[4]

Unlike Odysseus, Napoleon sheds no tears over his fate. But while ceasing to fight his enemy Hudson Lowe, the hero gives himself up increasingly to his friends. The fusion continues and becomes complete within the group. At the end of the *Mémorial*, Napoleon passes the reins to others, especially to Las Cases and his pen. We then see the Emperor as a romantic figure, tortured by a secret melancholy that is hidden from all, even from himself. Only

Las Cases—his alter ego, his soul brother, his pen—is able to divine it. The struggle to the death for recognition, integrated into the substance of the text itself, would be pursued beyond his death. Here the "beautiful" or heroic death is no longer like that of Achilles; it is not Napoleon's cadaver that endured those offenses, it is the living man. In many respects the *Mémorial* attempts to invert the objective of the beautiful death that Jean-Pierre Vernant has described so well.[5] Granted, it is always a matter of "transforming his death into imperishable glory"; but instead of seeking, like Achilles, to "turn the lot common to all creatures into a good that is his own and whose brilliance would be his forever,"[6] the Napoleon of the *Mémorial*, choosing to fight on the front of the simple everyday, takes up the common cause of all modern men, those for whom the frontline is no longer that of war.

No one understood better the importance and the consequences of this changing of the front than the author of *La Comédie humaine*. In *Le Colonel Chabert*, Balzac puts the reader in the midst of a ravaged economy of glory and the downfall of those who refuse to face the new reality: the miraculously saved hero of the battle of Eylau wanders like a ghost, "rejected from the world of the living."[7]

> Though he was eager in pursuit of his military distinction, of his fortune, of himself, perhaps it was in obedience to the inexplicable feeling, the latent germ in every man's heart, to which we owe the experiments of alchemists, the passion for glory, the discoveries of astronomy and of physics, everything which prompts man to expand his being by multiplying himself through deeds or ideas. In his mind, the *Ego* was now but a secondary object, just as the vanity of success or the pleasure of winning become dearer to the gambler than the object he has at stake.

> S'il courait après son illustration militaire, après sa fortune, après lui-même, peut-être est-ce pour obéir à ce sentiment inexplicable, en germe dans le cœur de tous les hommes, et auquel nous devons les recherches des alchimistes, la passion de la gloire, les découvertes de l'astronomie, de la physique, tout ce qui pousse l'homme à se grandir en se multipliant par les faits ou par les idées. L'*ego*, dans sa pensée, n'était plus qu'un objet secondaire, de même que la vanité du triomphe ou le plaisir du gain devient plus cher au parieur que de l'est l'objet du pari.[8]

Balzac understands how a concern with self could be compatible with disinterestedness: he admits this blending explicitly, and it is certainly at the heart of the drama of his own life. For Chabert, just as for Napoleon in the *Mémorial*, the only worthwhile stake is that of recognition. This ghost of the Empire could have made general Pelleport's statement his own: "I date only from myself."[9] He expresses it, moreover, in his own way:

> I am but a workhouse child, a soldier, whose sole fortune was his courage, whose sole family is mankind at large, whose country is France, whose only protector is the Almighty — Nay, I am wrong! I had a father — the Emperor! Ah! If he were but here, the dear man!

> [J]e suis un enfant d'hôpital, un soldat qui pour patrimoine avait son courage, pour patrie la France, pour tout protecteur le bon Dieu. Je me trompe! J'avais un père, l'Empereur! Ah! S'il était debout, le cher homme![10]

Having started from nothing, he became a colonel, a high-ranking officer in the Legion of Honor and a comte d'Empire. Thus, the person of Colonel Chabert contains all the complex bonds of self-assertion and legitimacy, bonds that end up suffocating the man of "generous nature" and "primitive virtues," marked by classic "simplicity."[11] "I no longer wish to be me," he cries out; "The sense of my rights is killing me."[12] Colonel Chabert, who is self-made thanks to the politics of fusion, falls victim to that politics precisely because his wife manages to benefit from it by marrying the comte de Ferraud. Ultimately, it is not only in relation to other nations that the economy of glory proves to be a zero-sum game: here, either Chabert benefits from it, or his wife does. *Le Colonel Chabert* thus represents a response to a *Mémorial* whose lesson has no currency in the post-imperial society. The colonel dies from his inability to find a place for himself in a world in which greed, wickedness, and fierce selfishness triumph,[13] where there is no longer any possible connection between glory and legitimacy. Here we are in full "Napoleon effect," in the sense that precisely those who benefited from the regime of glory are discredited. When, years later, the lawyer Godeschal meets him, the old colonel is one of the unfortunate poor lodged in the Hospice de la Vieillesse. "I am no longer a man, I am No. 164, room 7."[14] In this world, moral currency, once so precious, is clearly out of circulation.

When Odysseus returns to Ithaca, he too is reputed to be dead, and those who benefit from the situation have an interest that he remain so. Like Chabert, he is a poor wretch, or at least he pretends to be. But adopting that ruse means that the king of Ithaca — in the scene that disgusted Napoleon — would have to fight like a wretch. Odysseus is a warrior in a world of warriors, and it is with weapons that he regains his place. But in the modern world, as Napoleon notes, it is no longer by physical force that the hero can triumph. Recognition no longer comes by that route or, Balzac seems to add, from "primitive virtues" or a "generous nature."

Imagining an Incontestable Legitimation

What François Furet so aptly describes as a "theatrical succession of sovereigns" and the "repetition of scenes and regimes" allows us to see nineteenth-century France as a political laboratory in which pathological forms of government were cultivated.[15] In *Le Sacre du citoyen*, Pierre Rosanvallon observes: "It was a unique universalism that French democracy was proposing: far from incarnating a model, it constituted a repertory of the aporias of political modernity."[16] Legitimacy, having been aspired to in such a radical fashion, remained elusive. What is more, the visible gap between true merit and the vanity of those holding high positions continued to be a problem that defied a lasting solution. The Second Empire would, in fact, derive its legitimacy from the legend of Napoleon. As for the monarchy, it seemed to cede the field of glory to the Emperor. Rather than placing value on its immemorial glory, the restored monarchy sought to depict itself as a victim and enjoyed displaying its suffering. But the *Mémorial* succeeded in countering evocations of the king as martyr with its pathetic description of Napoleon as martyr.

Following the Revolution of 1830, the politics of fusion returned under other names: "Let all these unfortunate divisions be erased!" exclaims King Louis-Philippe before the delegates of Montpellier, "We shall form a single family!"[17] To the delegates of Nîmes he asserts: "The spirit of reconciliation is necessary where there are differences of opinion and religion."[18] The historical museum of Versailles became a pictorial illustration of the politics of fusion. Napoleon had begun to restore the château and dreamed of adorning the gardens with vast panoramas of his victories; the restored Bourbons dreamed of moving back there; Louis-Philippe turned it into a public museum devoted to "all the glories of France." The *Journal des débats* of 10 June 1837 saw it as a "vast Pantheon of all the exploits and all the heroes of the *patrie*," into which the king "has gathered the great historical family of France, has reunited all the various epochs, reconciled everyone, whatever their origins."[19] In many respects, the historical museum of Versailles—a polyphonic museum that sought to reduce the revolutionary fracture by assembling France's glories— relied on an approach similar to that of Girodet in his painting *The Apotheosis of French Heroes Who Died for Their Country*. At Versailles, however, Napoleon is situated in the continuity of national glory; he no longer plays the role of guarantor and arbiter. Therein lies the strength and weakness of the July monarchy: the political edifice appears to have been built on broader and more solid foundations, but it is missing the keystone of legitimacy needed to hold all the elements of social construction in place.

Emerging from the violence and the popular heroism of the Trois Glorieuses, the July monarchy relied on the thinking of the Doctrinaires in order to ground itself conceptually. Guizot developed and propagated the idea of a sovereignty of reason and a society governed by those who had the greatest "capacity."[20] The Doctrinaires inherited from the Enlightenment a vision of history as the advent of reason; from the Revolution, a conception of the rights of man as civil equality; and from Napoleon, an administrative rationalism as well as the pretention, espoused by some members of the elite, of incarnating disinterested authority and thus of designating themselves keepers of the general interest. In his famous Sorbonne lectures of 1828, Victor Cousin, after returning from eight years of exile imposed by the "ultraroyalist" government, expounded teachings that amounted to an apology for the Charter — "our Constitution"—while revealing the foundations of "true philosophy," which "embraces religion, art, the State, and labor" and aims to "reconcile and bring everything together."[21] The Constitution represents "the real fusion of the king and the people, seeking together the best way to govern."[22] Besides the Chamber of Peers, Cousin also sees the Charter as guaranteeing

> the accessibility of all French to all positions; from which it follows that the lowliest soldier [. . .] has the makings of a maréchal de France: the lowliest Frenchman in any career can arrive at the very foot of the throne.

> l'accessibilité de tous les Français à toutes les places; d'où il suit que le dernier des soldats [. . .] porte son bâton de maréchal de France dans sa giberne: le dernier des Français peut dans toutes les carrières arriver au pied même du trône.[23]

Thus, the Constitution and French laws "contain all the contrasting elements"—throne and country, monarchy and democracy, order and freedom, aristocracy and equality—"blended in a harmony" with a spirit of a "true eclecticism."[24]

Corresponding to this politics of fusion is a philosophy that reflects it, which Cousin sets forth in his courses:

I ask whether, when everything around us is mixed, complex, blended, when all contrasts live and live very well together, it is possible for philosophy to escape the general spirit; I ask whether philosophy can avoid being eclectic when everything around it is.

Je demande si, quand tout autour de nous est mixte, complexe, mélangé, quand tous les contraires vivent et vivent très bien ensemble, il est possible à la philosophie d'échapper à l'esprit général; je demande si la philosophie peut n'être pas éclectique quand tout l'est autour d'elle.[25]

For philosophy alone makes possible a full understanding of the necessary, providential course of humanity and civilization; it alone enables each person to escape any exclusive preoccupation, "to embrace all elements of thought, and thus to reconstruct all of humanity."[26] In the drama of history, humanity — that is "the masses" — is represented by "a few eminent individuals," the great men.[27] And it is precisely with them that glory returns as an essential measure of man. "Glory is an undeniable testimony to the importance of man's true greatness."[28] It permits Cousin to reconcile providential necessity and human greatness. In this philosophy of fusion, it is glory that illuminates the path of history:

The two greatest things in the world are to act and to think, on the battlefield or in life in an office. The two greatest ways to serve humanity are to have it take a step on the path to truth, by raising the ideas of the time to their highest expression, pushing them to their greatest metaphysical heights, or to imprint those ideas by the sword on the face of the world and have them make vast conquests. One might hesitate between the destiny of an Aristotle and that of an Alexander, between Columbus and Vasco de Gama, or Bacon and Descartes.

Les deux plus grandes choses qui soient dans le monde, c'est agir et penser, le champ de bataille ou la vie du cabinet. Les deux plus grandes manières de servir l'humanité, c'est de lui faire faire un pas dans la route de la vérité, en élevant les idées d'un temps à leur expression la plus haute, en les poussant à leurs dernières extrémités métaphysiques, ou d'imprimer ces idées avec son épée sur la face du monde et de leur faire faire de vastes conquêtes. On peut hésiter entre la destinée d'Aristote et celle d'Alexandre, entre Colomb ou Vasco de Gama, et Bacon ou Descartes.[29]

For Cousin, "the struggle among heroes," whether in war, politics, or philosophy, "is thus not so difficult to imagine," for victory always falls to the one who deserves it; and no matter who loses, humanity wins. In this triple apology for victory, power, and glory,

> war is but an exchange of ideas, using swords and canons; a battle is but the combat between error and truth; [. . .] victory and conquest are but the victory of the truth of the day over the truth of the day before, having become the error of today.

> la guerre n'est pas autre chose qu'un échange d'idées, à coups d'épée et à coups de canon; une bataille n'est pas autre chose que le combat de l'erreur et de la vérité; [. . .] la victoire et la conquête ne sont pas autre chose que la victoire de la vérité du jour sur la vérité de la veille, devenue l'erreur d'aujourd'hui.[30]

In such a spiritualist perspective, war takes on the characteristics of a trial by ordeal:

> History with its great events is but the judgment of God over humanity, [. . .] war is but the pronouncement of that judgment, and [. . .] the conquered is always the one who should be so.

> L'histoire avec ses grands événements n'est pas autre chose que le jugement de Dieu sur l'humanité, [. . .] la guerre n'est pas autre chose que le prononcé de ce jugement, et [. . .] le vaincu est toujours celui qui doit l'être.[31]

The great man thus incarnates "the highest possible individuality," but he is at the same time a product of history and comes "in order to represent an idea insofar as that idea has strength and deserves to be represented."[32] Incarnating the ideal of a people and an era, the great man is ultimately nothing more than "the people, which has become man."[33] As a judgment of humanity and moral currency, glory represents "the price for the services that humanity recognizes having received from glory, and that it pays for with its most precious possession, its esteem."[34]

Following Cousin's career, one can only admire the degree to which he put his own philosophy to work. Imposing his ideas through an eloquence — or grandiloquence — to which our ears are no longer attuned, he accumulated positions of authority: member of the Conseil royal de l'Instruction publique, director of the École normale supérieure, president in perpetuity of the Jury d'agrégation de philosophie, member of the Académie française, commander in the Legion of Honor, conseiller d'État, a Peer of France — all of which helped him create what he called "his regiment." Working closely with Guizot, who recognized the great importance of education, Cousin made a lasting impact on the teaching of philosophy in France.[35]

But the reflection on glory that Cousin undertook in 1828 also illustrates the double weakness that haunted the July monarchy. Glory, the judgment of humanity, should be infallible: "The daughter of great and obvious deeds, it is itself a manifest fact, as clear as day," and we must love it "because it means loving great things, extensive work, effective services rendered unto the nation."[36] Anyone can acquire a reputation, a false glory that is merely "the judgment of a few."[37] True glory is the judgment of the masses — of the greatest number. Thus, for Cousin, glory confers an incontestable legitimacy, for if "great results are irrefutable," so is glory.[38] Here we recognize the logic of the *Mémorial,* and at the same time we find what seems to be a powerful argument against tax-based voting requirements that enfranchised only the wealthy. Officials elected under this system acquired their positions from the votes of a small number, an *aristoi* claiming to have the greatest "capacity."[39] The legitimacy of the great man, on the other hand, comes from neither a contractual construction nor from any sort of electoral process:

> The root of a great man's power is much better than humanity's purposeful consent, which is quite often doubtful and disloyal; it is the intimate, spontaneous, irresistible belief that this man *is* the people, that he *is* the era.

> La racine de la puissance du grand homme est bien mieux que le consentement exprès de l'humanité, lequel est fort souvent douteux et infidèle; c'est la croyance intime, spontanée, irrésistible, que cet homme, c'est le peuple, c'est l'époque.[40]

On the eve of the 1830 Revolution, Cousin seems to be describing the very impasse in which the July monarchy would end up, while at the same time outlining the logic of Louis Bonaparte's rise to power.

Indeed, by surpassing himself, the Cousinian hero no longer belongs to himself. As the product of history, of an era, of a people, he becomes something other than himself. Cousin's reasoning concerning glory as the result of surpassing oneself is familiar to us. Strangely, however, he takes pains to strip the hero of his individuality, which remains mired in the insignificance and pettiness of the everyday; in the details of his life and in his behavior, the hero remains full of vice and almost contemptible.[41] For it is undeniable, Cousin maintains, that the intentions of the great men of history are "almost always the [. . .] pettiest."[42] In this vision of things, any projection of glory onto daily life is unthinkable. And in this sense, the *Cours d'introduction à l'histoire de la philosophie* rejects the entire focus of the *Mémorial*, though it does reveal a careful reading of that work. By seeking to turn history into an epic struggle in which ideas confront each other, by seeking the legitimacy of philosophy in an essentially military ethic, Cousin leaves his readers, whom he is attempting to inspire to greatness, in a state of fundamental ignorance about what they are doing, and of scorn for their own individuality as it manifests itself in everyday reality. The Cousinian hero winds up alienated, dispossessed of himself. Thus the philosopher condemns romantic drama precisely because it "takes man in his entirety, not only in his general side, but in his individual side." According to Cousin, the history of philosophy rises above these indignities; it rejects the specific qualities that anchor the individual in the real; "it omits, it ignores the purely individual and biographical side of the great man."[43] The gap that separates the great man from himself is to be attributed to the fact that his will is mired in the everyday; it is the gap between what a person believes he is doing and what he actually is doing, but it is also the gap that separates the great man from the masses who admire him. In that world, the only way to remain faithful to oneself is to rise — however unconsciously — above one's lesser self, to make one's mark on the world and to dominate it for the time allotted by history and the movement of events. The entire lesson of the *Mémorial*, on the other hand, lies in its rootedness in the real, in the idea of a glory that can be derived from the very pettiness of the everyday, in the possibility of reducing the gap between a great man and the lowliness of his individuality. In both cases, however, glory remains a fundamental legitimizing value, a valid individual and collective aspiration.

Cousin might well have affirmed that we should disdain reputation, think only of doing and not of appearing,[44] but he also teaches that we are often otherwise than what we appear, even with regard to ourselves. We might even see Cousin himself as an emblem of the strengths and weaknesses of the ideal of glory in its ability to motivate people as well as to blind them. In this perspective, the continuity of the ideology of glory should be seen as an essential element of a certain national specificity that turned nineteenth-century France into a laboratory exploring the political aporias of modernity.[45] Renan's famous passage in *Qu'est-ce qu'une nation?* (1882) eloquently testifies to the persistence of the ideal of glory and of its fundamental value during the Third Republic:

> The nation, like the individual, is the result of a long history of endeavor, sacrifice, and devotion. The cult of ancestors is the most legitimate of all; ancestors have made us what we are. A heroic past, great men, glory (I mean true glory), this is the social capital upon which a national idea rests. To have had common glory in the past, a common will in the present; to have done great things together, to want to do them again, these are the essential conditions for being a people.

> La nation, comme l'individu, est l'aboutissant d'un long passé d'efforts, de sacrifices et de dévouements. Le culte des ancêtres est de tous le plus légitime; les ancêtres nous ont faits ce que nous sommes. Un passé héroïque, des grands hommes, de la gloire (j'entends de la véritable), voilà le capital social sur lequel on assied une idée nationale. Avoir des gloires communes dans le passé, une volonté commune dans le présent; avoir fait de grandes choses ensemble, vouloir en faire encore, voilà les conditions essentielles pour être un peuple.[46]

This is not the place to retrace all the avatars of glory in France up to the present. We set out to explore the conditions of Napoleonic glory in the light of the collective *longue durée*. We have seen how a value passed on by antiquity and claimed by France from the country's origins was transformed through time; by the end of the Enlightenment it had acquired the force of a coherent ideology that held out the promise of resolving the conflict between virtue and self-interest. In France, the ideology of glory competed successfully with the model of a society based on the "natural" harmony of self-interest. Glory became a principle of political legitimation and a mechanism for governing, an essential element in the self-constitution of the individual and the nation. In the nineteenth century, France not only had overthrown an immemorial monarchy in the name of the sovereignty of the people, but was the only country that had ever tried to institute a *political and social* economy of glory. Under the impulse of war, this experiment quickly assumed gigantic proportions. Napoleon was the man of the hour, the one who, at the dawn of modernity, made it possible for the nation to project itself into the realm of myth and thus enable a return to history. But the collapse of the economy of glory did not wipe out the ideal, as Cousin demonstrated. For if glory—as an ideal that was put to the test of reality—was at the heart of France's political weakness in the nineteenth century, it was also at the heart of its literary strength. Ultimately, it was through literature that France rethought itself and that French specificity again found its connection with the universal.

The Ebbing of Glory

French writers in the first half of the nineteenth century were imbued with the *Mémorial de Sainte-Hélène*.[47] Writers were, of course, not the only ones: historians, too, were obviously influenced by it. But historians—whether Thiers, Michelet, Quinet, or Taine—were trapped in the logic of "for or against."[48] Literary authors, precisely because of their poetic engagement and their vision of the writer's role,[49] proved capable of viewing the "Napoleon effect" in a more productive light. We will look at only a few works here—among the best known—that bear the mark of an aesthetics of fusion, whether in their themes or in their formal elements. Taken together they illustrate a surprising range of genres in which this aesthetics comes into play.

Just before the advent of the July monarchy, Victor Cousin asserts with grandiloquence that one has to *do* rather than *appear*. But he also teaches that one is often other than what one appears or even what one wants to be. Glory is what enables Cousin to bridge the gap between virtue and self-interest, between the social grandeur of results and the pettiness of individual intentions. The void that opens between the great man and his own individuality in some way reflects the void above which the regime of the Doctrinaires would continue precariously to hover. It is precisely that void that the *Mémorial de Sainte-Hélène* seeks to fill or to bridge in its own way. The projection of glory onto the everyday, the grandeur and dignity of misery and isolation, the poetics of polyphony constitute elements of an aesthetics of fusion governing some of the greatest works of French romanticism.

Both Stendhal and Balzac step into an emptiness that characterize the ebbing of glory. Taking up the theme of fusion, Stendhal describes an ambitious young hero who uses the *Mémorial* as "the one guide of his conduct and object of his enthusiasm."[50] Stendhal does not hide his scorn for the narrowness and pettiness of a society characterized by "the most brutal callousness to everything except financial gain, precedence, or orders"[51] and dominated by a public opinion that keeps society in the most lamentable mediocrity. The tragedy of Napoleon on the island of Saint Helena is indeed the tragedy of all men of spirit:

The ordinary trend of the nineteenth century is that when a noble or a powerful individual encounters a man of spirit, he kills him, imprisons him, or so humiliates him that the other is foolish enough to die of grief.

La marche ordinaire du XIXe siècle est que, quand un être puissant et noble rencontre un homme de cœur, il le tue, l'emprisonne ou l'humilie tellement, que l'autre a la sottise d'en mourir de douleur.[52]

But it is the narrator of *The Red and the Black* who sees this, not Julien Sorel; a narrator who often takes the opportunity to step away from his hero and uses the techniques of polyphony to avoid amalgamating his voice with Julien's point of view.[53]

Modeling itself, as we have seen, on the core lesson of the *Mémorial*, Julien's ambition takes the form of a struggle for recognition; hence, the novel becomes a long illustration of the disastrous effects of the projection of glory onto the everyday. If Julien incarnates the democratization of the ideal of glory, Mathilde de La Môle personifies the aristocratic legacy of that ideal. Julien's siege and conquest of Mathilde follow the logic of the struggle for recognition, so that the love of the young woman is in fact a recognition of the grandeur and nobility of the young commoner's character. It takes the entire novel for Julien to understand his foolishness and the profound incompatibility between the strategies of glory and those of personal happiness in the society in which he lives. But that lesson is learned thanks to a strange fusion of democratic and aristocratic values. While the identification of a worker's son with the Emperor is the novel's point of departure, the story tells how, to be yourself, you cannot live like another, how emulation necessarily leads you astray. Julien Sorel is indeed a fusional character, but only after many stumbles does he learn how to be truly himself, that is, a man of spirit or, rather, of heart. It was with the pen that Napoleon took hold of Julien's mind; it was by the pen that Stendhal frees himself of that same hold.[54]

Julien's liberation comes about through the love of a woman. It is by stripping himself of all ambition that he discovers himself, that he achieves the joy of pure love — not for God, but for a woman. Julien Sorel is portrayed as the reverse image of Napoleon, precisely because he is not on a desert island but in the midst of society. The *Mémorial* manages to project glory onto the everyday, thanks to the purity of Napoleon's fight to the death for recognition. It is from the moment when he proves his ability for abnegation, when the only true stakes are no longer anything but recognition, that Napoleon launches into that struggle, building around him a "moral barrier," from behind which "he defends himself inch by inch."[55] The battle that unfolds on the island of Saint Helena is a battle between men. If there are any women, they are, so to speak, out of place, at least in the story told in the *Mémorial*. On the island of Saint Helena the only loving bond (*lien amoureux*) established between two beings is the fraternal and fusional one between Napoleon and Las Cases; the Emperor's only true passion is that which he bears for France. It is this sentimental stripping down of Napoleon and the sheer wickedness of Lowe that ensure the primordial nature of a battle between men unfolding "outside the boundaries of human laws."[56] Carried out through civil and social relationships that are those of 1830 France, the will for recognition that animates Julien Sorel can amount to nothing more than the pursuit of vainglory and self-alienation.

"A hateful era!" cries Dr. Benasis in *The Country Doctor*; "You must bow down before mediocrity, frigidly polite mediocrity that you despise, and obey."[57] His story seems to be that of all romantics. Everything is there: dreams of glory, the life of a student, amorous adventures, the weight of boredom, broken hearts. Enrolled in the École de médicine, the southern provincial student quickly lets himself be corrupted by the ways of Parisian life. "Rapt man, longing for social distinctions," he soon tires of pursuing glory, however, "because it is too slow."[58] For in Paris, at that age, he sees glory merely as "moral currency" to be used in obtaining the immoral pleasures that attract him:

> Looking on study and glory as too slow a means of arriving at the pleasures that tempted me, drawn one way by my inward scruples, and another by evil examples [. . .], I passed my days in wretchedness, overwhelmed by a surging tumult of desires, and of indolence of the most deadly kind, utterly cast down at times, only to be suddenly elated.

> [R]egardant l'étude et la gloire comme une voie trop tardive pour procurer les plaisirs qui me tentaient; flottant entre mes pudeurs secrètes et les mauvais exemples, [. . .] je passai de tristes jours, en proie au vague des passions, au désœuvrement qui tue, à des découragements mêlés de soudaines exaltations.[59]

His long descent into despair passes through many broken lives and leads Benassis to the brink of suicide before he finds the consolation of a Christianity that teaches resignation and expiation. Tempted to retreat to a monastery, he discovers in the depths of the cloisters of the Grande-Chartreuse a sort of "sublime egoism" that he rejects so as to "devote his life of expiation" to the service of his fellow man.[60] And it is this sense of mission that leads him to settle in the "large town" nearby.

With the idea of a repentance beneficial to the social world, the good doctor settles in this backwater canton; he transforms life there, to the point of becoming "the local oracle" of the canton.[61] *The Country Doctor* unfolds as if Balzac had assigned himself the task of showing on a very concrete level what the projection of glory onto the smallness of the everyday might mean. The novel's structure is, moreover, a strange reflection of that of the *Mémorial*. Balzac opens the tale with the arrival of Captain Genestas into the town of which Benassis has become mayor. This "unostentatious kind of Bayard" is—like the very moving captain Renaud in Alfred de Vigny's *Military Servitude and Grandeur*—one of those simple soldiers constantly eulogized in the *Mémorial*. After having "borne [his] part on every battlefield where Napoleon commanded," this courageous, loyal, and upright man had accompanied the Emperor to Paris and again to Rochefort.[62] Were it not for the orphan for whose upbringing he had assumed responsibility, he would have accompanied the fallen Emperor to the island of Saint Helena. On his departure, Napoleon, observing that the captain had never asked anything of him, gives him, as a sign of recognition, an object from his everyday life: the snuff box he had used in his last campaign.[63] Toward the end of his career, the captain winds up in that remote canton and enters into what we might call a fusional relationship with Benassis, to whom he ultimately confers his adoptive son, who has fallen ill and needs the doctor's care.

The conversations between the two men, each of whom in his own way incarnates disinterestedness and abnegation, deal with all the great issues of the time. Benassis explains that he quickly understood that he could assist the poor people in the canton only "through an appeal to their selfish interests, and by schemes for their immediate well-being."[64] This is why he places so much importance on the economic development of the canton. But to be effective, he asserts, it is not enough to have ideas; one must have the will—and the audacity—to act:

> In my opinion, a man who has thought out a political system, and who is conscious that he has within him the power of applying it in practical politics, should keep his mind to himself, seize his opportunity, and act.

À mon avis, un homme qui conçoit un système politique doit, s'il se sent la force de l'appliquer, se taire, s'emparer du pouvoir et agir.⁶⁵

A person must make his mark through the effectiveness of his actions rather than through his eloquence:

> The people need infallibility [. . .]; the same rules hold good for the great conqueror and for the provincial mayor, and a nation or a commune is much the same sort of herd.

> Avec le peuple, il faut toujours être infaillible. [. . .] Au maire de village et au conquérant, mêmes principes: la Nation et la Commune sont un même troupeau.⁶⁶

During a dinner gathering of notables including the mayor, the justice of the peace, the priest, and the soldier, each man exposes his vision of society. But when the good captain intervenes at the end to propose military organiza-tion as a true model for any good civil society, his words provoke friendly, condescending laughter:

> The justice of the peace laughed softly. "Captain," he said, "an old lawyer once said that empires began with the sword and ended at the writing desk; we have reached the desk stage by this time.

> "Capitaine, répondit en riant le juge de paix, un vieil avocat a dit que les empires commençaient par l'épée et finissaient par l'écritoire; nous en sommes à l'écritoire."⁶⁷

Ultimately, then, the sword is replaced by the pen—in the hands of justices of the peace, lawyers, and legislators, of course, but also in the hand of the novelist.

In spite of serving as Balzac's spokesman, Benassis, as an apostle of ab-negation and silent effectiveness, entertains a paradoxical relationship with the novel of which he is the hero. But the fusional relationship between the doctor and the soldier resolves this paradox, for it makes possible an exchange that escapes the logic of recognition and self-affirmation. It is in a context of shared friendship that Benassis insists that Captain Genestas relate "some heroic trait": "When a man is quite sure that he will not be misunderstood,

should he not find a kind of pleasure in saying 'I did thus?'"[68] Genestas then
relates an episode that occurred during the debacle of the Russian campaign.
The captain was forced to kill a soldier in the Grande Armée in order to save
a shelter in which he himself was staying with many others, including some
high-ranking officers. Benassis notes that Genestas has nothing to be ashamed
of, that it was an act of legitimate defense, relied upon by the whole group. The
old soldier then observes that many of the people he saved now live opulently
and "without feeling their hearts oppressed by gratitude." Immediately the
doctor raises the question of motivation and, from there, the idea of glory
as moral currency: "Then would you only do people a good turn in order to
receive that exorbitant interest called gratitude?" notes Benassis, laughing.
"That would be asking a great deal for your outlay." The ensuing exchange
neatly describes the moral impasse of the recognition of a virtuous self:

> "Oh, I know quite well" [replied Genestas] "that all the merit of a good deed
> evaporates at once if it benefits the doer in the slightest degree: If he tells the
> story of it, the toll brought in to his vanity is a sufficient substitute for grati-
> tude. But if every doer of kindly actions always held his tongue about them,
> those who reaped the benefits would hardly say very much either. Now the
> people, according to your system, stand in need of examples, and how are
> they to hear of them amid this general reticence? [. . .]" "Perhaps the rules of
> morality cannot be absolute," Benassis answered, "though this is a danger-
> ous idea, for it *leaves the egoist free to settle cases of conscience in his own favor.*"

> "Ah! Je sais bien," répondit Genestas, "que le mérite d'une bonne action
> s'envole au moindre profit qu'on en retire; la raconter, c'est s'en constituer
> une rente d'amour-propre qui vaut bien la reconnaissance. Cependant si
> l'honnête homme se taisait toujours, l'obligé ne parlerait guère du bienfait.
> Dans votre système, le peuple a besoin d'exemples; or, par ce silence général,
> où donc en trouverait-il? [. . .]" "Peut-être n'y a-t-il rien d'absolu en morale,"
> répondit Benassis, "mais cette idé est dangereuse, *elle laisse l'égoïsme interpré-
> ter les cas de conscience au profit de l'intérêt personnel.*"[69]

Genestas defends the idea that some concern with self in narrative form is
not only legitimate but important for the well-being of society. Indeed, the
novel illustrates the legitimacy and usefulness of certain heroic tales. Take,
for example, the famous scene in which a "Napoleon of the people" emerges;
the old soldier Goguelat tells of the golden legend of the Emperor:

Keep this well in your minds, that as every soldier stood a chance of having a throne of his own (provided he showed himself worthy of it), a corporal of the Guard was by way of being a sight to see, and they gaped at him as he went by; for everyone came by his share after a victory, it was made perfectly clear in the bulletin.

Vous entendez bien que chaque soldat ayant la chance de chausser un trône pourvu qu'il en eût le mérite, un caporal de la Garde était comme une curiosité: on l'admirait passer, parce que chacun avait son contingent dans la victoire, parfaitement connu dans le bulletin.[70]

Through this act of recounting, the peasant world emerges from its resigned silence, goes beyond the calculations of immediate self-interest and well-being, and reenchants the world through a narrative imbued with a marvel-ous that is always simple and an impossibility that is almost credible. This is the story of Napoleon protected by God, carrying out the Divine will as long as he is accompanied by the mysterious Red Man. We are not very far from the vision of great men as providential vehicles in the movement of history, but this popular tale, Balzac makes clear, manifests "the immense influence that poetry exerts over every mind." Like Las Cases in the *Mémorial*, the faith-ful Genestas survives, and the tale of the everyday hero continues to be made known. "His life will make a grand story to tell, eh?" says Genestas to the old soldier after the death and burial of Dr. Benassis. "Yes," responds Goguelat, "he was the Napoleon of our valley, barring the battles."[71]

In *The Country Doctor*, we find not only a fusion of very diverse, indeed contrasting, types of tales, but also a place where grandeur and the marvel-ous can exist in a society of calculation and self-interest. Indeed, *La Comédie humaine* as a whole is brilliant proof of such coexistence.

The Polyphony of *Passeurs*

Of all nineteenth-century writers, Chateaubriand and Victor Hugo went per-haps the farthest in the aesthetics of fusion. On one level, *Memoires d'outre-tombe* and *Les Misérables* seem to be total contrasts. After all, Chateaubriand describes himself as the last torchbearer of an aristocratic ideal, whereas in Hugo's *Les Misérables* the torch has been passed to the heroes perched on the barricades of a popular insurrection. Yet, on another level, the two works have much in common; in particular, they both present reflections on the ideal of glory, the role of recognition, and the meaning of disinterestedness. Each in its own way, on both the thematic and the formal levels, voices an *apologia* for freedom; each grants a large place to spirituality; and each is constructed from the experience of exile. Above all, they resemble each other in their epic scope as well as in their polyphony. And each in its own way inherits its poetics from the *Mémorial de Sainte-Hélène*.

Chateaubriand clearly attempts to establish similarities between his own life and that of the Emperor. On many points, his life takes on meaning only *in relation* to that of Napoleon:

> I was at the time, like Bonaparte, a thin, quite unknown second lieutenant; we were both starting out from obscurity at the same time, I, to seek my fame in solitude, he, his glory among men.

> J'étais alors, ainsi que Bonaparte, un mince sous-lieutenant tout à fait inconnu; nous partions, l'un et l'autre, de l'obscurité à la même époque, moi pour chercher ma renommée dans la solitude, lui sa gloire parmi les hommes.[72]

In a long back-and-forth between "the poet and the emperor," to borrow Marc Fumaroli's phrase,[73] the author of *Mémoires d'outre-tombe* would lead a rear-guard battle, lost in advance against Napoleon's hold over the entire period. Napoleon unwittingly becomes the evil Hudson Lowe, because his tyranny and absolute domination prevented Chateaubriand from being himself.[74] The tyrant was not content to fill all the available space while he was alive; from beyond the grave he continues to impose himself via his legend:

> Bonaparte is no longer the real Bonaparte, he is a legendary figure [. . .]. That fantastic hero will remain the true figure [. . .]. Bonaparte belonged so strongly to absolute domination that after enduring his personal despotism, we must now endure the despotism of his memory. The latter is more dominating than the former.

> Bonaparte n'est plus le vrai Bonaparte, c'est une figure légendaire [. . .]. Ce héros fantastique restera le personnage réel [. . .]. Bonaparte appartenait si fort à la domination absolue, qu'après avoir subi le despotisme de sa personne, il nous faut subir le despotisme de sa mémoire. Ce dernier despotisme est plus dominateur que le premier.[75]

To carry out his fantasy joust, the Chateaubriand of *Mémoires d'outre-tombe* settles in the margins of history, on the edges of the halo of glory, where he lives a life that seems to be a long series of exiles. As in the *Mémorial*, *ennui* is a major motif in the *Mémoires*; as in the epic narrative of the *Mémorial*, Napoleon in the *Mémoires* rises above the unrelenting succession of days leading eventually to the grave. The books devoted to the life of Napoleon, as Jean-Claude Berchet notes, form "an almost autonomous ensemble, a true narrative interlude."[76] Napoleon's life is fascinating, and Chateaubriad has to struggle against that seduction and against the temptation to become a tyrant himself, arbitrarily condemning his enemy. He battles daily to be himself: it is the battle of freedom confronting tyranny in all its forms.

Chateaubriand's ego incarnates and drives the fusion of the nobility's tradition of liberties with the tradition of the Declaration of the Rights of Man: "I prefer my name to my title."[77] As a young man, he sought the glory of an explorer as he headed to America in hopes of discovering the northwest passage. With his pen, Chateaubriand becomes a *passeur*, a conveyor, between what François Hartog calls two "regimes of historicity."[78] He succeeds by assimilating his personal story with that of his time. To the amalgam of genres — memoires, history, epic — is added a polyphony of voices — citations of authors, correspondence, documents, archives, passages from his own works, and more. Like Las Cases, Chateaubriand proves a past master of the paratext. The telescoping of time is made concrete through a dizzying interplay of dates, emphasizing gaps between the first draft and the next, between two states of self, with the text itself carrying out the fusion. The first chapter of the twenty-fifth book is dated thus: "Paris, 1839. *Revised on 22 February 1845.*" The title: "Change in the World." The famous opening of this book functions as a prelude to all that will follow.

> To fall from Bonaparte and the Empire to that which followed them is to fall from reality into nothingness, from the top of a mountain into a chasm. Did not everything end with Napoleon? Should I have spoken of something else? What other figure besides him can be of interest? Who or what can be a subject of interest after such a man? [. . .] How can we name Louis XVIII in the Emperor's stead? I blush to think that I must now drivel on about a swarm of little creatures of whom I am one, doubtful, nocturnal beings that we were, in a landscape whose huge sun had disappeared.

> Retomber de Bonaparte et de l'Empire à ce qui les a suivis, c'est retomber de la réalité dans le néant, du sommet d'une montagne dans un gouffre.

Tout n'est-il pas terminé avec Napoléon? Aurais-je dû parler d'autre chose? Quel personnage peut intéresser en dehors de lui? De qui et de quoi peut-il être question, après un pareil homme? [. . .] Comment nommer Louis XVIII en place de l'empereur? Je rougis en pensant qu'il me faut nasillonner à cette heure d'une foule d'infimes créatures dont je fais partie, êtres douteux et nocturnes que nous fûmes d'une scène dont le large soleil avait disparu.[79]

So as not to sink into the abyss of pettiness, Chateaubriand sets himself up as the defender of the fundamental values he proclaims in the "Summary of My Life":

In the divine order, religion and freedom; in the human order, honor and glory (which are the human offspring of religion and freedom): this is what I have desired for my country.

Dans l'ordre divin, religion et liberté; dans l'ordre humain, honneur et gloire (qui sont la génération humaine de la religion et de la liberté): voilà ce que j'ai désiré pour ma patrie.[80]

In this context, to cite oneself becomes a way of retrospectively demonstrating the importance of literature, the power and grandeur of the pen, even in the turpitude and baseness that characterized the entire July monarchy. The end of the *Mémoires* seems to echo the end of the *Mémorial*. Like Las Cases, Chateaubriand wanders from place to place defending a lost cause, that of legitimacy. But his peregrinations begin to look like comic opera. "We were rather like a wandering French troupe."[81] An epic of self, an epic of an era, the *Mémoires d'outre-tombe* is also a mock epic in which Chateaubriand agrees to play the role that has fallen to him. To Bonaparte goes the grandeur of the shooting star:

All our earlier glories were united [. . .] and made their last explosion in Bonaparte.

[T]outes nos gloires d'autrefois se réunirent [. . .] et firent leur dernière explosion dans Bonaparte.[82]

The glory to which Chateaubriand lays claim is that of incarnating an immense, historic fusion and playing the essential role of *passeur*:

It seems that the old world is ending, and the new one beginning. I see the reflections of a dawn from which I will not see the sun rise.

[O]n dirait que l'ancien monde finit, et que le nouveau commence. Je vois les reflets d'une aurore dont je ne verrai pas se lever le soleil.[83]

The role of Jean Valjean is also that of *passeur*, but to achieve it the hero must take to the sewers. *Les Misérables* illustrates the tendency toward disproportion inherent in the aesthetics of fusion. Epic, novel, melodrama, and idyll: all come together to form the story of humanity, the nation, and Victor Hugo himself, a story echoing the languages of all classes, all ages, all political tendencies. Hence, Hugo's famous novel represents the novel par excellence of the grandeur of the insignificant, of the ordinary, of the miserably vulgar. From his voluntary exile Hugo derides Napoleon III as "Napoléon le Petit," the one who reduced the *Mémorial de Sainte-Hélène* to a political program[84] and took advantage of universal suffrage to seize power by force and install the Second Empire. With *Les Misérables*, Hugo seeks to create the myth of a legitimizing heroism that can take glory from Napoleon and return it to the Republic, to leave the romantic problematics of the struggle for recognition behind.

Marius's father, like Hugo's, was a hero of the imperial wars. It was during the battle of Waterloo that Napoleon promoted him to colonel and named him baron and officer of the Legion of Honor. We know the story: he was saved by Thénardier, his titles were not recognized, and he died in near-poverty. When he received letters addressed to the *commandant Pontmercy* from the authorities, he would send them back unopened. The narrator's clarification is revealing:

At the same moment, Napoleon at Saint Helena was treating in the same fashion the missives of Sir Hudson Lowe addressed to *General Bonaparte*. Pontmercy had ended, may we be pardoned the expression, by having in his mouth the same saliva as his Emperor.

En ce même moment, Napoléon à Sainte-Hélène traitait de la même façon les missives de sir Hudson Lowe adressées *au général Bonaparte*. Pontmercy avait fini, qu'on nous passe le mot, par avoir dans la bouche la même salive que son empereur.[85]

In *The Country Doctor*, Captain Genestas declines to set off for Saint Helena because he has undertaken to raise an orphan who had been put in his care; the same sense of duty and generosity inspires Pontmercy to give his child to his dead wife's father because the grandfather imperiously claims the boy and threatens to disinherit him if the father doesn't comply. Raised by Monsieur Gillenormand, who, like Hugo's mother, was a Voltairian royalist, Marius discovers, too late, the identity of his real father. And so he makes inquiries; he reads *Le Moniteur*, histories, the *Mémorial*, memoirs, newspapers, proclamations, and so forth. While reading the bulletins of the Grande Armée, "those heroic strophes penned on the field of battle," Marius, gasping with emotion,

> all at once, *without himself knowing what was in him, and what impulse he was obeying*, [. . .] sprang to his feet, stretched both arms out of the window, gazed intently into the gloom, the silence, the infinite darkness, the eternal immensity, and exclaimed, "Long live the Emperor!"

> tout à coup, *sans savoir lui-même ce qui était en lui et à quoi il obéissat*, [. . .] se dressa, étendit ses deux bras hors de la fenêtre, regarda fixement l'ombre, le silence, l'infini ténébreux, l'immensité éternelle, et cria: "Vive l'empereur!"[86]

This scene of conversion certainly has a comic element that prevents the reader from taking Marius seriously and thus undermines the fictional legitimacy of the character. In the name of his father, Marius thus joins the struggle for recognition. He has calling cards printed, bearing the title of baron. That means, he declares to Monsieur Gillenormand at the moment of their break-up, "that I am the son of my father."[87] He defends Napoleonic glory among his Republican friends:

> Let us be just, my friends! What a splendid destiny for a nation [. . .] to be in Europe a sort of nation gilded through glory, [. . .] to conquer the world twice, by conquest and by dazzling, that is sublime; and what greater thing is there?

> Soyons justes, mes amis! Être l'empire d'un tel empereur, quelle splendide destinée pour un peuple! [. . .] être en Europe une sorte de peuple doré à force de gloire, [. . .] conquérir le monde deux fois, par la conquête et l'éblouissement, cela est sublime; et qu'y a-t-il de plus grand?

Combeferre's biting response — "to be free" — sums up the entire problem. Marius lowers his head: "that cold and simple word had traversed his epic effusion like a blade of steel."[88] The time for oversized glory is past.

But before Marius discovers the awesome grandeur of the Napoleonic armies, the novel has already sung of it in recounting the battle of Waterloo. That reality surpasses understanding; it originates in the marvelous, the epic, and erases the distinctions between Ancients and Moderns:

> The cuirassiers replied by crushing them. Their great horses reared, strode across the ranks, leaped over the bayonets and fell, gigantic, in the midst of these four, living walls [. . .]; the bayonets plunged into the bellies of these centaurs.

> Les cuirassiers répondaient par l'écrasement. Leurs grands chevaux se cabraient, enjambaient les rangs, sautaient par-dessus les bayonnettes et tombaient, gigantesques, au milieu de cds quatre murs vivants [. . .] Les bayonnettes s'enfonçaient dans les ventres de ces centaures.[89]

In this battle — "the hinge of the nineteenth century" — Napoleon, with his fiery and very romantic way of waging war, is defeated by a classic Wellington:

> The counter-revolution was involuntarily liberal, in the same manner as, by a corresponding phenomenon, Napoleon was involuntarily revolutionary. On the 18th of June, 1815, Robespierre on horseback was hurled from his saddle.

> La contre-révolution était involontairement libérale, de même que, par un phénomène correspondant, Napoléon était involontairement révolutionnaire. Le 18 juin 1815, Robespierre à cheval fut désarçonné.[90]

Yet the true event lies elsewhere. The narrator fixes his gaze on the last formation of Napoleon's army so as to project the light of glory onto the obscurity of the infinitely small and to underscore Cambronne's famous "word." The scene is well known. Ordered by the British to surrender, Cambronne, in Hugo's account, responds: "Shit." This word of "titanic" scorn contains an "Aeschylean grandeur!" Indeed, "this Cambronne, this man spending his last hour, this unknown soldier, this infinitesimal of war" proves to be "the winner of Waterloo."[91] Thus, the last words become the first; Napoleon's defeats, romanticism, and freedom ultimately prevail through Cambronne's word.

The process of projecting glory onto the infinitely small characterizes the entire novel. Within each man is a certain epic grandeur. By rebelling in the name of his father against Monsieur Gillenormand, Marius experiences poverty and suffering. He endures humiliation, mockery, vexation, and bitterness, which are the lot of the poor; from the crucible of misfortune one emerges infamous or sublime, "outlaw" or "half-god." In a revealing passage, the narrator explains the meaning of Marius's tribulations:

> For many great deeds are performed in petty combats. There are instances of bravery, ignored and obstinate, which defend themselves step by step in that fatal onslaught of necessities and turpitudes. Noble and mysterious triumphs which no eye beholds, which are requited with no renown, which are saluted with no trumpet blast. Life, misfortune, isolation, abandonment, poverty, are the fields of battle which have their heroes, who are, sometimes, grander than the heroes who win renown.

> Car il se fait beaucoup de grandes actions dans les petites luttes. Il y a des bravoures opiniâtres et ignorées qui se défendent pied à pied dans l'ombre contre l'envahissement fatal des nécessités et des turpitudes. Nobles et mystérieux triomphes qu'aucun regard ne voit, qu'aucune renommée ne paye, au'aucune fanfare ne salue. La vie, le malheur, l'isolement, l'abandon, la pauvreté, sont des champs de bataille qui ont leurs héros; héros obscurs plus grands parfois que les héros illustres.[92]

Throughout the novel, Hugo aims to illuminate and legitimize the heroism that is unseen but is imbued with the marvelous of the everyday. Marius is charged with bearing the novelist's vision, yet he has trouble asserting himself as a hero. The dangers he confronts are those of reverie and laziness — hardly, in the eyes of readers, the stuff of heroes. He ends on the barricades mainly by reason of unrequited love: "He said to himself that, since Cosette was gone, all that there was left for him was to die."[93] Marius manages to make his mark at the end of the novel, but borne — literally — on the shoulders of the towering figure of Jean Valjean.

In this polyphonic novel, the life of Jean Valjean — like that of Chateaubriand in *Mémoires d'outre-tombe* — is set up in counterpoint to the Napoleonic epic:

> On the 22nd of April, 1796, the victory of Montenotte, won by the general-in-chief of the army of Italy, whom the message of the Directory to the Five Hundred, of the 2nd of Floréal, year IV, calls Buona-Parte, was announced in Paris; on that same day a great gang of galley-slaves was put in chains at Bicêtre. Jean Valjean formed a part of that gang.

Le 22 avril 1796, on criait dans Paris la victoire de Montenotte remportée
par le général en chef de l'armée d'Italie, que le message du Directoire aux
Cinq-Cents, du 2 floréal an IV, appelle Buona-Parte; ce même jour une grande
chaîne fut ferrée à Bicêtre. Jean Valjean fit partie de cette chaîne.[94]

Jean Valjean would be freed in October 1815; on 15 October of the same year,
Napoleon arrived at Saint Helena. The ex-convict enters Digne "by the same
street which, seven months previously, had witnessed the passage of the
Emperor Napoleon on his way from Cannes to Paris."[95] This inverse journey leads Jean Valjean to Montreuil-sur-Mer, where he eventually becomes
mayor under the name of Monsieur Madeleine. Like the mayor Benassis in
the obscure valley near the Grande-Chartreuse, Monsieur Madeleine transforms the city of Montreuil, which prospers under his paternalistic leader-
ship but deteriorates as soon as he is no longer there. In pointing out these
murky connections with the Emperor, Hugo emphasizes that Napoleon, too,
was marked by a fundamental illegitimacy. Jean Valjean, a model of sacrifice
and disinterestedness constantly put to the test, makes Les Misérables into
an epic of obscure heroism. Cambronne found the word; Jean Valjean finds
the deed. He enacts the work of *passeur* by carrying Marius, an unconscious
hero in every sense of the word, toward the realization of the bourgeois idyll.

    In the vast fusion this novel attempts to establish and portray, we redis-
cover all the aspirations and contradictions of a society that needed glory as
a legacy but proved unable to integrate it into its functioning. Perhaps this
is why Hugo's great fresco became, in a sense, the fictional symbol not only
of the Republic but also of a certain modernity. For it plumbs the depths of a
problematic particular to all of French history: the aspiration to universality.
As the last hurrah of romanticism, Les Misérables, in its strengths and in its
weaknesses, depicts the confluence of a politics of fusion with an aesthetics
of fusion. Hugo performs a giant experiment in projecting glory onto the
everyday, in all of its minutest, most pitiful elements. The denouement illustrates the impossibility of finding a happy medium in an economy of glory.
For even in this fictional world, Jean Valjean's glory—his heroic capital, so
to speak—prevents Marius from acquiring his own. We end up, then, in a
zero-sum version: Marius cannot accede to autonomy until Jean Valjean disappears from the scene, since the fictional glory of Jean Valjean continues
to be asserted at the expense of the fictional legitimacy of the young man.
So Jean Valjean's disappearance has to be absolute. In the fictional world of
the Misérables, there remains no trace, no memory of him. Valjean's tomb is
reduced to an empty stone, with no name inscribed on it. Through the heroic

but unseen action of that anti-Napoleon, Marius is freed from the despotism of memory. The aspiration to a glory that escapes the logic of moral currency is inscribed in the paradoxical space that extends from Jean Valjean's anonymous tomb to Victor Hugo's State funeral in 1885.[96]

For Renan, a heroic past, great men, and glory constitute the social capital upon which a national idea can be founded. France may be unique among nations in the path it has traced between the ideal of glory, the demands of virtue, and the necessities of self-interest.

NOTES

Introduction

1. ["Votre gloire est immense: l'Univers a peine à contenir, et la postérité croirait difficilement, les événements les plus authentiques de votre illustre carrière"; "Le langage de la flatterie nous est étranger! Celui du cœur est le seul digne du GRAND-NAPOLÉON"]

2. ["invention funeste, où se confondent la vérité et la flatterie, l'hypocrisie et la bonne foi"] A.-C. Thibaudeau, *Le Consulat et l'Empire, ou Histoire de la France et de Napoléon Bonaparte* (Paris: Renouard, 1834–1835), vol. 2, p. 214.

3. Ibid., pp. 214–215.

4. *Le Moniteur*, no. 6 (6 January 1806), p. 28 (emphasis mine).

5. ["(I)l faut aussi *révolutionner la gloire* et la reverser *comme la fortune* sur les nombreux bataillons, sur les modestes citoyens qui combattent tous les jours pour la République"] *Rapport et projet de décret, présentés au nom des comités de salut public et de la guerre, sur les places à décerner par la Convention nationale aux défenseurs de la patrie qui seront distingués.* Session of 1 Thermidor Year II of the French Republic one and indivisible (19 July 1794) (Paris: Imprimerie nationale, 1794) (emphasis mine).

6. On this subject, see Annie Jourdan, *Napoléon: Héros, imperator, mécène* (Paris: Aubier, 1998).

7. ["j'admirai, je reconnus, j'aimai Napoléon, et dès ce moment je devins français jusqu'au fanatisme"] Emmanuel de Las Cases, *Mémorial de Sainte-Hélène*, edited by Joël Schmidt, preface by Jean Tulard (Paris: Seuil, "Points," 1968), vol. 1, p. 488 (Wednesday, 27 March 1816). Hereafter cited as E. de Las Cases, *Mémorial de Sainte-Hélène* (ed. Schmidt).

8. I refer to the article by Jean Tulard, "Le retour des cendres," in *Les Lieux de mémoire, II: La nation—3*, edited by Pierre Nora (1986; Paris: Gallimard, "Quarto," 1997), vol. 2, pp. 1729–1754.

9. Since there are so many such works, I will cite a selection: Georges Lefebvre, *Napoléon* (Paris: F. Alcan, 1935, repr. 2005); Jean Tulard, *Napoléon, ou le mythe du sauveur*, new and revised ed. (1977; Paris: Fayard, 1989); José Cabanis, *Le Sacre de Napoléon: le 2 décembre 1804* (Paris: Gallimard, 1970; new ed. 2007); Jacques Bainville, *Napoléon* (Paris: Fayard, 1931; new ed. with preface by Patrice Guenniffey, Paris: Gallimard, 2005); Annie Jourdan, *L'Empire de Napoléon* (Paris: Flammarion, 2000); Thierry Lentz, *Nouvelle Histoire de l'Empire* (Paris: Fayard, 2002–2004; Steven Englund, *Napoleon: A Political Life* (Cambridge, MA: Harvard University Press, 2005).

10. Again, I mention just a few here: Philippe Gonnard, *Les Origines de la légende napoléonienne: L'œuvre historique de Napoléon à Sainte-Hélène* (Paris, 1906; Geneva: Slatkine-Magariotis Reprints); Jules Deschamps, *Sur la légende de Napoléon* (Paris: Champion, 1931); Pieter Geyl, *Napoleon, For and Against* (New Haven: Yale University Press, 1949); Jean Tulard, *L'Anti-Napoléon: La légende noire de l'Empereur* (Paris: Julliard, 1965); Natalie Petiteau, *De la mythologie à l'histoire* (Paris: Seuil, 1999); Sudhir Hazareesingh, *The Legend of Napoleon* (London: Granta, 2005); David Bell, *The First Total War: Napoleon's Europe and the Birth of Warfare as We Know It* (Boston: Hougthon Mifflin, 2007).

11. ["le caractère général"; "génie"] See, e.g., Montesquieu's *Essai sur les causes qui peuvent affecter les esprits et les caractères*, in *Œuvres complètes*, ed. Caillois (Paris: Gallimard), vol. 2, pp. 58–59. See also *De l'esprit des lois*, III, 19 "Des lois dans le rapport qu'elles ont avec les principes qui forment l'esprit général, les mœurs et les manières d'une nation."

12. See P. Geyl, *Napoleon, For and Against*.

13. Voltaire, "La Tactique," *Œuvres complètes* (Oxford, Voltaire Foundation, 2009), vol. 75A, pp. 341–385.

14. P. Bénichou, *Morales du Grand Siècle* (Paris: Gallimard, 1948); A. O. Hirschman, *The Passions and the Interests: Political Arguments for Capitalism before Its Triumph* (Princeton: Princeton University Press, 1977).

15. P. Rosanvallon, *Le Capitalisme utopique: Histoire de l'idée de marché* (Paris: Seuil, 1979; new ed. "Points," 1999), p. 61; see also Marcel Gauchet, *La Religion dans la démocratie. Parcours de la laïcité* (Paris: Gallimard, 1998), pp. 85–87; and Pierre Manent, *Les Libéraux* (Paris: Hachette, 1986).

16. P. Rosanvallon, *Le Capitalisme utopique*, pp. 11–33; see also M. Gauchet, *Le Désenchantement du monde: Une histoire politique de la religion* (Paris: Gallimard, 1994); Charles Taylor, *Sources of the Self: The Making of the Modern Identity* (Cambridge: Cambridge University Press, 1992), esp. parts 3 and 4; Jerome Schneewind, *The Invention of Autonomy: A History of Modern Moral Philosophy* (Cambridge: Cambridge University Press, 1997), esp. parts 3 and 4.

17. John G. Pocock, *The Machiavellian Moment: Florentine Political Thought and the Atlantic Republican Tradition* (Princeton, Princeton University Press, 2003); and "Virtues, rights, and manners: A model for historians of political thought," in *Virtue, Commerce and History: Essays on Political Thought and History, Chiefly in the Eighteenth Century* (Cambridge: Cambridge University Press, 1985); Catherine Larrère, *L'Invention de l'économie au XIXe siècle: Du droit naturel à la physiocratie* (Paris: PUF, 1992).

18. See, e.g., Dale Van Kley, *The Religious Origins of the French Revolution: From Calvin to the Civil Constitution, 1560–1791* (New Haven, Yale University Press, 1996); Catherine Maire, *De la cause de Dieu à la cause de la nation: le jansénisme au XVIIIe siècle* (Paris: Gallimard, 1998); Norbert Elias, *The Civilizing Process: Sociogenetic and Psychogenetic Investigations* (Oxford UK: Blackwell Publishing, 2000).

19. See Pierre Force, *Self-Interest before Adam Smith: A Genealogy of Economic Science* (Cambridge: Cambridge University Press, 2003); Marisa Linton, *The Politics of Virtue in Eighteenth-Century France* (Basingstoke: Pelgrave, 2001); John Shovlin, *The Political Economy of Virtue: Luxury, Patriotism, and the Origins of the French Revolution* (Ithaca: Cornell University Press, 2006).

20. The expression belongs to P. Rosanvallon, *Le Sacre du citoyen: Histoire du suffrage universel en France* (Paris: Gallimard, 1992, p. 601).

21. For a good general study of the subject, see Maria Rosa Lida de Malkiel, *La idea de la fama en la edad media castellana* (México: Fondo de Cultura Económica, 1952); French ed.: *L'Idée de la gloire dans la tradition occidentale: Antiquité, Moyen Age occidental, Castille*, translated by S. Roubaud (Paris: Klincksieck, 1968).

Chapter 1

1. See James M. Redfield, *Nature and Culture in the* Iliad: *The Tragedy of Hector* (Chicago: University of Chicago Press, 1975), pp. 32–33, and chap. 3, pp. 99–127. Redfield discusses the relationship between *kleos* ("reputation" or "renown"), *timē* ("honor, status"), and *kudos*, which is a sort of *mana*, or luminosity, or magical splendor, often the gift of a god (pp. 32–33). See also Jean-Pierre Vernant, "La belle mort et le cadavre outragé," in *L'Individu, la mort, l'amour* (Paris: Gallimard, "Folio," 1989), pp. 41–79; "La belle mort d'Achille," in *Entre mythe et politique* (Paris: Seuil, 1996), pp. 501–510; "La mort héroïque," in *La Traversée des frontiers* (Paris: Seuil, 2004), pp. 69–86, notably the wonderful section on the *kleos aphthiton* (sung, everlasting glory), pp. 75–84; and Dean A. Miller, *The Epic Hero* (Baltimore: Johns Hopkins University Press, 2000), p. 5. There is also *doxa*, "which honored less the individual than the citizen," as Étienne Tiffou explains in his *Essai sur la pensée morale de Salluste à la lumière de ses prologues* (Paris: Klincksieck, 1973), p. 76.

2. R.-A. Gauthier, *Magnanimité: l'idéal de la grandeur dans la philosophie païenne et dans la théologie chrétienne* (Paris: Vrin, 1951), p. 36.

3. The French precedes the English in this quotation because it is Corneille's translation that is being discussed: *Les Métamorphoses d'Ovide mises en vers françois par T. Corneille de l'Académie Françoise* (À Paris: chez Jean Baptiste Coignard, 1697, avec privilège de Sa Majesté), vol. 3, p. 414. Here are Ovid's verses: "*nomenque erit indelebile nostrum, / quaque patet domitis Romana potentia terris, / ore legar populi, perque omnia saecula fama, / siquid habent veri vatum praesagia, vivam.*" Thomas Corneille thus translates *fama* as "glory." Étienne Tiffou underscores the abundance of glory-related terms in Latin: *gloria, claritas, fama, decus, laus, honos*. See also the recent work by Jean-François Thomas, *Gloria et Laus: Étude sémantique* (Louvain: Peeters, 2002), esp. chap. 5, "La synonymie de *Gloria* et de *Laus*: le sens de 'Gloire,'" pp. 294–358.

4. Aristotle, *Nicomachean Ethics*, translated and edited by Roger Crisp (Cambridge: Cambridge University Press, 2000), book IV, chap. 3, p.71 (emphasis mine).

5. Ibid. (emphasis mine).

6. The expression "reward for truth" comes from Marcel Hénaff, *Le Prix de la vérité: Le don, l'argent, la philosophie* (Paris: Seuil, "La couleur des idées," 2002).

7. See Françoise Joukovsky, *La Gloire dans la poésie française et néolatine du XVIe siècle: Des Rhétoriqueurs à Agrippa d'Aubigné* (Geneva, Droz, 1969).

8. Cited by Maurice Testard in his edition of Saint Ambrose's *Les Devoirs* (Paris: Belles Lettres, 1984), vol.1, p. 266, n.1.

9. Cicero, *De Officiis*, with an English translation by Walter Miller (Cambridge, MA:

Harvard University Press, 1975), I, xix, 65, p. 67. Cicero also wrote a text on glory, which has disappeared.

10. Ibid., II, xii, 42, p. 211.

11. Ibid., I, xix, 62, p. 65. On the place of the all-powerful emperor in relation to glory, see Paul Veyne, *L'Empire gréco-romain* (Paris: Seuil, 2005), pp. 29–30. To understand the collective nature of the Roman concept of glory, this text by Claude Nicolet is particularly helpful: "the Roman (every Roman) is above all a warrior, or rather a soldier, that is, less a fighter hungry for individual exploits than a disciplined citizen incorporated into a machine whose fearsome efficiency comes from its coherence." *Le Métier de citoyen dans la Rome républicaine* (Paris: Gallimard, 1988), p. 123.

12. Cicero, *De Officiis*, II, ix, 31, pp. 199–200.

13. Ibid., II, xii, 43, p. 211.

14. On this point, see Andrew R. Dyck, *A Commentary on Cicero De Officiis* (Ann Arbor, University of Michigan Press, 1996), pp.32, 422–425.

15. Montesquieu, *Considérations sur les causes de la grandeur des Romains et de leur décadence* (Paris: "Classiques Garnier," 1967), p. 65.

16. Étienne Tiffou, *Essai sur la pensée morale de Salluste*, p. 103.

17. ["une espèce de transcendance dans l'immanence"] I am citing here the excellent phrase by Tiffou, Ibid., p. 41.

18. Saint Ambrose, *De Officiis*, edited and translated by Ivor J. Davidson (New York: Oxford University Press, 2001), I, xxxiv, 175, p. 219 (emphasis mine).

19. "Here is true courage, the kind possessed by the athlete of Christ, who 'does not receive the crown unless he has competed according to the rules'[II Tim. 2:5]," Ibid., I, xxxvi, 183, p. 225); "So, no one can receive the prize unless he has competed according to the rules, and there is no glory in victory except where the contests have cost real effort," Ibid., I, xv, 58, p. 151).

20. Ibid., I, xxxv, 177, p. 221.

21. Here Ambrose is citing the words of Saint Paul (I Tim. 6:10) ; Ibid., II, xvii, 87, p. 317; see also Ibid., I, xxxviii, 191, p. 229.

22. Ibid., I, xl, 196, pp. 231–233.

23. Ibid., I, xli, 200, p. 235.

24. Ibid., I, xli, 202, p. 235.

25. Ibid., II, 2, p. 269. Ambrose is citing Matthew 6:2.

26. Ibid., II, 3, p. 269, and II, 18, p. 279.

27. Ibid., III, 23, p. 367 (emphasis mine).

28. Saint Augustine, *The City of God against the Pagans*, edited and translated by R. W. Dyson (Cambridge: Cambridge University Press, 1998), book 5, chap. 13, p. 212.

29. Ibid., book V, chap. 12, p. 208.

30. Thus, Augustine cites the *Catilina* of Sallust (V, 12) before launching into the passion for glory that animated the Romans: "'They were avid for praise, generous with their wealth, and desired boundless glory and riches with honor.' This glory they loved most ardently. They chose to live for it, and they did not hesitate to die for it. They suppressed all other desires in their boundless desire for this one thing." Ibid., V, 12, p. 207.

31. Ibid., chap. 15, p. 216. Augustine is citing the same passage of Matthew 6:2 cited earlier by Ambrose.

32. Ibid., chap. 16, p. 216.

33. Ibid., chap. 18, p. 219 (he cites Virgil, *The Aeneid*, book VI, verse 823).

34. Ibid., chap. 14, p. 214.

35. Ibid.

36. Ibid., chap. 12, p. 210.

37. Ibid.

38. See Reinhard Kosellek, *Le Futur passé: Contribution à la sémantique des temps historiques* (Paris: EHESS, 1990), pp. 209–210.

39. Saint Augustine, *City of God*, book V, chap. 13, p. 213 (emphasis mine).

40. In *The Semantic Development of* Gloria *in Early-Christian Latin* (Nijmegen: Dekker & van de Vegt, 1956), A. J. Vermeulen follows the evolution of this aspect of *gloria* from Tertullian: *gloria martyrum* and the martyr as victorious *miles Christi*; see esp. chap. 2, "The Origin of a New Christian Concept: Glory or Renown in the Eyes of God," part C ("*Gloria martyrum*") and D ("*Gloria martyrum* in its wider sense"), pp. 53–104.

41. Saint Thomas Aquinas, *Summa Theologica*, Latin text and English Translation, Introductions, Notes, Appendices, and Glossaries (New York: McGraw Hill, 1964), II, 132.

42. Ibid., p. 145. Of note, as well, is the distinction that Thomas makes between "glory" and "honor": "praise and honourable recognition are related to glory as causes from which glory proceeds. So glory is related to them as their end. It is because of glory that a person loves recognition and praise, since he believes that through it he will have renown in the sight of others." Ibid., p. 157.

43. Ibid., p. 147.

44. Ibid.

45. Ibid., pp. 155–157.

46. Ibid., II–II, Q.36.

Chapter 2

1. Jacques Le Goff, *Saint Louis* (Paris: Gallimard, 1996), p. 502; quoted from Gareth Evan Gollrad's translation *Saint Louis* (Notre Dame, IN: Notre Dame University Press, 2009), p. 402. This involves a discussion of the thesis that Walter Ullmann develops in *The Individual and Society in the Middle Ages* (Baltimore: Johns Hopkins University Press, 1966). Le Goff points out the difference between the French and English cases.

2. Yvonne Robreau, *L'Honneur et la Honte: Leur expression dans les romans en prose du Lancelot-Graal (XIIe–XIIIe siècles)* (Geneva: Droz, 1981), part 2, chap. 1, "*Gloire* et les mots de la même famille," and chap. 2, "*Nom, renom, renomée* et *los*," pp. 75–102.

3. See Dominique Boutet, *La Chanson de geste: Forme et signification d'une écriture du Moyen Age* (Paris: PUF, 1993).

4. *La Chanson de Roland*, verses 83–84. English translation drawn from *The Online Medieval and Classical Library*, http://omacl.org/Roland/.

5. ["Jamais on ne le reprochera à mes parents"; "l'on ne doit pas sur (nos combats) chanter de mauvaise chanson"] Ibid., verse 112: '*Male chançun n'en deit estre cantee*. On the "bad song," see the article by Edmond Faral, "Sur trois vers de la *Chanson de Roland* (vers 1016, 1465, 1517)," *Modern Philology*, vol. 38, no.3 (February 1941), pp. 235–242.

6. ["gestes vains; gestes necessaries"] Alphonse Dupront, *Le Mythe de croisade* (Paris: Gallimard, 1997), vol. 1, p. 53.

7. Jacques Le Goff explores these contradictions brilliantly in *Saint Louis*.

8. In a sense, this is this paradox Ernst Kantorowicz explores in his famous work *The King's Two Bodies* (Princeton, Princeton University Press, 1997).

9. A. Dupront, *Le Mythe de croisade*, vol. 1, p. 199.

10. ["commerce de gloire, avec, source des valeurs, la guerre sainte"] Ibid., vol. 2, p. 664.

11. François-René de Chateaubriand, *Mémoires d'outre-tombe*, edited by J.-C. Berchet (Paris: Classiques Garnier, 1998), book 19, chap. 16, v. 1, pp. 901-911.

12. ["les Français semèrent en Égypte ces germes de civilisation que Méhémet a cultivés: la gloire de Bonaparte s'accrut; un rayon de lumière se glissa dans les ténèbres de l'Islamisme, et une brèche fut faite à la barbarie"] Ibid., p. 911.

13. Éginhard, *Vie de Charlemagne*, edited by L. Halphen (Paris: Belles Lettres, 1981), pp. 2-3.

14. François de Belle-Forest Comingeois, *L'Histoire des Neuf Roys Charles de France: contenant la fortune, vertu, & heur fatal des Roys, qui sous ce nom de Charles ont mis à fin des choses merveilleuses* (Paris: l'Olivier de P. L'Huillier, 1568), p. 35.

15. On the myth of the Gallic Hercules, see Robert E. Hallowell, "Ronsard and the Gallic Hercules Myth," *Studies in the Renaissance*, vol. 9 (1962), pp. 242-255; Claude-Gilbert Dubois, *Celtes et Gaulois au XVIe siècle: Le développement littéraire d'un mythe nationaliste* (Paris: Vrin, 1972); Philippe Desan, *Penser l'histoire à la Renaissance* (Caen: Paradigme, 1993).

16. See Norbert Elias, *The Civilizing Process: Sociogenetic and Psychogenetic Investigations* (Oxford,: Blackwell Publishing, 2000).

17. Montaigne, *Essais*, II, 16, "De la gloire." English version quoted from *The Complete Essays of Montaigne*, translated by Donald M. Frame (Stanford, Stanford University Press, 1958), "Of Glory," p. 477.

18. Montaigne, *Essays*, I, 31, "Of Cannibals"; see also, e.g., II, 7, "Of Honorary Awards."

19. See Marc Fumaroli, "L'héroïsme cornélien et l'idéal de la magnanimité," in *Héroïsme et création littéraire sous les règnes d'Henri IV et de Louis XIII, Actes et Colloques* no. 16 (Paris: Klincksieck, 1974), pp. 53-88, here p. 68; reprinted in *Héros et Orateurs: Rhétorique et dramaturgie cornéliennes* (Geneva: Droz, revised ed., 1996), pp. 323-348, here p. 340.

20. M. Fumaroli, *Héros et Orateurs*, p. 339. On Horace, see also Michel Prigent, *Le Héros et l'État dans la tragédie de Pierre Corneille* (Paris: PUF, 1986), pp. 127-128; and William A. Nitze, "Vertu as Patriotism in Corneille's Horace," *PMLA*, vol. 67, no. 7 (December 1952), pp. 1167-1172.

21. Pierre Corneille, *Horace*, act 5, scene 3. English version quoted from Pierre Corneille, *Horace*, translated by Alan Brownjohn (London: Angel Books, 1996), p. 86.

22. Nicolas Faret, *L'Honnête homme, ou l'art de plaire à la cour* (Paris: Toussaincts du Bray, 1630), pp. 44 and 78-79.

23. E. H. Kantorowicz, *The King's Two Bodies*.

24. Louis XIV, *Mémoires pour l'instruction du dauphin* (Paris: Libraire Académique, 1860), p. 541, cited by Olivier Chaline in *Le Règne de Louis XIV* (Paris: Flammarion, 2005); see the wonderful text "La gloire du roi," pp. 99-112; see also Ran Halévi, "Savoir politique et 'mystères de l'État': Le sens caché des *Mémoires de Louis XIV*," *Histoire, Économie et Société*, 2000, no. 4, pp. 451-468; and "Testament de la royauté: L'éducation politique de Louis XVI," in *Le Savoir du prince du Moyen Age aux Lumières*, edited by Ran Halévi (Paris: Fayard, 2002), pp. 311-361. See also Peter Burke, *The Fabrication of Louis XIV* (New Haven, Yale University Press, 1994).

25. On the magnanimity/humility relationship, see the commentary by P. Tarquinio Galluzzi on the description of the magnanimous in Aristotle's *Nicomachean Ethics*, "An

Magnanimitas sit Virtus et utrum sit Humilitatis contraria," in *In Aristotelis libros quinque priores [quinque posteriores] Moralium ad Nicomachum nova interpretatio, commentarii, quaestiones* (Paris: Sumptibus S. & G. Cramoisy, 1645), vol. 1, pp. 766–771, a text cited by M. Fumaroli, who provides a very relevant analysis of it in the context of the Cornelian hero, "L'héroïsme cornélien et l'éthique de la magnanimité," in *Héros et Orateurs*, pp. 335–340.

26. *De la vie et des actions d'Alexandre le Grand.* The legend of Alexander was revived and reinvigorated under the reign of Louis XIII for the needs of royal propaganda. There were three translations of it at the beginning of the century (Séguier, 1614, 1622; Soulfour, sieur de Glatigny, 1629; Lesfargues, 1639). Vaugelas's translation appeared posthumously. Conrart and Chapelain published a first version of it in 1653; Patru published another in 1659. Vaugelas's text was published many times in the seventeenth and eighteenth centuries. See the thesis by Fabrice Butlen, *Vaugelas et sa traduction de Quinte-Curce: Un grammairien traducteur,* École des Chartes, defended in 1999; and *Les Remarques de l'Académie française sur le* Quinte-Curce *de Vaugelas, 1719–1720: Contribution à une histoire de la norme grammatical & rhétorique en France,* critical edition by Wendy Ayrès-Bennett and Philippe Caron (Paris: Presses de l'École normale supérieure, "Études & documents en Histoire de la langue française," 1997).

27. ["cette production d'esprit la plus excellente & la plus merveilleuse de tous les Siecles, qui a proprement et principalement formé Alexandre, & qui l'a rendu Maistre du Monde"] Jean de Lartigue, *La Politique des conquérants* (Paris: chez Guillaume de Luyne, 1662, avec privilege du roi). On Lartigue, see the essential work by Lionel Rothkrug, *Opposition to Louis XIV: The Political and Social Origins of the French Englishtenment* (Princeton, Princeton University Press, 1965), pp. 111–130.

28. ["La grandeur d'un Prince à proprement parler n'est autre chose que la ruine ou la diminution de ses voisins"; "comme si c'estoit Aristote luy-mesme qui la donnât au public"; "Car, il n'y a point de condition ni de genre de vie qui s'approche plus d'une severe & parfaite Vertu"] Jean de Lartigue, *La Politique des conquérants,* pp. 3, 35. As Rothkrug points out, the historical dictionary of Moréri describes Jean de Lartigue as being from a family of old nobility, "lord of Caplice, priest, doctor in theology, and Premontré; he was then received doctor of Sorbonne in Paris: to which his merits and his works had drawn him: he was well known and esteemed by scholars. His mind was as deep as it was fine and subtle: to be distinguished among a number of writings that he produced are those on the *immortality of the soul; the politics of the conqueror; on the flux and reflux of the sea,* and others: he was then a historiographer of France, and died after 1569." *Grand dictionnaire historique, ou le Mélange curieux de l'Histoire sacrée et profane,* Louis Moréri (Paris: Libraires associés, 1759), vol. 6, p. 167.

29. ["en leur fermant la porte aux Charges les plus grandes par autre voye que par la voye des Armes, comme il s'est veu parmy les Nations où la domination & la puissance ont esté recherchées"] Jean de Lartigue, *La Politique des conquérants,* p. 43.

30. ["pour la Patrie, & le service de la Republique par une vertu toute extraordinaire, on a voulu faire revivre leur merite & leur vertu en leurs Enfans"] Ibid., p. 70.

31. ["luy inspire des pensées hautes par des principes generaux qui sont d'autant plus excellens qu'ils sont plus universels, & plus separez des particularitez inutiles, ou peu seantes"] Ibid., p. 81.

32. ["[l]'opinion présente que les nations ont des affaires de l'Estat, de sa puissance, de ses armes, de sa bonne conduite, & de toute la bonne disposition où il se trouve aujourd'huy"] Ibid., p. 128.

33. Ibid., p. 131.

34. Ibid., p. 109.

35. ["le consentement universel de toutes les Nations & de tous les peuples, non seulement les plus anciennes & les plus éclairez, mais encore les plus sauvages & les plus stupides, les Philosophes & le vulgaire l'ont authorisée d'une voix"] Ibid., p. 59.

36. Jean de Lartigue, *La Seconde Partie de la politique des conquerans accommodée au gouvernement de la France et à l'estat present des affaires*, B.N.: Fds. Fr., MS 4165, f. 2v.

37. ["dans un milieu et dans une juste proportion au regard des qualités du prince"] Ibid., f. 6r.

38. ["Grand roi, cesse de vaincre, ou je cesse d'écrire [. . .]. Je m'arrête à l'instant, j'admire et je me tais"] Epistle VIII.

39. ["Il faut, sans oser plus, voir, se taire, admirer"] *Mercure galant,* November 1682.

40. March 1686; passages cited by Bernard Magné, *Crise de la littérature française sous Louis XIV: Humanisme et nationalisme* (Lille: Atelier Reproduction des thèses, Université de Lille III), p. 236. On this theme, see esp. Jean-Pierre Néraudau, *L'Olympe du Roi-Soleil: Mythologie et idéologie royale au Grand Siècle* (Paris: Belles Lettres, 1986); but also Chantal Grell and Christian Michel, *L'École des Princes, ou Alexandre disgracié: Essai sur la mythologie monarchique de la France absolutiste* (Paris: Belles Lettres, 1988); and Jean-Marie Apostolidès, *Le Roi-machine: Spectacle et politique au temps de Louis XIV* (Paris: Éditions de Minuit, 1981).

41. "The new pantheon, or the relationship of the divinities of paganism, the heroes of Antiquity, and the so-called great princes with the virtues and actions of Louis-the-Great."

42. For recent interpretations of the quarrel between the Ancients and the Moderns, see "Les abeilles et les araignées," by Marc Fumaroli, introduction to *La Querelle des Anciens et des Modernes* (Paris: Gallimard, 2001); the study by Larry Norman, "Homère entre Anciens et Modernes, 1670–1770," *Lalies*, vol. 25 (2005), pp. 60–108; and "La philosophie à l'assaut de l'héroïsme dans la *Querelle d'Homère*," *L'Héroïsme au XVIIIe siècle*, in *Cahiers parisiens/Parisian Notebooks* (Paris: The University of Chicago Center in Paris, 2007), no. 3, pp. 303–320.

43. Paris: chez J. Morel, 1686; first ed. entitled *Parallèle de Louis-le-Grand avec les princes qui ont été nommés grands* (Paris: chez J. Le Febvre, 1685), cited in J.-P. Néraudau, *L'Olympe du Roi Soleil*, p. 111.

44. "*Nec viget quidquam simile aut secundum,*" Horace, *Carmina*, I, xii, 17–18; J.-P. Néraudau, *L'Olympe du Roi-Soleil*, p. 55. English translation by A. S. Kline, 2003: http://www.poetryintranslation.com/PITBR/Latin/HoraceOdesBkI.htm#_Toc39402018.

45. Olivier Chaline, *Le Règne de Louis XIV* (Paris: Flammarion, 2005), p. 107.

46. ["l'affirmation glorieuse ne vaut pas mieux que la cupidité"] Paul Bénichou, *Morales du Grand Siècle* (Paris: Gallimard, 1948), cited from the "Folio" ed. (Paris: Gallimard, 1998), p. 134.

47. *Réflexions ou sentences et maximes morales*, in *Moralistes du XVIe siècle* (Paris: Robert Laffont, "Bouquins," 1992), p. 134.

48. On this question, see Vincent Descombes, *Le Complément du sujet: Enquête sur le fait d'agir de soi-même* (Paris: Gallimard, 2004), p. 239.

49. ["toutes sortes de biens, d'honneurs, de plaisirs [. . .]. Il se fait le centre de tout: il voudrait dominer sur tout, & que toutes les créatures ne fussent occupées qu'à le contenter, à le louer, à l'admirer"] Pierre Nicole, "De la charité et de l'amour-propre," in

Essais de morale, contenus en divers traités sur plusieurs devoirs importants (Paris: Guillaume Desprex, 1733), v. 3, Second treatise, p. 132.

50. Christian Lazzeri formulates this contrast in *Force et justice dans la politique de Pascal* (Paris: PUF, 1993), pp. 15–17. See the pioneering article by Marcel Raymond, "Du jansénisme à la morale de l'intérêt," in *Mercure de France*, vol. 330 (1957), pp. 238–255. On Pierre Nicole, see the insightful study by Dominique Weber, "Le 'commerce d'amour-propre' selon Pierre Nicole," in an issue entitled "Le philosophe et le marchand" of the journal *Astérion—Philosophie, histoire des idées, pensée politique*, no. 5 (July 2007), pp. 169–196. On the morality of interest and the development of a concept of society as composed entirely of individuals motivated by interest and *amour-propre*, see Marcel Gauchet, "De l'avènement de l'individu à la découverte de la société," in *Annales E.S.C*, 34 (May–June 1979), pp. 451–463; E. J. Hundert, *The Enlightenment's Fable: Bernard Mandeville and the Discovery of Society* (Cambridge: Cambridge University Press, 1994); Keith Baker, "Enlightenment and the Institution of Society: Notes for a Conceptual History," in *Civil Society: History and Possibilities*, ed. S. Kaviraj and S. Khilnani (Cambridge: Cambridge University Press, 2001), pp. 84–104.

51. P. Nicole, "De la grandeur," in *Essais de morale*, vol. 2, part 1, chap. 6, p. 170.

52. Saint Augustine, *The City of God against the Pagans*, book 5, chap 13, p. 213.

53. The importance of the concept of public opinion during the eighteenth century has been studied many times. See Jürgen Habermas, *L'Espace public Archéologie de la publicité comme dimension de la société bourgeoise*, translated by M.-B. de Launay (Paris: Payot, 1978). For its role in the rise of the Revolution, see the work by Keith Baker, *Inventing the French Revolution: Essays on French Political Culture in the Eighteenth Century* (Cambridge: Cambridge University Press, 1990); and Mona Ozouf's article "l'Esprit publique," in *Dictionnaire de la Révolution française*, edited by François Furet and Mona Ozouf (Paris: Flammarion, 1988), pp. 711–719.

54. Pierre le Pesant de Boisguilbert, *Factum de la France, contre les demandeurs en delay, pour l'exécution du projet traité dans le Détail de la France, ou le Nouvel ambassadeur arrivé du pays du peuple* in *Pierre de Boisguilbert, ou la naissance de l'économie politique*, vol. 2, *Œuvres, manuscripts et imprimés* (Paris: Institut national d'études démographiques [INED], 1977), pp. 741–818, here pp. 748–749; *Le Détail de la France* dates from 1695, the *Factum*, an unpublished manuscript conserved in the Archives of the Minister of Foreign Affairs, bears the date 1705 but, according to INED, it was written before that date (vol. 2, p. 579).

55. Mercantilist thought in France had, of course, already formulated the idea of interest as a principal motivation for all merchants, but according to this vision, the ends of commerce were to be essentially the same as those of the State, which was the same as saying that it was in the service of the glory of the prince. See Henry C. Clark, *Compass of Society: Commerce and Absolutism in Old-Regime France* (Plymouth, Lexington Books, 2007), part 1, chap. 2: "Louis XIV and the two kinds of trade," pp. 27–72.

56. Pierre de Boisguilbert, *Mémoire sur l'assiette de la taille et de la capitulation*, in *Pierre de Boisguilbert, ou la naissance . . .* , vol. 2, p. 665; this text would thus date from 1705.

57. *England's Glory; or, The Great Improvement of Trade in general, by a Royal Bank, or Office of Credit, to be erected in London* (London, 1694), p. 17.

58. *England's Glory*, p. 23. On the image of bees, see James W. Johnson, "That Neo-Classical Bee," *Journal of the History of Ideas*, vol. 22, no.2 (April–June, 1961), pp. 262–266.

Johnson notes that, for the Egyptians, the bee was divine. In the context of the history of France, in 1653 more than three hundred pieces of jewelry were found in the form of bees in the tomb of Childéric, the father of Clovis. Moreover, Louis XII took the bee as a symbol, with the motto: "non utitur aculeo rex cui peremur" ("the king to whom we have submitted abstains from using his stinger") during his incursions into Italy. On this subject, see Nicole Hochner, "Louis XII and the porcupine: transformations of a royal emblem," *Renaissance Studies*, vol. 15, no.1 (2000), pp. 17-36, on bees, pp. 27-32; and Deonna Waldemar, "L'abeille et le roi," *Revue belge d'Archéologie et d'Histoire de l'Art*, vol. 25 (1956), pp. 105-131. It was Cambacérès who advised Napoleon to adopt the bee; he might have studied the *Histoire critique de l'établissement de la monarchie françoise dans les Gaules* by Jean-Baptiste Dubos, who says that in Childéric's tomb were discovered "a great number of golden Medals, all of which are stamped on the corner with Roman Emperors, and bees of natural size, also made of solid gold. Childéric, to all appearances, wore these little figures sewn to his ceremonial robes, because the Tribe of the Francs, over whom he reigned, had taken the bee as their symbol . . . I even believe that our bees through the acts of Painters and Sculptors became our Fleurs de lys when, in the XIIe century, France and the other States of Christendom began to carry weapons with coats of arms" (Paris: Ganeau, 1742), vol. 3, chap.16, pp. 473-474). For an excellent discussion of bee imagery in the English context, see Adrian Johns, *The Nature of the Book: Print and Knowledge in the Making* (Chicago, University of Chicago Press, 1998), pp. 266-272.

59. See Steven Pincus, "Whigs, Political Economy and the Revolution of 1688-89," in *Cultures of Whiggism*, edited by D. Womersley (Newark, University of Delaware Press, 2005), pp. 62-87; and, by the same author, *1688: The First Modern Revolution* (New Haven, Yale Univrsity Press, 2009), chap. 12, "Revolution in Political Economy," pp. 366-399.

60. ["un pays inconnu du peuple de commerçants et d'ouvriers"] *Factum de la France*, in *Pierre de Boisguilbert, ou la naissance . . .* , vol. 2, pp. 761-762. The "nation" of the privileged was composed of those who bought titles "that one [. . .] wants only with the revenue on the current price of an ordinary rent," in a society where "the land remains abandoned [and] commerce ceases." Boisguilbert abstains from criticizing religion or the law, "provided that they join their voters to destroy another nation that costs, alone, half of the goods of France without any profit for anyone." From this pejorative use of the word "nation" he launches into a series of reflections in which he places himself as an ambassador and interpretor of the "unknown country of merchants and workers" (vol. 2, p.768).

61. ["consiste à déguiser continuellement ses véritables sentiments, [à] trahir sa conscience en la vérité, en sorte que l'on appelle le blanc noir, et le noir blanc, lorsqu'il est question de faire sa cour, et que cela contribue à sa fortune"] Ibid., vol. 2, p. 765.

62. ["C'est uniquement la politesse qui a produit tout le désordre, qui ruin[e] entièrement la ligne de communication qui doit être entre tous les membres d'un État [. . .]"] Ibid., vol. 2, p. 764.

63. Ibid., vol. 2, p. 767.

64. ["pays inconnu du peuple des commerçants et d'ouvriers"; "impostures engen-drées par l'intérêt."

65. *Dissertation de la nature des richesses, de l'argent et des tributs, où l'on découvre la fausse idée qui règne dans le monde à l'égard de ces trois articles*, in Ibid., vol. 2, p. 992; text written in 1704 (emphasis mine).

66. See Joseph J. Spengler, "Les théories économiques de Boisguilbert comparées à celles de réformateurs de son temps," in Ibid., vol. 1, pp. 1-40. On Boisguilbert's thought,

notably in relation to Adam Smith, see Gilbert Faccarello, *Aux origines de l'économie poli-tique libérale: Pierre de Boisguilbert* (Paris: Anthropos, 1986). In "Le circuit et l'équilibre de Boisguilbert dans le courant de l'analyse économique," Jean-Louis Billoret notes that the diagnostics of John Law would be for the most part those of Boisguilbert. *Boisguilbert parmi nous: Actes du colloque international de Rouen, 22–23 mai 1975*, edited by Jacqueline Hecht (Paris: INED, 1989), pp. 59–81, here p. 73. See also the essential work by Catherine Larrère, *L'Invention de l'économie au XVIIIe siècle* (Paris: PUF, 1992), on Boisguilbert, pp. 99–100. On Boisguilbert's place vis-à-vis the politics of Louis XIV, see L. Rothkrug, *Opposition to Louis XIV*, chap. 6, "Secular Reform: Utilitarian Philosophy and Agrarian Theory," pp. 299–371.

67. Fénelon, *Explication des maximes des saints sur la vie intérieure*, in *Œuvres* (Paris: Gallimard, "Bibliothèque de la Pléiade," 1983), vol.1, pp. 1000–1095, here p. 1024.

68. Ibid., p. 1005.

69. ["jamais ôter à une âme le soutien des motifs intéressés, quand on commence suivant l'attrait de sa grâce à lui montrer le pur amour"] Ibid., p. 1019.

70. ["tous les mots intéressés de crainte et d'espérance"] Ibid., p. 1059. On the ties between Salesian contemplation and Rousseauist reverie, see Robert Morrissey, *La Rêverie jusqu'à Rousseau: Recherches sur un topos littéraire* (Lexington, KY: French Forum, 1984), pp. 58–62.

71. ["se laisser gouverner par les lois"] François de Fénelon, *Les Aventures de Télé-maque* (Paris: Classiques Garnier, 1994), book 5, p. 205. Quoted from English-language edition: *Telemachus, Son of Ulysses*, edited and translated by Patrick Riley (Cambridge: Cambridge University Press, 1994), p. 67.

72. ["n'est digne de la royauté qu'autant qu'il s'oublie lui-même pour se sacrifier au bien public"] Ibid., p. 61. The same idea returns in the eighteenth book.

73. See Jean-Claude Bonnet, *La Naissance du Panthéon: Essai sur le culte des grands hommes* (Paris: Fayard, "L'Esprit de la cité," 1998), chap. 2, "La métamorphose de la gloire."

74. ["se montroit infatigable dans les plus rudes travaux de la guerre"] Fénelon, *Telemachus*, book 13, p. 236.

75. Ibid., book 11, p. 196; Mentor expresses the same idea in book 10, p. 154: "'Care,' he said, 'must be taken of population in time of peace; but, lest the whole nation should sink into effeminacy, and ignorance of the art of war, it is proper that the young nobility be sent to the wars abroad. These will be sufficient to keep up the whole nation in an emulation of glory, in the love of arms, in a contempt of hardship and death itself, and in experience of military art.'"

76. ["ne doit point avoir plus de richesses et de plaisirs, mais plus de sagesse, de vertu et de gloire que le reste des hommes"] Ibid., book 5, p. 61.

77. ["Mais voulez-vous empêcher l'ingratitude des hommes? [. . .] [A]ppliquez-vous à redresser leurs mœurs"] Ibid., book 18, pp. 324–325.

78. ["par ses exemples et par son autorité, à les rendre bons"] Ibid.

79. See Robert Morrissey, *L'Empereur à la barbe fleurie: Charlemagne dans la mythologie et l'histoire de France* (Paris: Gallimard, "Bibliothèque des histoires," 1997). English-language ed.: *Charlemagne and France: A Thousand Years of Mythology* (Notre Dame, IN, University of Notre Dame Press, 2003).

80. ["héros du premier ordre, & sans contredit le plus grand Roi [. . .] qui ait regné jusqu'à présent en France"; "le génie du souverain"; "desintéressement personnel, qui faisoit en quelque sorte le caractere particulier du siecle de Charlemagne; ce Prince

ne voul[ait] rien pour lui, qui ne fut à l'avantage de la Nation entiere"; "cette union de sentiments & de volontez"] Henri de Boulainvilliers, *Histoire de l'ancien gouvernement de France, avec XIV lettres historiques sur les parlements ou états généraux* (La Haye et Amsterdam, aux dépens de la Compagnie, 1727), pp. 240 and 245.

81. Lucien Karpik, "Le désintéressement," *Annales E.S.C.*, 44 (May-June 1989), pp. 733-751; see also David Bell, *Lawyers and Citizens: The Making of a Political Elite in Old Regime France* (Oxford, Oxford University Press, 1994), p. 64.

82. ["prolonger les ouvrages ordonnés par les rois"] *Encyclopédie, ou dictionnaire raisonné des sciences, des arts et des métiers, etc.*, edited by Denis Diderot and Jean le Rond d'Alembert (University of Chicago: ARTFL Encyclopédie Project [Spring 2013 edition], ed. Robert Morrissey, http://encyclopedie.uchicago.edu/.), article "Encyclopédie," vol. 5, p. 636. All quotations are from this edition.

83. D'Alembert, "Avertissement des éditeurs," in Ibid., vol. 3, p. xiv. For the projection of universal values onto the entity of the nation and the role that the editors attributed to their own disinterestedness, see Robert Morrissey, "The *Encyclopédie*: Monument for a Nation," *Studies on Voltaire and the Eighteenth Century [SVEC]*, vol. 5 (2002), pp. 143-161.

Chapter 3

1. Montesquieu, *The Spirit of Laws*, translated by Thomas Nugent, revised by J. V. Prichard; based on a public domain edition published in 1914 by G. Bell & Sons, Ltd., London. Rendered into HTML and text by Jon Roland of the Constitution Society, http://www.constitution.org/cm/sol.txt,part 1, book 3, chap 7.

2. ["L'honneur fait mouvoir toutes les parties du corps politique; il les lie par son action même et il se trouve que chacun va au bien commun, croyant aller à ses intérêts particuliers"] Ibid.

3. On this point, see the wonderful book by Céline Spector, *Montesquieu: Pouvoirs, richesses et sociétés* (Paris: PUF, 2004), pp. 156-159. See also Henry Clark, *Compass of Society: Commerce in Old-Regime France* (Lanham, MD: Lexington Books, 2007), pp. 123-127.

4. Montesquieu, *The Spirit of Laws*, part 2, book 11, chap.7.

5. Ibid., part 4, book 20, chap. 2. On Montesquieu and commerce, see M. Hénaff, *Le Prix de la vérité*, pp. 460-473.

6. [à faire toutes les actions difficiles, et qui demandent de la force, sans autre récompense que le bruit de ces actions"] Montesquieu, *The Spirit of Laws*, part 1, book 3, chap. 7.

7. [cette passion générale que la nation française a pour la gloire"] Montesquieu, *Persian Letters: With Introduction and Notes, Now Completely Done Into English* (1901; Google Books online edition), letter 91, from Usbek to Ibben. In this context, there is a critique of the point of honor and the practice of the duel.

8. Ibid., Letter 90, from Usbek to Ibben.

9. ["produit dans les hommes un certain sentiment de la justice exacte, opposé d'un côté au brigandage, et de l'autre à ces vertus morales qui font qu'on ne discute pas toujours ses intérêts avec rigidité, et qu'on peut les négliger pour ceux des autres"] Montesquieu, *Spirit of the Laws*, part 4, book 20, chap. 2.

10. [à la gloire des citoyens, de l'État et du prince"] Ibid., part 2, book 11, chap. 7, "Of the Monarchies we are acquainted with."

11. See C. Spector, *Montesquieu: Pouvoirs, richesses et sociétés*, chap. 2, "Paradigme du Commerce et paradigme des Manières: Les figures de la société civile," pp. 145-220.

12. In an article entitled "La campagne des philosophes contre l'honneur," John Pappas looks at what he calls "the decadence of the concept of honor," intimately linked with the "theme of the decline and the moral debasement of the nobility" and to the idea of the "social prejudice," *SVEC*, vol. 205 (Oxford, Voltaire Foundation, 1982), pp. 31–44, here pp. 32, 35, 36; see also Louis Althusser, who, in *Montesquieu, la politique et l'histoire* (Paris: PUF, "Sup," 1969), pp. 76–79, stresses the degree to which "honor has nothing to do with truth, nor with morality"; it is "the passion of a social class."

13. Jean-Paul Marat, *The Chains of Slavery: A work wherein the clandestine and villainous attempts of princes to ruin liberty are pointed out, and the dreadful scenes of despotism disclosed; to which is prefixed, an address to the electors of Great Britain, in order to draw their timely attention to the choice of proper representatives in the next Parliament* (London, J. Almon, 1774), p. 36. On the publication dates, see Rachel Hammersley, "Jean-Paul Marat's *The Chains of Slavery* in Britain and France 1774–1833," *Historical Journal*, vol. 48, no. 3 (2005), pp. 641–660. She situates the English version in the context of English republicanism described by Caroline Robbins in *The Eighteenth-Century Commonwealthman* (Cambridge, MA: Harvard University Press, 1959); as for the French version, she dates it to 1793. The reader will note that the French and English editions do not always correspond.

14. ["éteindre l'amour de la gloire"] J.-P. Marat, *The Chains of Slavery*, p. 36.

15. See David Bien, "The Army in the French Enlightenment: Reform, Reaction and Revolution," *Past and Present*, vol. 85, no. 1 (1979), pp. 68–98; Chaussinand-Nogaret, *La Noblesse au XVIIIe siècle: De la féodalité aux Lumières*, edited by. E. Le Roy Ladurie (Brussels, Complexe, 1984); Jay Smith, *The Culture of Merit: Nobility, Royal Service, and the Making of Absolute Monarchy in France, 1600–1789* (Ann Arbor: University of Michigan Press, 1996); Rafe Blaufarb, *The French Army, 1750–1820: Careers, Talent, Merit* (Manchester: Manchester University Press, 2002).

16. ["nous rendre tous vertueux"] Mirabeau, *Ami des hommes, ou Traité de la population* (Avignon, 1756), part 2, p. 51; on the relationship between *Ami des hommes* and the thinking of Montesquieu, see Marco Platania, *Montesquieu e la virtù: Rappresentazioni della Francia di Ancien Régime et dei governi repubblicani* (Turin: Utet, 2007), pp. 193–194.

17. ["le désir de se distinguer dans sa profession paroît la plus naturelle des ambitions"] Mirabeau, *Ami des hommes*, part 2, p. 106.

18. ["l'émulation se tourne [. . .] vers la richesse, or l'émulation de la richesse n'est autre que la cupidité"] Ibid.

19. Ibid., p. 107.

20. K. Baker has analyzed this phenomenon in "Transformations of Classical Republicanism in Eighteenth-Century France," *Journal of Modern History*, vol. 73 (March 2001), pp. 32–53; see also the important book by François Hartog, *Anciens, Modernes, Sauvages* (Paris: Galaade Éditions, 2005).

21. J.-P. Marat, *The Chains of Slavery*, p. 24.

22. Ibid.

23. Marat submitted a tribute to Montesquieu (*Éloge de Montesquieu*) to the Academy of Bordeaux for the essay competition the Academy announced in 1782. His essay was registered by the Academy in 1785.

24. ["la gloire n'est jamais compagne de la servitude"] Montesquieu, *Persian Letters*, Letter 90, p. 165.

25. [[e]n mécanique, on préfère les machines qui produisent les plus grands effets par les plus petits moyens. En politique, on doit faire de même"] Antoine-Léonard

Thomas, *Essai sur les éloges* [1773], in *Œuvres complètes* (Paris: Desessarts, 1802), vol. 3, p. 4 (on Thomas's influence, see the important work by J. -C. Bonnet, *La Naissance du Panthéon*, chap. 4, "Enfin parut Thomas . . .", pp. 67–82). This passage by Thomas recalls the famous passage by Montesquieu in *Persian Letters*, Letter 80.

26. A.-L. Thomas, *Essai sur les éloges*, p. 4.

27. Ibid., p. 5.

28. Paul-Henri Dietrich d'Holbach, *La Morale universelle, ou les devoirs de l'homme fondés sur sa nature* (Amsterdam, Marc-Michel Rey, 1776), vol. 1, p. 73.

29. ["un pouvoir qu'ils approuvent"] Ibid., p. 129.

30. Ibid., p. 197.

31. Ibid.

32. E. de Las Cases, *Mémorial de Sainte-Hélène* (ed. Schmidt), vol. 2, p. 1573.

33. ["la vertu et le génie souvent opprimés se réfugient loin du monde réel, dans un monde imaginaire, comme dans un asile où la justice est rétablie"] A.-L. Thomas, *Essai sur les éloges*, p. 7.

34. [par l'exemple, par l'opinion publique qui, prêtant des forces continuelles aux imaginations ardentes, les déterminent à des actions qui, souvent, paroissent surnat-urelles"] D'Holbach, *Morale universelle*, p. 192.

35. The expression *"merveilleux chrétien"* referred to the depiction in literary works of divine intervention, that of the saints, the devil, or of miracles and the like. It was the subject of great debate in seventeenth-century France.

36. ["le concert unanime & soutenu d'une admiration universelle"; *"le merveil-leux . . . [ce qui] s'élève ou semble s'élever au-dessus des forces de la nature"*] The article "Gloire" is by Marmontel (*Encyclopédie*, vol. 7, pp. 716–721); the article "Gloire, glorieux, glorieusement, glorifier" (also in vol. 7) is by Voltaire (emphasis mine).

37. Ibid.

38. ["Les hommes nés pour la gloire, l'ont cherchée où l'opinion l'avoit mise"] Ibid.

39. [la gloire, comme la lumière, se communique sans s'affaiblir: celle du souverain se répand sur la nation"; "genre de merveilleux le plus funeste"; "il n'est point de gloire comparable à celle des guerriers; car celle même des législateurs exige peut-être plus de talens, mais beaucoup moins de sacrifices."] Ibid.

40. Ibid., p. 720.

41. [asservis [. . .] à une espèce de routine"] D'Alembert, "Discours préliminaire," *Encyclopédie*, vol. 1, p. xiv.

42. ["Hé quoi," dit-il, "l'on ne m'entend point?" *"L'on vous entend, s'écrie une voix; mais qu'appelez vous douze hommes de bonne volonté? Nous le sommes tous, vous n'avez qu'à choisir"*; (*"mets-le sur mon dos, dit[-il], du-moins s'il y a un coup de fusil à recevoir, je le lui épargnerai"*] Ibid.

43. See Introduction, note 3.

44. ["Une conquête peut détruire les préjugés nuisibles et mettre, si j'ose parler ainsi, une nation sous un meilleur génie"] Montesquieu, *The Spirit of Laws*, part 2, book 10, chap. 4 (http://www.constitution.org/cm/sol.htm).

45. ["[t]out fut uni par la force de son génie [qui] se répandit sur toutes les parties de l'empire"] Montesquieu, *The Spirit of Laws*, part 6, book 31, chap. 18. On Alexander, see Pierre Briant, "Alexandre, héros des Lumières," *L'Héroïsme au XVIIIe siècle*, in *Cahiers parisiens/Parisian Notebooks*, 2007, no.3, pp. 321–335; and "Montesquieu, Mably et Alexandre le Grand: Aux sources de l'histoire hellénistique," *Revue Montesquieu* 8 (2005–2006), pp. 151–185; see also Chantal Grell and Christian Michel, *L'École des princes,*

ou Alexandre disgracié (Paris: Belles lettres, 1988); and C. Volpilhac-Auger, "Montesquieu et l'impérialisme grec: Alexandre ou l'art de la conquête," *Montesquieu and the Spirit of Modernity* (Oxford: Voltaire Foundation, SVEC, 2002), pp. 49-60.

46. Montesquieu, *The Spirit of Laws*, part 2, book 10, chap. 14.

47. ["Il respecta les traditions anciennes et tous les monuments de la gloire ou de la vanité des peuples"] Ibid.

48. ["jetèrent dans la Grèce le premier germe de la Philosophie"; "un arbre immense dont les rameaux s'étendant d'âge en âge & de contrées en contrées"] Ibid.

49. See Jacques Proust, *Diderot et l'Encyclopédie* (1962; Paris: Albin Michel, 1995), p. 257.

50. See the article "Éclectisme," in *Encyclopédie*, vol. 5, pp. 570-593; Paolo Casini, "Diderot et le portrait du philosophe éclectique," *Revue internationale de philosophie*, nos. 148-149 (1984), pp. 35-45; and Donald Kelley, "Eclecticism and the History of Ideas," *Journal of the History of Ideas*, vol. 62, no. 4 (October 2001), pp. 577-592.

51. "Grecs (philosophie des)," in *Encyclopédie*, vol. 7, pp. 911-912.

52. On Count de Guibert and his role in the reform of the army, see R. Blaufarb, *The French Army, 1759-1820*, chap. 1, "The Merits of Birth: Lineage and Professionalism in the Old Regime," pp. 12-42; and D. Bien, "The Army in the French Enlightenment"; see also Jay M. Smith, *Nobility Reimagined: The Patriotic Nation in Eighteenth-Century France* (Ithaca: Cornell University Press, 2005).

53. ["où faire fortune ne signifie plus acquérir de la réputation, mais amasser des richesses"] Guibert, *Essai général de tactique, précédé d'un discours sur l'état actuel de la politique et de la science militaire en Europe; avec le plan d'un ouvrage, intitulé La France politique et militaire* (London [Liege], chez les libraries associés, 1773), "Discours préliminaire," p. xxxiv.

54. ["l'enflure pour la puissance, le luxe pour la richesse, l'éclat pour la gloire"] Ibid., p. xii.

55. Ibid., p. iv.

56. Ibid., p. iii.

57. ["esprits supérieurs et universels, qui font la gloire et les destins des empires"] Ibid., p. i.

58. Ibid., pp. xvi-xvii.

59. Ibid., p. xxxvii.

60. Ibid., p. xxi.

61. ["qui anime tous les Arts, qui relève toutes les professions: car toutes tiennent à la gloire d'une nation, soit par rapports de grandeur, soit par des rapports d'utilité publique"] Guibert's "Discours inaugural" took place on 13 February 1786. On emulation in the eighteenth century, see Jack Iverson, "Voltaire's Heroes: Violence and Politics in the Age of Enlightenment" (diss., University of Chicago, December 1998), Introduction: "Voltaire and the Age of Emulation," and chap. 1, "Social Virtue and Individual Grandeur: Voltaire and the Ethics of Glory," pp. 1-93.

62. See Raymond Mas, *"L'Essai général de tactique* (1770) de Guibert, ou le rationalisme des Lumières face à la guerre," in *La Bataille, l'Armée, la Gloire. 1745-1871—Colloque International de Clermont-Ferrand*, edited by Paul Viallaneix and Jean Ehrard (Clermont-Ferrand: Association des Publications de la Faculté des Lettres et Sciences Humaines de Clermont-Ferrand, 1985), vol. 1, pp.19-132; on the genius leader, pp. 123-124.

63. ["une sorte de dignité publique qui manquait à son pays"; "il faut bien qu'il donne à sa nation, à ses manufactures, à ses artistes des études et des modèles"] *Éloge*

du roi de Prusse, par l'auteur de l'Essai général de tactique was published in London in 1787; I am quoting from the *Choix d'éloges français les plus estimés* (Paris: Hautel, 1812), vol. 2, pp. 78-79.

64. ["conçoit, il exécute le projet d'un code général, et l'introduit à la fois et d'une manière uniforme, dans tant de pays morcelés"] Ibid., p. 82.

65. ["cette étonnante machine où tout paroissoit de pièces de rapport et prêt à se décomposer"] Ibid., p. 120.

66. ["la diriger avec succès, comme si elle eût été composée des matériaux les plus parfaits et les plus homogènes"] Ibid., p. 118.

67. ["sont presque toutes datées de ses camps, et composées au milieu du tumulte des armes; elles ont toutes ce ton de force et de simplicité, cette logique droite et noble qui convient si bien à un roi guerrier, mais qui ne peuvent appartenir en même temps qu'à un grand caractère et à un esprit distingué"] Ibid., pp. 73-74.

68. Ibid., p. 137.

69. ["cette consistance de gloire et de renommée"] Ibid., p. 175.

70. ["le prestige de gloire, comme une vapeur divine, étoit répandu sur sa Personne & l'environnoit toute entiére"] Ibid., p. 221.

71. Ibid., p. 235.

72. ["cet homme prodigieux fut bien plus son propre ouvrage que celui de la nature"] Ibid., p. 227.

73. Guibert, *Essai général de tactique*, p. iv.

74. ["fixent les opinions, ils répandent leur méthode et leur génie sur la science entière"] Ibid., p. xvii.

75. ["tactique complète"; science vaste et sublime"] Ibid., pp. i, iii.

76. Guibert, *Éloge du roi de Prusse*, p. 192.

77. Gabriel-François Coyer, *La Noblesse commerçante* (London: Duchesne, 1756), p. 141; a note in the BNF catalogue specifies that the London address is false, that the text was "published in Paris by Nicolas-Bonaventure Duchesne from the tacit permission granted to him on 25 June 1756"; on the subject see Daniel Roche, *La France des Lumières* (1993; Paris: Fayard, 2003), chap. 12.

78. ["Le désir de mériter l'estime publique est [. . .] un frein nécessaire à la passion des richesses"] Sieyès, *Qu'est-ce que le Tiers État? précédé de l'Essai sur les privilèges* (Paris: chez Alexandre Correard, 1822), p. 37, passage cited by Shovlin, in *The Political Economy of Virtue*, p. 223. See also "Forum: Emulation in France, 1750-1800," edited by Jack Iverson, special issue of *Eighteenth-Century Studies*, vol. 36, no. 2 (winter 2003), pp. 213-248.

79. Sieyès, *Qu'est-ce que le Tiers État?* p. 25; on Sieyès, see William Sewell, *A Rhetoric of Bourgeois Revolution: The Abbé Sieyès and* What is the Third Estate?, (Durham: Duke University Press, 1994), esp. pp. 150-189.

80. Sieyès, *Essai sur les privilèges*, pp. 12-13.

81. ["monnaie morale"] Ibid., p. 16. The expression is found in a note: "Among an enslaved people, moral currency is always false, regardless of the hand that distributes it."

82. See above, chap. 3, note 13.

83. ["en calculant sans cesse ses intérêts avec rigueur [chacun] contracte un caractère d'équité stricte [. . .] ennemi [. . .] de toute noblesse de procédés, de toute élévation d'âme."] Here is the passage as it appeared in English in the 1774 edition: "Careless of the good of the public, they then attend to their private interests only; the love of one's patria is extinguished in every heart; the citizen disappears, and the man

remains." As can be seen, Marat has considerably modified the passage in the French 1792 edition.

84. ["le prix du mérite en tout genre, le salaire de tous les services rendus à la patrie"] Marat, *Les Chaînes de l'esclavage*, pp. 73, 29, 88; see also *Chains of Slavery*.

85. On the transformation of love of self in Salaville, see James Livesey, *Making Democracy in the French Revolution* (Cambridge, MA: Harvard University Press, 2001), pp. 57–58.

86. ["La liberté est dans l'homme le principe du désintéressement et de la généosité, par conséquent de toute sociabilité, de toute moralité humaine"] Jean-Baptiste Salaville (1755–1832), *L'Homme et la Société, ou nouvelle théorie de la nature humaine et de l'état social* (Paris: chez Carteret, year VII [1798]), p. 302.

87. Ibid., pp. 33–34.

88. ["un être, pour ainsi dire, surnaturel, ou qui est hors des lois naturelles du monde, et qui habite ce monde sans être soumis à l'ordre [de] nécessité qui le règle et le dirige; d'où il suit que cet être est libre par sa nature"] Ibid., p. 133.

89. Ibid., p. 340.

Chapter 4

1. On Napoleon's relationship with money, see the excellent study by Pierre Branda, *Le Prix de la gloire: Napoléon et l'argent* (Paris: Fayard, 2007); on the question of the budgets of allied countries, pp. 329–333, "Les finances des alliés au service de la France."

2. On the ideal of the nation as it was developed in France, see David Bell, *The Cult of the Nation in France: Inventing Nationalism, 1680–1820* (Cambridge, MA: Harvard University Press, 2001); Edmund Dziembowski, *Un nouveau patriotisme français, 1750–1770: La France face à la puissance anglaise à lépoque de la guerre de Sept Ans* (Oxford, Voltaire Foundation, *SVEC*), 1998.

3. "Rapport fait par Robespierre au nom du comité de salut public sur les rapports des idées religieuses et morales avec les principes républicains et sur les fêtes nationales," National Convention, session of 7 May 1794 (18 Floréal Year II), in *Œuvres de Maximilien Robespierre*, notice historique, edited by Laponneraye (chez l'éditeur, 1840), vol. 3, pp. 611–612. On the question of the relationship between the logic of war and Republican ideology, see Sophie Wahnich, *La Longue Patience du peuple: 1792, naissance de la République* (Paris: Payot, 2008), esp. chap. 19, "Fierté républicaine," pp. 429–451; on honor and the Republic, see Anne Simonin, *Le Déshonneur dans la République. Une histoire de l'indignité, 1791–1958* (Paris: Grasset, 2008), part 1, "L'honneur, principe du gouvernement républicain."

4. Many studies deal with this theme, including: Albert Mathiez, *Les Origines des cultes révolutionnaires. 1789–1792* (Paris: Alcan, 1904); J.-C. Bonnet, *Naissance du Panthéon*; Jacques Guilhaumou, *La Mort de Marat (1793)* (Brussels: Complexe, 1989); Philippe Bordes, *La Mort de Brutus, de Pierre-Narcisse Guérin* (Vizille: Musée de la Révolution française, 1996); Raymonde Monnier, *Républicanisme, patriotisme et Révolution française* (Paris: L'Harmattan, 2005).

5. In a remarkable issue of the *Annales historiques de la Révolution française*, "Louis Charles Antoine Desaix: Officier du roi, Général de la République," no. 324 (2001), pp. 113–125, Raymonde Monnier analyzes what she calls "the Marengo moment" in her article "Vertu antique et nouveaux héros: la presse autour de la mort de Desaix et d'une bataille légendaire."

6. See Bernard Gainot, "Les mots et les cendres. L'héroïsme au début du Consulat," *AHRF*, no. 324 (2001), pp. 127-138, and, in the same issue, Annie Jourdan, "Bonaparte et Desaix, une amitié inscrite dans la pierre des monuments?" pp. 139-150.

7. *Gazette nationale, ou Le Moniteur Universel*, 18 messidor year VII of the Republic (6 July 1800), p. 1162.

8. *Le Moniteur*, 18 messidor year VII, p. 1163; passage cited by B. Gainot, "Les mots et les cendres," in *AHRF*, no. 324 (2001), p. 127 (emphasis mine).

9. ["Allez dire au Premier Consul que je meurs avec le regret de n'avoir pas assez fait pour vivre dans la postérité."] *Archives parlementaires: Recueil complet des débats législatifs et politiques des Chambres françaises de 1800 à 1860* (Paris: Librairie administrative de Paul Dupont, 1862), vol. 1, p. 1: from 22 Frimaire to 24 Ventôse year VIII, session of 3 Messidor, p. 594.

10. Ibid. On this passage, see B. Gainot, "Les mots et les cendres," *AHRF*, no. 324 (2001), p. 136; and R. Monnier, "Vertu antique et nouveaux héros," ibid., pp. 120-121.

11. *Archives parlementaires*, session of 16 Messidor, p. 599.

12. ["guerrier sans peur et sans reproche"] Ibid., p. 600.

13. *Choix de rapports, opinions et discours prononcés à la Tribune nationale depuis 1789 jusqu'à ce jour, recueillis dans un cadre chronologique et historique*, vol. 17, book 1, of the Consulat, of year 8 to year 10 (1799-1802), pp. 184-185; on the transfer of the ashes of Turenne, see Christine Helfrich, "L'Empereur et l'Hôtel des Invalides," in *Napoléon, de l'histoire à la légende: Actes du colloque des 30 novembre et 1er décembre 1999 organisé par le Musée de l'Armée, Hôtel national des Invalides* (Paris: Maisonneuve & Larose, 2000), pp. 155-166, here pp. 163-164; and Bronislaw Baczko, *Politiques de la Révolution française* (Paris: Gallimard, "Folio," 2008), chap. 7, "Turenne au Temple de Mars," pp. 492-534.

14. *Choix de rapports*, p. 185.

15. "Citizens, your eyes are fixed on the remains of the great Turenne. Here is the body of this warrior so dear to all the French, to any friend of glory and of humanity." Ibid., p. 184.

16. ["sut faire disparaître l'éclat de son rang par celui de ses victoires, et l'on ne vit plus en lui que le grand homme."]

17. Ibid., p. 186 (emphasis mine).

18. [sa gloire ne doit point être séparée de celle de ces héros républicains"] *Choix de rapports*, p. 186.

19. ["un corps moral et collectif"] Jean-Jacques Rousseau, *Du contrat social*, I, vi, "Du pacte social," in *Œuvres complètes*, edited by B. Gagnebin et M. Raymond (Paris: Gallimard, 1964), vol. 3, p. 361.

20. As A. Jourdan has said: "Fundamentally ahistorical, the parallel neglects framework and circumstances to favor vague analogies that falsify historical truth. Too influenced by Plutarch, the serious historian Napoleon wanted to be was unable to extract himself from those vague analogies." *Napoléon: Héros, imperator, mécène*, p. 55.

21. On the question of the experience of time, see the work by François Hartog, *Régimes d'historicité: Présentisme et experiences du temps* (Paris: Seuil, 2003).

22. *Choix de rapports*, "Discours prononcé par le president du Tribunat (Andrieux) devant les tribuns en séance pour célébrer l'anniversaire de la foundation de la République, le 1er vendémiaire an 9 (23 september 1800), p. 187.

23. ["qu'exalter l'égoïsme, la cupidité, l'ambition des honneurs frivoles, et une stu-

pide prédilection pour soi-même, [. . .] une profonde indifférence pour le bien général"]
Ibid., p. 188.

24. Ibid.

25. Ibid., pp. 188–189.

26. ["tout nous a jetés dans les exagérations"] Ibid., p. 189.

27. Ibid.

28. ["retracent les anciennes *administrations provinciales*, don't l'idée patriotique est
due à Turgot, ce ministre citoyen et vraiment ami du peuple"] Ibid., p. 192.

29. ["Il faut remonter jusqu'à Charlemagne pour trouver la France aussi vaste en
territoire, aussi puissante par la force des armes"] Ibid., p. 194. On the role of Lucien
Bonaparte in the development of the image of Napoleon as a new Charlemagne, see
R. Morrissey, *Charlemagne and France.*

30. Ibid., p. 200: "Discours prononcé dans le temple de Mars par Lucien Bonaparte,
ministre de l'Intérieur, le 1er vendémiaire an IX , pour la Fête de la fondation de la
République" (emphasis mine).

31. On the genre of funeral elegies, see J.-C. Bonnet, *Naissance du Panthéon*, chap. 2,
"Le triomphe d'un genre," pp. 83–111: "Far from being a dusty rhapsody turned exclu-
sively to the past, the elegy genre proved to be a little machine of power that concerned
the most immediate present and the future of the state" (p.111).

32. *Séances des Écoles normales, recueillies par des sténographes et revues par les profes-
seurs*, new ed. (Paris: Imprimerie du Cercle-social, year 9 of the French Republic [1800]),
vol. 1, p. 168. On the formation of opinion among the Sensualists and the Ideologues see
Jan Goldstein, *The Post-Revolutionary Self: Politics and Psyche in France, 1750–1850* (Cambridge, MA: Harvard University Press, 2005), chap. 2, "The Revolutionary Schooling of
the Imagination," pp. 60–100.

33. On constitutional developments, see Marcel Gauchet, *La Révolution des pouvoirs:
La souveraineté, le peuple et la représentation, 1789–1799* (Paris: Gallimard, 1995); within
the context that concerns us here, see chap. 3, "Brumaire: Sacre et disgrace du tiers-
pouvoir," pp. 186–255.

34. ["l'amour de la gloire le mobile de toute action véritablement grande, [. . .] qui
détourne de toute action lâche, injuste, oppressive, immorale"] *Archives parlementaires*,
vol.1, session of 3 Messidor, p. 594.

35. ["cette probité sévère et ces vertus généreuses qui embellissent tant l'héroïsme
et la victoire dans toute l'histoire des républiques anciennes"] D.-J. Garat, *Éloge funèbre
des généraux Kléber et Desaix, prononcé le 1er vendémiaire an IX à la place des Victoires, par le
citoyen Garat* (Paris: Imprimerie de la République, year IX), p. 31; see B. Gainot, "Les mots
et les cendres," *AHRF*, no. 324, pp. 130–133.

36. ["avait reçu de la nature la taille des demi-dieux d'Homère"; "le fanatisme ne
peut que défigurer et exposer une liberté fondée sur la raison, et qui ne doit se défendre
que par les talens"] D.-J. Garat, *Éloge funèbre . . .*, p. 17.

37. ["les sentimens de la nature pour avoir les vertus d'un citoyen"; "à laquelle on
aurait bein pu pardonner ses ancêtres en faveur de son fils"] Ibid., pp. 12–13.

38. ["première loi de la République fondée sur la raison"; "délire de la liberté"] Ibid.,
pp. 26–28.

39. Ibid.

40. ["Quoi! Dans les républiques mêmes les disgrâces suivent donc si souvent et de
si près à la gloire"] Ibid., p. 23.

41. ["adouci par les mœurs générales, par les arts et par la philosophie, avait fait adopter et respecter"] Ibid., p. 25.

42. ["sans opinion arrêtée tous les deux sur les différents systèmes d'ordre social"] Ibid., p. 8.

43. ["à cette voix de chef que le soldat a coutume d'appeler le dieu Mars, le soldat croit entendre le maître de la Fortune et l'arbitre souverain des combats"] Ibid., p. 46.

44. ["croient qu'elle ne peut avoir ni le besoin ni les moyens de s'élever davantage"] Ibid.

45. Ibid., pp. 46-47.

46. Ibid., p. 47.

47. ["créer pour la gloire des solennités et des représentations dont l'éclat efface les insipides et fatigantes pompes du pouvoir"; "tous les regards de cette nation se portent et se fixent sur celui qui ne les attire que par son nom et par sa gloire"] Ibid., p. 78.

48. Ibid., p. 77.

49. Ibid., p. 78.

50. Ibid., pp. 52-53.

51. Ibid., p. 79.

52. ["démocrates par toutes leurs pensées, par tous leurs actes"; "La vraie démocratie respire plus encore dans le génie de ces princes absolus que dans les harangues turbulentes des tribuns de la république"] Ibid., p. 80.

53. Ibid., pp. 80-81.

54. ["ont eu les conceptions les plus législatives et les plus populaires"] Ibid., p. 83.

55. ["destructeur des lois et des droits de son pays"] Ibid., p. 88.

56. Ibid., pp. 88-89 (emphasis mine).

57. Ibid., p. 91.

Chapter 5

1. "In his works on metaphysics, Malebranche tried to unite images and ideas; but since his ideas were not right, one could sense only imperfectly the link he sought to establish between them and his brilliant images. Garat, in his *Leçons* at the Écoles normales, a model of perfection in this genre, and Rivarol, despite a few convoluted expressions, make fully conceivable the possibility of this concordance between the image drawn from physical nature and the idea that serves to form the chain of principles and their deductions in the moral order." Madame de Staël (Anne-Louise Germaine Necker, baronne de Staël-Holstein), *De la littérature considérée dans ses rapports avec les institutions sociales*, April 1800 *Seconde edition revue, corrigée et augmentée*, December 1800, edited by Gérard Gengembre and Jean Goldzink (Paris: Flammarion, 1991), p. 383.

2. Ibid., p. 328.

3. See Florence Lotterie, "Madame de Staël et l'esprit de Coppet: une littérature d'opposition?" in *L'Empire des Muses: Napoléon, les arts et les lettres*, edited by J.-Cl. Bonnet (Paris: Belin, 2004), pp. 133-149; on the political evolution of Madame de Staël, see Bronislaw Baczko, "Utopie salonnière et realisme politique," in *Politiques de la Révolution française*, chap. 6, pp. 142-491; on French liberalism, see Lucien Jaume, *L'Individu effacé, ou le paradoxe du libéralisme français* (Paris: Fayard, 1997), primarily the first chapter, "La constitution d'un libéralisme du sujet: Madame de Staël et Benjamin Constant," pp. 25-117, in which the author explores the relationships between Ideologues, Bonaparte, and Madame de Staël.

4. Madame de Staël, *De l'influence des passions*, followed by *Réflexions sur le suicide*, with preface by Chantal Thomas (Paris: Payot & Rivages, 2000), p. 56.

5. ["dans la force sur soi-même et l'amour de la réputation"] Madame de Staël, *De la littérature . . .* , p. 138.

6. ["par système ce que son amour-propre laisse échapper"; *mais il se formaient au dedans pour l'ostentation*] Ibid., p. 139 (emphasis mine).

7. Ibid.

8. ["l'homme du midi se perdait tout entier dans les jouissances de la volupté"; "de l'imagination, de la mélancolie, du penchant pour la mysticité"] Ibid., p. 165.

9. Ibid., pp. 206-207.

10. ["la tristesse passionnée des habitants d'un climat nébuleux"; "sans altérer la nature de leur courage, parvint à lui donner un autre objet"] Ibid., p. 167.

11. Ibid., pp. 168-169.

12. Ibid., p. 169; see also p. 298.

13. ["vulgarité du langage, des manières, des opinions"; ("l'urbanité des mœurs et celle de l'émulation"] Ibid., p. 299.

14. ["la liberté, la vertu, la gloire, les lumières, ce cortège imposant de l'homme dans sa dignité"] Ibid., p. 76.

15. ["par une égalité grossière et jalouse ce que distingue l'inégalité naturelle"] Ibid., p. 393.

16. Ibid., p. 394.

17. ["contenir la liberté par la vertu, l'ambition par la gloire. [. . . Car ce] que l'on admire dans les grands hommes, ce n'est jamais que la vertu sous la forme de la gloire"] Ibid., p. 411.

18. ["le sentiment douloureux de l'incomplet de sa destinée"] Ibid., p. 208.

19. Ibid.

20. ["source de toutes les passions généreuses comme de toutes les idées philosophiques"] Ibid.

21. Madame de Staël, *De l'influence des passions*, pp. 60-61.

22. ["arriver, par un raisonnement subtil, à représenter le dévouement le plus généreux comme un égoïsme bien entendu"] Madame de Staël, *De la littérature . . .* , p. 377.

23. Ibid.

24. ["Ce style de l'âme, si je puis m'exprimer ainsi, est un des premiers moyens de l'autorité dans un gouvernement libre"] Ibid., p. 390.

25. Ibid., p. 392.

26. ["ne faut rabaisser aucun genre d'exaltation"] Ibid., p. 393.

27. Ibid., pp. 81-82.

28. ["au-dessus du pouvoir quelconque qui les récompense"] Ibid., p. 324. P. Bénichou has brilliantly explored the avatars of what Malesherbes had so well formulated in 1775 in his inaugural speech at the Académie française: "There rose up a tribunal independent of all powers, and which all the powers respect, which appreciates all talents, which speaks on all genres of merit," cited by P. Bénichou, *Le Sacre de l'écrivain* (Paris: José Corti, 1973; new ed., Gallimard, 1999), p. 27. On Madame de Staël, who made writers the "preachers and . . . theologians of enthusiasm" and who, with Benjamin Constant, developed a morality of sacrifice, see pp. 228-244.

29. ["[l]'encouragement de la haute littérature [. . .] c'est la gloire, la gloire de Cicéron, de César même et de Brutus"; "par le charme de son style et l'élévation philos-

ophique dont ses lettres portent le caractère"] Madame de Staël, *De la littérature . . .*, p. 324.

30. ["de contenir la liberté par la vertu et l'ambition par la gloire"] Ibid., p. 411.

31. ["En effet, les hommes peuvent toujours cacher leur amour-propre et le désir qu'ils ont d'être applaudis sous l'apparence ou la réalité des passions plus fortes et plus nobles"] Ibid., pp. 333–334; on this subject, see Karen De Bruin, "'La femme supérieure': l'individu, le roman et la république libre de Germaine de Staël" (diss., University of Chicago, 2007).

32. ["à la plus absurde médiocrité"; "comme autrefois, un utile ascendant sur l'opinion"] Madame de Staël, *De la littérature . . .*, p. 336.

33. ["tout ce qui tient à l'humanité, à la générosité, à la délicatesse"] Ibid.

34. ["de la célébrité dont jouissait la France par l'art de plaire et de vivre en société"] Ibid., p. 337.

35. The full French title is *L'Apothéose des héros français morts pour la Patrie. Les ombres des héros morts pour la Patrie conduits par la Victoire viennent habiter l'Élysée aérien où les ombres d'Ossian et de ses valeureux guerriers s'empressent de leur donner dans ce séjour d'immortalité et de gloire la fête de la Paix et de l'Amitié* (The Apotheosis of French heroes who died for their country. The ghosts of the heroes who died for the Fatherland led by Victory come to the heavenly Elysium where the ghosts of Ossian and his brave warriors eagerly give them during this sojourn of immortality and glory a festival of Peace and Friendship).

36. ["se penche pour embrasser Desaix. Kléber tend une main à Fingal en signe d'alliance; de l'autre il porte avec Desaix un trophée d'armées enlevées aux mameluks"] See Sylvain Bellenger, "Ossian, nouvel Homère," in *Girodet 1767–1824* (Paris: Gallimard/ Musée du Louvre Éditions, 2005), pp. 234–247. This catalogue includes Girodet's description of the painting referred to above.

37. The Celtic Academy was founded in this context in 1801; its mission was to "discover the past of France, gather the archeological, linguistic, and everyday vestiges of the ancient Celtic civilization," passage cited by S. Bellenger in *Girodet*, p. 246, note 40; on the relationship of this painting to the political context, see B. Gainot, "Les mots et les cendres," *AHRF*, no. 234, pp. 134–135.

38. François-René de Chateaubriand, *Le Génie du christianisme* (Paris: Garnier-Flammarion), part 2, book 2, chap. 1, vol. 1, p. 246; part 4, book 1, chap. 4, vol. 2, p. 66.

39. See the dedication: "To the First Consul Bonaparte. Citizen First Consul, you have wanted to take under your protection this edition of the *Génie du christianisme*; it is a new testimony to the favor that you grant to the august cause that is triumphing in the shelter of your power. One cannot help but recognize in your destinies the hand of Providence, which has marked you from afar for the accomplishment of its prodigious plans. The people are watching you; France, growing through your victories, has placed its hopes in you, since you are constructing the foundations of the State and of your prosperities upon Religion. Continue to hold out a helping hand to thirty million Christians who are praying for you at the feet of the altars that you have returned to them. I am, with profound respect, Citizen First Consul, your very humble and very obedient servant, Chateaubriand." Jean-Claude Berchet stresses that "Napoleon was not insensitive to such a brilliant tribute, whose solemn expression was maintained at the head of the three printings of the third edition that came out between June and December 1803, and was only taken out in the fourth, in 1804." "Chateaubriand et Napoléon: une question de régime," *Cahiers parisiens/Parisian Notebooks*, 2005, no.1, pp. 67–80.

40. ["efface les distinctions nobiliaires qui plaçaient la gloire héritée avant la gloire acquise, et les descendans des grands hommes avant les grands hommes"] *Archives parlementaires publiées par J. Mavidal et É. Laurent: Recueil complet des débats législatifs et politiques des chambres françaises*, 2nd series (from 1800 to 1860) (Paris: Librairie Administrative de Paul Dupont, 1867), vol. 3. p. 685 (emphasis mine).

41. ["paie aux services militaires, comme aux services civils, le prix du courage qu'ils ont tous mérité; *elle les confond dans la même gloire*, comme la Nation les confond dans sa reconnaissance"] Ibid. (emphasis mine).

42. [les croix et les rubans sont les hochets de la monarchie"; "système diamétralement opposé aux principes professés pendant la révolution"] A.-C. Thibaudeau, *Le Consulat et l'Empire*, vol. 2, pp. 476, 480.

43. ["raisonner des siècles de barbarie aux temps actuels."] Ibid., p. 475.

44. Ibid., pp. 475–476.

45. Ibid., pp. 478–480.

46. J. Tulard, *Napoléon et la noblesse d'Empire* (Paris: Tallandier, 1979), p. 19. See also excellent articles by Claude Ducourtial-Rey and Jérôme Zieseniss on the Legion of Honor in the *Dictionnaire Napoléon*, edited by J. Tulard (Paris: Fayard, 1999), as well as that of J.-C. Bonnet, "Les honneurs de l'empire," in *L'Empire des Muses*, pp. 293–315.

47. ["Marcellus, l'épée de Rome, avait érigé un temple à l'Honneur, où l'on n'arrivait qu'en passant par celui de la Vertu"; "fit un rapprochement oratoire entre Marcellus, *l'épée de Rome*, et Napoléon Bonaparte, *l'épée de France*, se rencontrant dans la même idée. L'enthousiasme s'empara de l'assemblée; on battit des mains pendant dix minutes."] Pierre-Louis Roederer, *Œuvres* (Paris: Firmin Didot Frères, 1854), vol. 3, pp. 441–442.

48. Ibid., p. 341.

49. ["ne se conduisent que par la raison ou le sentiment d'intérêt personnel"] Ibid., p. 331.

50. Ibid., p. 334.

51. *Le Moniteur*, no. 307, 7 Thermidor, Year III (Saturday 26 July 1795) (reprint, Paris: Plon, 1862), vol.25, p. 292.

52. F. Furet speaks of Sieyès's "clock-making inspiration" in *La Révolution française, de Turgot à Jules Ferry* (Paris: Hachette, 1988; new ed., Gallimard, "Quarto," 2007), p. 441.

53. P.-L. Roederer, *Œuvres*, p.338 (emphasis mine).

54. N. Petiteau, *Lendemains d'Empire: Les soldats de Napoléon dans la France du XIXe siècle* (Paris: La Boutique de l'histoire, 2003).

55. J.-P. Bertaud, *Quand les enfants parlaient de gloire: L'armée au cœur de la France de Napoléon* (Paris: Aubier, 2006).

56. A.-C. Thibaudeau, *Le Consulat et l'Empire*, vol. 2, p. 208; on Thibaudeau's attitude toward Napoleon, see Isser Woloch, *Napoleon and His Collaborators: The Making of a Dictatorship* (New York: Norton, 2001).

57. ["Car vous devez comprendre que je ne me sépare pas de mes prédécesseurs et que, depuis Clovis jusqu'au Comité de Salut publique, je me tiens solidaire de tout"]. Letter dated 21 December 1809, *Lettres inédites de Napoléon*, ed Léon Lecestre (Paris: Plon, 1897), vol. 1, p. 383.

58. ["Je suis le tuteur de leur gloire [. . .]. Je ne laisserai pas périr leurs noms"] E. de Las Cases, *Mémorial de Sainte-Hélène* (ed. Schmidt), vol. 1, p. 246.

59. A. Jourdan, *Napoléon: Héros, imperator, mécène*.

60. ["Certes, je serais fier et heureux de descendre de généreux citoyens ayant su maintenir nationalement leurs titres, comme nous avons conquis les nôtres sur les

champs de bataille, mais il n'en est rien: *je ne date que de moi*"] Pierre de Pelleport, *Souvenirs militaires et intimes du général vicomte de Pelleport de 1793 à 1853, publiés par son fils sur les manuscrits originaux, les lettres, notes et documents officiels laissés par l'auteur* (Paris: Didier, 1857), vol. 1, p. 4, cited by N. Petiteau in *Élites et militaires: la noblesse d'Empire au XIXe siècle (1808-1914)* (Paris: Boutique de l'histoire, 1997), p. 155.

61. ["Des ancêtres, pourquoi faire: je suis un ancêtre"] Cited in Edmond Pierson, *Étude de la noblesse créée par Napoléon Ier* (Orleans: Desjardins, 1910), p. 11, and by N. Petiteau in *Élites et militaires*, p. 155.

62. J.-P. Bertaud, *Quand les enfants parlaient de gloire*, p. 78. For the figures, see the article by Jérôme Zieseniss on the "Noblesse d'empire," in the *Dictionnaire Napoléon*, pp. 404-405; for an interpretation of the figures, see N. Petiteau, *Élites et militaires*; and Jean Tulard, *Napoléon et la noblesse d'Empire* (Paris: Tallandier, 1979).

63. ["Donner des appuis à la dynastie présente, *faire oublier* la noblesse (ancienne); voilà le but qu'on a voulu atteindre"] Note from 14 June 1810, cited by J. Zieseniss in "Noblesse d'Empire," *Dictionnaire Napoléon*, vol. 2, p. 402 (emphasis mine).

64. *Le Moniteur*, no. 112, 22 Nivôse year XII (13 January 1804), p. 446.

65. ["droits imprescriptibles"; "qui par là redevint véritablement l'assemblée de la nation"] Gabriel Bonnot de Mably, *Observations sur l'histoire de France* (1765; Paris: Bossange, Masson et Bresson, 1997), p. 164. On Mably, see Johnson Kent Wright, *The Political Thought of Gabriel Bonnot de Mably, 1709-1785* (Stanford: Stanford University Press, 1997).

66. ["consentir à n'avoir que les mêmes inérêts [et à] former un seul corps"] Mably, *Observations sur l'histoire de France*, p. 182.

67. Ibid., p. 167.

68. Ibid., p. 171.

69. ["hydre féodale"] Népomucène Lemercier evokes the "feudal hydra" in his *Âges Français: Poème en quinze chants* (Paris: Barba, year XI [1803]), p. 166.

70. ["notre ancienne gloire à notre gloire présente"; "le Gouvernement de la République soit confié à un empereur"] Ibid.

71. *Le Moniteur*, no. 221, 11 Floréal, year XII (1 May 1804), p. 1004. Curée delivered his speech on 10 May.

72. ["par un mouvement spontané, par une volonté unanime [. . .] s'écrièrent: Que l'égalité s'établisse, que les privilèges disparaissent, et que la nation soit tout ce qu'elle doit être"] Ibid.

73. ["redemander la place que depuis quatorze siècles elle a occupée parmi les nations"] Speech by C. Duvidal, *Le Moniteur*, no. 223, 13 Floréal, year XII (3 May 1804), p. 1012.

74. Ibid.

75. Madame de Staël, *De la littérature . . .* , p. 328.

76. Cicero, *De officiis*, II, xii, 42, p. 211 (see chap 1 above).

77. Fénelon, *Explication . . .* , p. 1019 (see chap. 2, n. 67, above).

78. ["on devient pour soi-même un modèle en quelque sorte et un émule"] Garat, *Éloge funèbre . . .* , p. 46.

79. ["Les destinées de la France vont s'accomplir; [. . .] une carrière immense de succès et de gloire s'ouvre devant elle"] *Le Moniteur*, no. 232, 22 Floréal year XII (12 May 1804), p. 1056; the authors of the letter are identified as "the government of Paris: the generals stationed in this city, and the troops comprising the garrison of the first military division."

80. A.-C. Thibaudeau, *Le Consulat et l'Empire*, vol. 7, p. 139.

81. ["une invention funeste, où se confondent la vérité et la flatterie, l'hypocrisie et la bonne foi"] Ibid., vol. 2, p. 215.

82. ["nos espérances ne connaîtront point de bornes sous les auspices du héros qui ne connaît point d'obstacles"] *Le Moniteur*, no. 232, 22 Floréal year XII (12 May 1804), p. 1056.

83. *Le Moniteur*, no 270, 30 Prairial year XII (19 June 1804), p. 1234.

84. On these lines, see above, chap. 2, nn 38–39.

85. ["est un homme dont le noble caractère n'est ni craintif ni flatteur. Il n'aurait pas parlé ainsi si ce n'eût été son sentiment"] Laure Junot d'Abrantès, *Mémoires de Madame la duchesse d'Abrantès, ou souvenirs historiques sur Napoléon, la Révolution, le Directoire, le Consulat, l'Empire et la Restauration*, (Paris: chez Madame-Delaunay, 1833), vol. 10, p. 178.

86. ["les souffrances intérieures se taisaient ou disparaissaient devant la gloire. L'absence de la liberté était compensée par la grandeur et la suprématie de la nation"] A.-C. Thibaudeau, *Le Consulat et l'Empire*, vol. 5, p. 310.

87. ["Je crois que l'histoire moderne n'offre aucun exemple d'une semblable humiliation"] Laure Junot d'Abrantès, *Mémoires de Madame la duchesse d'Abrantès*, vol. 10, p. 175.

88. The attempt took place on 13 October 1810 during a review of troops in Schoenbrunn, and the execution on 17 October.

89. ["l'Empereur n'aurait jamais consenti de lui-même à rétrograder, à descendre, c'était contre sa nature"] A.-C. Thibaudeau, *Le Consulat et l'Empire*, vol. 6, p. 475.

90. [Vous m'ôtez mon passé"; "je veux le conserver. Il faut que la nouvelle constitution se rattache aux anciennes; elle aura la sanction de plusieurs années de gloire"] Cited by B. Constant, *Mémoires sur les Cent-Jours*, edited by O. Pozzo di Borgo (Paris: J.-J. Pauvert, 1961), p. 141.

91. On using the intersection of the right of the people and natural law to establish in France the status of outlaw during the trial of the king and afterwards, see Dan Edelstein, *The Terror of Natural Right: Republicanism, the Cult of Nature, and the French Revolution* (Chicago: University of Chicago Press, 2009), pp. 146–163.

92. Emphasis mine.

Chapter 6

An earlier version of this chapter was published as "The *Mémorial de Sainte-Hélène* and the Poetics of Fusion" in an issue of *MLN* entitled "The Specter of Napoleon," edited by David Bell, vol. 120 (2005), pp. 716–732.

1. ["Quel roman pourtant que ma vie"] E. de Las Cases, *Mémorial de Sainte-Hélène* (ed. Schmidt), vol. 1, p. 896.

2. ["la patrie, ses destinées, ses doctrines, son avenir tenaient à [sa] seule personne!"; "Mais sire, [. . .] c'est bien aussi ce que chacun disait, et plusieurs nuances de partis vous en faisaient le reproche, ajoutant avec aigreur: 'Mais pourquoi s'est-il donc mis dans le cas de tout rattacher à sa seule personne?'"; "Accusation banale et vulgaire"] E. de Las Cases, *Mémorial de Sainte-Hélène*, vol. 1, pp. 1181–1182.

3. ["est sorti le héros d'une cause dont il demeure le messie"] Ibid., p. 94.

4. ["a dédaigné de mêler des intérêts personnels avec les grands intérêts dont il avait constamment l'esprit occupé"] Ibid., p. 201.

5. See P. Bénichou, *Le Sacre de l'écrivain*.

6. ["petit jeune homme [. . .] faible en apparence, avec des traits irréguliers, mais

délicats, et un nez aquilin"; "regardait tous les autres livres du monde comme menteurs, et écrits par des fourbes pour avoir de l'avancement"] Stendhal, *Le Rouge et le noir*, edited by Anne-Marie Meininger (Paris: Gallimard, "Folio," 2000), pp. 63, 66.

7. E. de Las Cases, *Mémorial de Sainte-Hélène*, edited by Marcel Dunan (1951; Paris: Flammarion, 1983). Hereafter cited as *Mémorial de Sainte-Hélène* (ed. Dunan). Regarding the editions, see the excellent introduction by Dunan, pp. xv–xvii.

8. E. de Las Cases, *Mémorial de Sainte-Hélène* (ed. Schmidt; see above, chap. 1, n. 5). In his foreword, Joël Schmidt stresses the degree to which the 1830–1832 edition "remains faithful to the spirit of the first edition" (p. 38). Unless otherwise indicated, all citations are to this edition.

9. Ibid., vol. 2, p. 1803.

10. Marc Fumaroli has written an excellent text on the memoir genre in *Chateaubriand: Poésie et Terreur* (Paris: De Fallois, 2003), pp. 667–674.

11. On 15 July 1815, from the Island of Aix, Napoleon set sail on the English ship Bellérophon, which took him to Plymouth. On 7 August, he boarded the Northumberland, which took him to Saint Helena. The Northumberland set anchor there on 15 October 1815, and Napoleon disembarked on 16 or 17 October.

12. ["le cœur des enfants était toujours le plus disposé à l'enthousiasme"] E. de Las Cases, *Mémorial de Sainte-Hélène* (ed. Schmidt), vol. 1, p. 117.

13. Ibid.

14. [A l'âge de la puberté, Napoléon devint morose, sombre"] Ibid., vol. 1, p. 119.

15. ["n'en avoue presque aucune"] Ibid., vol. 1, p. 120. As Dunan notes in his edition, this version of the birth already circulated under the Empire. In his historical essay devoted to "Madame Mère," the baron Larrey describes the mother's reaction to this story: "It is a fable; to have him be born on Caesar's head! Did he need that? . . . And anyway, we don't have carpets in our houses in Corsica, even less in summer than in winter," *Madame Mère* (Paris: Dentu, 1892), vol. 1, p. 54; passage cited in a note by Dunan in *Mémorial de Sainte-Hélène* (ed. Dunan), vol. 1, p. 91.

16. ["propre dictée de l'Empereur; on verra plus tard quand et comment"] E. de Las Cases, *Mémorial de Sainte-Hélène* (ed. Schmidt), vol. 1, p. 119.

17. [après en avoir parcouru deux ou trois lignes, c'est-à-dire après l'avoir reconnu, il s'en éloignait ou parlait d'autre chose sans avoir touché ce sujet] Ibid., vol. 2., p. 1317.

18. Ibid., vol. 1, p. 202 (Sunday 22 to Tuesday 24 October 1815).

19. Ibid., vol. 1, pp. 296–297 (15–16 December 1815).

20. Ibid., vol. 1, pp. 297–298.

21. ["unissant dans ses bizarreries tout ce qu'il y a de plus élevé et de plus vil parmi les mortels; [. . .] une espèce de *Jupiter Scapin*"].Ibid., vol. 1, pp. 298, 15–16 December 1815. Dominique-Georges Dufour de Pradt, bishop of Poitiers, then of Malines. Napoleon sent him as ambassador to Poland; Las Cases cites his *Histoire de l'ambassade dans le grand-duché de Varsovie en 1812*.

22. "The people have accused my ambition for all these wars; but were they my choice; were they not always in the nature and force of things, always in that struggle between the past and the future, in that constant and permanent coalition of our enemies . . . ?" E. de Las Cases, *Mémorial de Sainte-Hélène* (ed. Schmidt), vol. 2, p. 1182.

23. ["réconcilier la France avec l'Europe [. . . et d']amalgamer entièrement la France nouvelle avec la France ancienne"] Ibid., vol. 2., p. 1530.

24. ["le héros d'une cause dont il demeure le messie"] Ibid., vol. 1, p. 94.

25. This is what he called his arrest, then his expulsion from the island, for having tried clandestinely to deliver two letters.

26. Ibid., vol. 1, p. 82.

27. Ibid.

28. Ibid., vol. 1, p. 488.

29. [j'ennoblis tous les Français: chacun peut être fier"] Ibid., vol. 1, p. 846.

30. ["nous les avons entrelacés de lustre, de monuments, de prodiges; nous en avons noyé les premières souillures dans des flots de gloire"] Ibid., vol. 1, p. 510.

31. Ibid., vol. 1, p. 846.

32. ["J'amalgamais"] Ibid., vol. 1, p. 519.

33. Ibid., vol. 1, p. 95.

34. Ibid., vol. 1, p. 897.

35. ["L'Empereur, qui s'était promis d'abord de s'en tenir au plus complet stoïcisme, s'en émeut néanmoins et s'en exprime fortement"] Ibid.

36. Georg Wilhelm Friedrich Hegel, *Phänomenologie des Geistes*, translated by A.V. Miller (Oxford: Oxford University Press, 1977), B, IV, A.

37. ["en dehors des lois humaines"] E. de Las Cases, *Mémorial de Sainte-Hélène*, vol. 2, p. 1743.

38. ["une continuité de vents, de nuages, d'humidité, toujours une température modérée et monotone qui présente du reste peut-être plus d'ennui que d'insalubrité"] Ibid., vol. 1, p. 292 (Monday, 11–Thursday, 14 December 1815).

39. ["*L'Empereur se fixe à Briars. Description. Situation misérable*"] Ibid., vol. 1, p. 194.

40. ["*Uniformité. Ennui. Solitude de l'Empereur. Caricatures*"] Ibid., vol. 1, p. 414.

41. Ibid., vol. 1, pp. 200, 243, 495–496; vol. 2, pp. 1256, 1548.

42. ["Il nous est arrivé plus d'une fois d'avoir à leur donner bataille après le dessert."] Ibid., vol. 1, p. 875 (26 June 1816); p. 876 (27 June 1816).

43. ["*Uniformité. Ennui. L'Empereur se décide à écrire ses* Mémoires"] Ibid., vol. 1, p. 148.

44. ["une petite élévation d'où il paraissait comme sur un piédestal, au milieu des ruines"] Ibid., vol. 1, p. 368.

45. ["de la peine à retrouver le monstre insensible, dur, méchant, cruel, en un mot le tyran dont on l'a si souvent, si longtemps entretenu"] Ibid., vol. 1, p. 369.

46. ["du *cœur* et de la sensibilité réelle de Napoléon"] Ibid.

47. Ibid., vol. 1, pp. 371–372.

48. Ibid., vol. 1, pp. 365–366.

49. Les Cases eliminated these fragments starting with the 1840 edition, which gives the text a clearly more political slant.

50. Ibid., vol. 1, pp. 377.

51. [*on n'avait pas de temps à perdre*"] Ibid., vol. 1, p. 378.

52. Ibid., vol. 1, p. 395.

53. ["monotone, insalubre; mais la température, il fallait en convenir, était douce"] Ibid., vol. 1, p. 405.

54. Ibid., vol. 1, p. 458.

55. Ibid., vol. 1, pp. 464–465.

56. ["Il me serait difficile d'employer quatre mots à exprimer, durant ces quatre jours, aucune déviation quelconque de notre vie accoutumée"] Ibid., vol. 1, p. 417.

57. ["La plupart de nos journées se ressemblaient beaucoup; si elles nous semblaient

longues en détail, elles perdaient rapidement dans le passé, et ne nous laissaient que des souvenirs vagues"] Ibid., vol. 1, p. 424.

58. As Marcel Dunan points out, in the first edition this summary was placed after the days of 30–31 March 1816; in the 1824 reprint it always constituted the end of the second volume, which, this time, ended with the days of 21–22 March. In later editions, it remained interspersed with that date. *Mémorial de Sainte-Hélène* (ed. Dunan), vol. 1, p. 477, note 1. Dunan returned it to its original location, following the days 30–31 March.

59. E. de Las Cases, *Mémorial de Sainte-Hélène* (ed. Schmidt), vol. 1, p. 479.

60. Ibid., vol. 1, p. 480 (emphasis mine).

61. ["en un mot, nous retrouvions l'Empereur, et tout Napoléon"] Ibid., vol. 1, p. 481.

62. It is in this sense that the *Mémorial* can be seen as playing a significant role in the inversion at the heart of what Jacques Rivières calls "the aesthetic revolution." Essential to this revolution is "the glory of the ordinary" ("la gloire du quelconque"). The *Mémorial*'s treatment of the everyday is key to understanding the fundamental modernity of the Napoleonic myth. On the "glory of the ordinary," see Jacques Rancière, *Le partage du sensible, esthétique et politique* (Paris: La Fabrique, 2000), p. 50.

63. Ibid., pp. 70, 299.

64. On this subject see Frank Bowman, *Le Christ romantique* (Geneva: Droz, 1953), chap. 5, "Napoléon et le Christ," pp. 171 ff.

65. ["il avait été sévèrement enjoint de ne lui donner d'autre qualification que celle de *général*, et de ne le traiter qu'à l'avenant"] E. de Las Cases, *Mémorial de Sainte-Hélène*, vol. 1, p. 91 (Monday, 7 August 1815).

66. [*qu'ils m'appellent comme ils voudront, ils ne m'empêcheront pas d'être moi*1"] Ibid., vol. 1, p. 92 (emphasis mine, except for "moi"/"myself," which Las Cases underlined).

67. Ibid., vol. 1, p. 200; vol. 2, pp. 1224–1225, 1620.

68. ["Quelle ignoble et sinistre figure que celle de ce gouverneur!"; "Dans ma vie je ne rencontrai jamais rien de pareil!"] Ibid., vol. 1, p. 564.

69. Ibid., vol. 2, p. 1392.

70. ["veut forcer l'Empereur à descendre, disait Napoléon, dans la fange de ses besoins, pour les discuter vis-à-vis de lui"] Ibid.

71. ["il avait l'air triste, ennuyé"]Ibid., vol. 1, p. 555.

72. ["transiger avec cette indépendance sacrée, qui, non moins que l'honneur, est aussi *une île escarpée et sans bords*"; "il est noble et courageux de surmonter l'infortune"; "L'île est trop petite pour moi"; "Tout ici respire un ennui mortel"] Ibid., vol. 1, pp. 561–562.

73. Ibid., vol. 1, p. 565.

74. ["saisit un drapeau, s'élança vers le pont et *l'y plaça*"; "aide de camp du général en chef, fut tué couvrant de son corps son général . . . Mort héroïque et touchante!"] Ibid., vol. 1, p. 589.

75. ["sans toutefois la spécifier davantage"] Ibid., vol. 2, p. 1043.

76. ["au moment même de l'impression de ce volume"; "une entreprise vraiment nationale"] Ibid. The eyewitness was general Jean-Jacques Germain Pelet, who between 1824 and 1828 published his *Mémoires sur la guerre de 1809 en Allemagne, avec les opérations particulières des corps d'Italie, de Pologne, de Saxe, de Naples et de Walcheren*. In his critical edition of the *Mémorial*, Marcel Dunan makes the connection between the title as Las Cases notes it and the erroneous title of Pelet's *Mémoires*: *Mémoires sur les guerres de Napoléon en Europe, depuis 1796 jusqu'en 1815*. See *Mémorial de Sainte-Hélène* (ed. Dunan), vol. 2, p. 143.

77. E. de Las Cases, *Mémorial de Sainte-Hélène* (ed. Schmidt), vol. 2, p. 1077.

78. Ibid., vol. 2, p. 1078.

79. Ibid., vol. 2, p. 1059.

80. Ibid., vol. 2, p. 1083.

81. M. Dunan explains that "after several reprintings at the time, these *Mémoires* were entered 'following the original manuscript communicated by Madame la comtesse de Montholon' into the *Œuvres de Napoléon à Sainte-Hélène*, in vol. XXXI of the *Correspondance*, as well as in the current editions of the Emperor's *Mémoires*." See *Mémorial de Sainte-Hélène* (ed. Dunan), vol. 2, p. 245.

82. E. de Las Cases, *Mémorial de Sainte-Hélène* (ed. Schmidt), vol. 2, p. 1391.

83. ["*Empereur change et s'affaiblit. Argenterie brisée*"; "s'affaiblit visiblement; sa démarche devient pesante; il a le pied traînant, ses traits s'altèrent"] Ibid., vol. 2, p. 1259.

84. ["limât les écussons, et qu'on brisât les pièces de manière à ce qu'elles ne présentassent aucun vestige qui pût montrer qu'elles lui avaient appartenu. [. . .] Quelques-uns pleuraient"] Ibid., vol. 2, p. 1260.

85. ["je devine ce qui m'affecte encore, je me mets à la place, c'est la crainte d'être rossé par un misérable"; "fait tout pour l'âme, et la favorise entièrement aux dépens du corps"] Ibid., vol. 2, pp. 1321–1322.

86. Ibid., vol. 2, p. 1493.

87. ["enlèvement"; "exigeait ma soumission pure et simple [. . .] je résistais héroïquement"] Ibid., vol. 2, p. 1068.

88. Ibid., vol. 2, p. 1530.

89. Ibid., vol. 2, p. 1172.

90. Ibid., vol. 2, pp. 512–513.

Conclusion

1. ["à compter du 18 brumaire, lorsque Napoléon arrive au pouvoir, son histoire est réellement celle de la France dans tous ses rapports intérieurs et extérieurs"] A.-C. Thibaudeau, *Le Consulat et l'Empire*, "Avertissement de l'édition," vol. 1, p. iii.

2. *Le Moniteur*, no. 6, Thursday 2 January 1806, p. 28.

3. Homer, *The Odyssey*, books 9–13.

4. E. de Las Cases, *Mémorial de Sainte-Hélène* (ed. Schmidt), "Résumé des trois mois," vol. 1, p. 897.

5. Jean-Pierre Vernant, "La belle mort et le cadavre outragé," in *L'Individu, la Mort, l'Amour* (Paris: Gallimard, "Folio," 1989, pp. 41–79; "La belle mort d'Achille," in *Entre mythe et politique* (Paris: Seuil, 1996), pp. 501–510; "La mort héroïque," in *La Traversée des frontières* (Paris: Seuil, 2004), pp. 69–86.

6. ["faire du lot commun à toutes les créatures un bien qui lui soit propre et dont l'éclat lui appartienne à jamais"] J.-P. Vernant, *L'Individu, la Mort, l'Amour*, p. 41.

7. Pierre Cascar, "Préface," H. de Balzac, *Le Colonel Chabert. El Verdugo. Adieu. Le Réquisitionnaire*, edited by P. Berthier (Paris: Gallimard, "Folio classique," 1974), p. 13. English-language edition: *La Comédie Humaine of Honoré de Balzac: Scenes from Country Life. 1. The Country Doctor. 2. The Vendetta. 3. Colonel Chabert*, edited by William Peterfield. Trent, New York, The Century, 1909. All quotations are from the English-language edition; French page numbers are in brackets. On Napoleon and Balzac, see Saint-Paulien, *Napoléon, Balzac et l'empire de la* Comédie humaine (Paris: Albin Michel, 1979).

8. H. de Balzac, *Le Colonel Chabert*, p. 358 [pp. 49–50].

9. ["Je ne date que de moi"] See chap. 4, n. 60, above.

10. Balzac, *Le Colonel Chabert*, p. 361 [p. 53].

11. Ibid., pp. 405, 321 [p. 105, 31].

12. ["Je ne voudrais plus être moi"; "le sentiment de mes droits me tue"] Ibid., p. 357 [p.47].

13. "Then, with the deep perspicacity given only by utter villainy, or by fierce worldly selfishness, she knew that she might live in peace on the word and the contempt of this loyal veteran." Ibid., p. 400 [p. 111].

14. ["Je ne suis plus un homme, je suis le numéro 164, septième salle"] Ibid., p. 405 [p. 118].

15. F. Furet, *La Révolution française*, p. 527.

16. P. Rosanvallon, *Le Sacre du citoyen: Histoire du suffrage universel en France* (Paris: Gallimard, 1992), p. 601.

17. ["Que toutes ces malheureuses divisions s'effacent!" "Ne formons qu'une seule famille!"] *Discours, allocutions et réponses de S. M. Louis-Philippe, roi des François, 1830*, audience of 22 September 1830 (Paris, 1830), p. 323, cited by Jean-Claude Caron in "Louis-Philippe face à l'opinion publique, ou l'impossible réconciliation des Français, 1830–1835," *French Historical Studies*, vol. 30, no. 4 (fall 2007), pp. 597–621, here p. 608.

18. ["L'esprit de conciliation est nécessaire là où existent des différences d'opinion et de religion"] *Discours, allocutions et réponses, 1830*, audience of 27 September 1830, p. 371, cited by J.-Cl. Caron, *French Historical Studies*, p. 608.

19. ["vaste Panthéon de tous les exploits et de tous les héros de la patrie"; "a rassemblé la grande famille française dans le passé, [. . .] a réuni tous les âges, réconcilié toutes les origines"] Cited by Thomas Gaehtgens, "Le musée historique de Versailles," in *Les Lieux de mémoire, II: La nation—2*, pp. 1781–1801, here p. 1798. English-language edition: *Rethinking France: Les Lieux de mémoire*, vol. 4: *Histories and Memories*, "The Historical Museum at Versailles," translated by Richard S. Levy, pp. 161–84; here p. 182. On the historical museum and the political significance of the paintings that make up the galerie des Batailles, see the excellent work by Gaehtgens, *Versailles: De la Résidence royale au musée historique*, translated by Patrick Poirot, Preface by Pierre Lemoine (Paris: Albin Michel, 1984).

20. P. Rosanvallon, *Le Moment Guizot* (Paris: Gallimard, 1985), chap. 3, "La nouvelle citoyenneté," pp. 75–106.

21. ["embrasse à la fois et la religion, et l'art, et l'État, et l'industrie"; "tout concilier et tout rapprocher"] Victor Cousin, *Cours d'introduction à l'histoire de la philosophie* (Paris: Pichon et Didier, 1828), lesson 1, pp. 30–31.

22. ["la fusion réelle du roi et du peuple, cherchant ensemble la meilleure manière de gouverner"] Ibid., lesson 13, p. 40.

23. Ibid.

24. Ibid., p. 42.

25. Ibid., p. 44; this passage is cited by J. Goldstein in *The Post-Revolutionary Self*, p. 154.

26. ["d'embrasser tous les éléments de la pensée, et de reconstruire ainsi l'humanité entière"] V. Cousin, *Cours d'introduction . . .*, lesson 7, p. 10.

27. Ibid., lesson 8, pp. 13–14.

28. ["La gloire est un témoin irrécusable de l'importance de la vraie grandeur des hommes"] Ibid., lesson 10, p. 34.

29. Ibid., pp. 36–37.

30. Ibid., lesson 9, p. 31.

31. Ibid., lesson 10, pp. 36–37.

32. ["pour représenter une idée tant que cette idée a de la force et vaut la peine d'être représentée"] Ibid., pp. 14–15.

33. ["que ce peuple qui s'est fait homme"] Ibid., p. 20.

34. ["le prix des services qu'elle reconnaît en avoir reçus, et qu'elle lui paie avec ce qu'elle a de plus précieux, son estime"] Ibid., p. 22.

35. See F. Furet, *La Révolution française*, p. 611; and, notably, J. Goldstein, *The Post-Revolutionary Self*, chaps. 4 and 5, pp. 139–232.

36. ["Fille de faits grands et évidents, elle est elle-même un fait manifeste, aussi clair que le jour"; "parce que c'est aimer les grandes choses, les longs travaux, les services effectifs rendus à la patrie"] V. Cousin, *Cours d'introduction . . .* , lesson 10, pp. 22–23.

37. Ibid., p. 21.

38. Ibid., p. 22.

39. On this issue, see the enlightening reflection by P. Rosanvallon in *Le Sacre du citoyen*, pp. 306–318.

40. V. Cousin, *Cours d'introduction . . .* , lesson 10, p. 20.

41. Ibid., p. 24.

42. ["presque toujours les [. . .] plus mesquines"] Ibid.

43. ["elle omet, elle ignore le côté purement individuel et biographique du grand homme"] Ibid., pp. 25–26.

44. Ibid., p. 23.

45. Pierre Rosanvallon, *Le Sacre du citoyen*, p. 601.

46. Ernest Renan, "Qu'est-ce qu'une nation?" in *Qu'est-ce qu'une nation? et autres écrits politiques*, edited by Raoul Girardet (Paris: Imprimerie nationale, 1996), chap. 3, p. 240.

47. On representations of Napoleon and his legend in literature, see Maurice Descotes, *La Légende de Napoléon et les écrivains français du XIXe siècle* (Paris: Minard, 196); and the section in the journal *Europe* entitled "Napoléon et la littérature," nos. 480–481 (April–May 1969).

48. On the historians, see esp. P. Geyl, *Napoleon, For and Against*.

49. See the essential work of P. Bénichou, notably *Le Sacre de l'écrivain*.

50. ["unique règle de sa conduite et objet de ses transports"] Stendhal, *Le Rouge et le noir* (Paris: Gallimard, "Folio," 2000), p. 104. English-language ed.: *The Red and the Black: A Chronicle of 1830*, translated by Horace B. Samuel (London: E. P. Dutton & Co., 1916), p. 53. All quotations are from the English-language edition; French page numbers are in brackets.

51. ["la plus brutale insensibilité à tout ce qui n'était pas intérêt d'argent, de préséance ou de croix"] Ibid., p. 38 [p. 87].

52. Ibid., p. 155 [p. 222].

53. On the use of masks in Stendhal, see Jean Starobinski, "Stendhal pseudonym," in *L'œil vivant* (1951; Paris: Gallimard, "Tel," 2001), pp. 231–284; see also Georges Blin, *Stendhal et les problèmes du roman* (Paris: José Corti, 1953).

54. On Stendhal and his time, see Michel Crouzet, *Stendhal, ou Monsieur moi-même* (Paris: Flammarion, 1990; see also the wonderful work Mona Ozouf, "*Lucien Leuwen*: ni l'un ni l'autre," in *Récits d'une patrie littéraire: Les aveux du roman* (Paris: Fayard, 2006), pp. 453–475.

55. ["enceinte morale derrière laquelle il se défend [. . .] pouce à pouce"] E. de Las Cases, *Mémorial de Sainte-Hélène* (ed. Schmidt), vol. 1, p. 480.

56. ["en dehors des lopis humaines"] Ibid., vol. 2, p. 1743.

57. ["Horrible époque! Où l'on se courbe devant un homme poli, médiocre et froid que l'on hait, mais à qui on obéit"] H. de Balzac, *Le Médecin de campagne*, preface by E. Le Roy Ladurie (Paris: Gallimard, "Folio," 1974), p. 265. English-language ed.: *The Country Doctor, The Quest for the Absolute, and Other Stories*, translated by Ellen Marriage (Philadelphia, Gebbie Publishing Co., 1899), p. 222. All quotations are from the English-language edition; French page numbers are in brackets.

58. ["[H]omme ardent, affamé de distinctions sociales"; "parce qu'elle marche d'un pied trop lent"] Ibid., p. 212 [p. 254].

59. Ibid., p. 209 [p. 252].

60. ["sublime egoïsme"; "rendre son repentir profitable au monde sociale"] Ibid., p. 244 [pp. 287-288].

61. ["l'oracle du canton"] Ibid., p. 30 [p. 73].

62. ["espèce de Bayard sans faste"; "labouré tous les champs où commanda Napoléon"].

63. On the place of everyday objects in the cult of Napoleon, see Sudhir Hazareesingh, *The Legend of Napoleon* (London: Granta, 2005), chap. 3: "A Cult of Seditious Objects," pp. 72-98.

64. ["par des calculs d'intérêt et bien-être immédiats"] Balzac, *The Country Doctor*, p. 40 [p. 83].

65. Ibid., p. 156 [p. 2010. On "exceptional beings" in the novel of the nineteenth century, see Thomas Pavel, *La Pensée du Roman* (Paris: Gallimard, 2003), pp. 245-253.

66. Balzac, *The Country Doctor*, pp. 64-65 [p. 108]. Let us recall the passage from Louis-Napoléon Bonaparte's *Idées napoléoniennes* (Paris: Paulin, 1839), pp. 41-42, in which the author insists on the importance of the communal administration: "The Emperor felt all the importance of a good communal administration; he said that one must indeed keep from destroying the municipal spirit. He often supported the mayors over the prefects [. . .] The communal spirit is an essentially conservative spirit [. . .] To regenerate the commune, it was necessary to deprive it temporarily of a part of its rights, until its education was done."

67. Balzac, *The Country Doctor*, p. 167 [p. 212].

68. ["Lorsqu'un homme est bien sûr d'être compris par ceux auxquels il se confie, ne doit-il pas éprouver une sorte de plaisir à dire: 'J'ai fait cela'?"] Ibid., p. 103 [pp. 146-47].

69. Ibid., p. 106 [pp. 148-49] (emphasis mine).

70. Ibid., p. 186 [pp. 230-31]; the old soldier tells of the benefits of the political economy of glory: "Then came the real triumph of the soldier. For everyone who could write became an officer forthwith, and pensions and gifts of duchies poured down in showers. There were fortunes for the staff that never cost France a penny, and the Legion of Honor was as good as an annuity for the rank and file; I still draw my pension on the strength of it." Ibid., pp. 184-185 [pp. 230-231].

71. ["'Oui,' reprit Goguelat, 'c'est, sauf les batailles, le Napoléon de notre vallée'"] Ibid., p. 279 [p. 323].

72. François-René de Chateaubriand, *Mémoires d'outre-tombe*, critical edition by Jean-Claude Berchet (Paris: Livre de poche/Classiques Garnier, "La Pochothèque"), vol. 1, p. 309.

73. M. Fumaroli, "L'empereur et le poète," in *La Vie de Napoléon* (Paris: De Fallois, 1999), pp. 8-48.

74. Jean-Paul Clément, in his *Chateaubraind: Biographie morale et intellectuelle* (Paris:

Flammarion, 1998), cites the work of Sainte-Beuve, who asserted that the figure of Napoleon "had literally become Chateaubriand's nightmare" (p. 215).

75. Chateaubriand, *Mémoires d'outre-tombe*, p. 1230.

76. J.-C. Berchet, in Chateaubriand, *Mémoires d'outre-tombe*, "Notice des livres XIII à XXIV," vol. 1, p. 601; the excellent preface by J.-C. Berchet explores in detail both the question of "the historical representation of self" and the polyphony of the *Mémoires*. See also Jean-Marie Roland, *Chateaubriand, l'exil et la gloire: du roman familial à l'identité littéraire dans l'œuvre de Chateaubriand* (Paris: Champion, 1994).

77. ["Je préfère mon nom à mon titre"] Chateaubriand, *Mémoires d'outre-tombe*, vol. 1, p. 121; on the essential question of freedom in Chateaubriand, see Marc Fumaroli, *Chateaubriand: Poésie et terreur*.

78. See François Hartog, *Régimes d'historicité*; he uses the term *passeur* in chap. 3, "Chateaubriand: entre l'ancien et le nouveau régime d'historicité," pp. 77–107.

79. Chateaubriand, *Mémoires d'outre-tombe*, vol. 2, p. 13.

80. "Récapitulation de ma vie," ibid., vol. 2, p. 1026.

81. ["Nous ressemblions pas mal à une troupe ambulante de comédiens français"] Ibid., vol. 2, p. 886.

82. Ibid., vol. 2, p. 1002.

83. Ibid. vol. 2, p. 1030.

84. See Louis-Napoléon Bonaparte, *Idées napoléoniennes*.

85. Victor Hugo, *Œuvres complètes, Roman II: Les Misérables* (Paris: Robert Laffont, 1985), III, 3, 2, p. 488. English-language ed.: *Les Misérables*, translated by Isabel F. Hapgood (New York: Thomas Y. Crowell Publishers, 1887), p. 36. All quotations are from the English-language edition; French page numbers are in brackets.

86. Ibid., p. 53 [pp. 501–502] (emphasis mine).

87. Ibid., p. 63 [p. 509]. On Marius, see Mona Ozouf, "Les Misérables," *Récits d'une patrie littéraire*, pp. 476–499.

88. ["[c]e mot simple et froid avait traversé comme une lame d'acier son effusion épique"] V. Hugo, *Les Misérables*, pp. 91–92 [pp. 533–534].

89. Ibid., p. 29 [p. 263].

90. Ibid., p. 45 [p. 277].

91. ["ce Cambronne, ce passant de la dernière heure, ce soldat ignoré, cet infiniment petit de la guerre"; "l'homme qui a gagné la bataille de Waterloo"] Ibid., pp. 37–38 [pp. 271–72].

92. Ibid., p. 96 [p. 537].

93. ["[I]l se dit que, puisque Cosette était partie, il n'avait plus qu'à mourir"] Ibid., p. 208 [p. 823].

94. Ibid. p. 81 [p. 69] On the correspondences between the chronology of Napoleon and that of Jean Valjean, see Yves Gohin, "Une histoire qui date," in *Lire* Les Misérables, edited by Anne Ubersfeld and Guy Rosa (Paris: Corti, 1985), pp. 30–57, notably pp. 48–49.

95. ["par la même rue qui sept mois auparavant avait vu passer l'empereur Napoléon allant de Cannes à Paris"] V. Hugo, *Les Misérables*, p. 56 [p. 49].

96. See Avner Ben-Amos, "Les funérailles de Victor Hugo: Apothéose de l'événement spectacle," in *Les Lieux de Mémoire, I: La République*, vol. 1, pp. 425–464.

GENERAL INDEX

Note: Page numbers in *italics* indicate illustrations.

INDEX OF CITED AUTHORS